Praise for *The Next Act*:
Realigning Your Mindset, Purpose, and Career

"*The Next Act* is a powerful collection of essays providing a broad-ranging discussion of career development opportunities for student affairs professionals within and outside student affairs and higher education. Each author bases helpful advice on personal and frank narratives. Should student affairs professionals aspire to a promotion within student affairs, should they take a second (or third) vice presidency, should they aspire to a presidency, or should they leave higher education altogether? The editors' insightful framing chapter and the decision matrix in the appendix are invaluable. While the intended audience of the book is student affairs professionals, other professionals, especially from higher education, will find transferable lessons as they consider career paths."

—**R. BARBARA GITENSTEIN,** President Emerita, The College of New Jersey; Senior Fellow, Senior Consultant, Association of Governing Boards

"Informed by their unique vantage points as leaders, coaches, scholars, and practitioners, Pina and Hecht have curated a remarkable anthology on career transformations. *The Next Act* is more than a guidebook for anyone charting their own path in student affairs—it is also essential reading for university leaders who are set on helping administrators flourish."

—**LINDA G. MILLS,** President, New York University

"Most professionals will make moves at various junctures in their careers—they should read this excellent book before doing so. *The Next Act* is impressively comprehensive and includes useful guidance for everyone at all career stages. This timeless text thoughtfully honors the importance of living in the present while simultaneously preparing for future transitions."

—**SHAUN HARPER,** Clifford and Betty Allen Professor, University of Southern California

"*The Next Act* is an invaluable resource for student affairs practitioners navigating the evolving landscape of higher education. The book's insightful exploration of career transitions, resilience, and adaptability is compelling and offers practical strategies that align strongly with TBD's commitment to empowering leaders with purpose and cultivating inclusivity. This book is a must-read for anyone seeking to realign their career with their values and aspirations, offering a roadmap to not just professional success, but personal fulfillment."

—**ANGELA E. BATISTA,** Founder and CEO, Transformation by Design (TBD)

"Across all professional levels, the student affairs workforce is facing unprecedented changes and challenges. This book beautifully captures these challenges and the many choices and opportunities for professionals in higher education. It is a book of hope and promise and is a must-read for every student affairs professional today."

—**KEVIN KRUGER,** President Emeritus, NASPA–Student Affairs Administrators in Higher Education

THE NEXT ACT

THE NEXT ACT

Realigning Your Mindset, Purpose, and Career

JASON B. PINA, AMY HECHT, & **ASSOCIATES**

Student Affairs Administrators
in Higher Education

Student Affairs Administrators
in Higher Education

Copyright © 2024 by the National Association of Student Personnel Administrators (NASPA), Inc. All rights reserved.

Published by
NASPA–Student Affairs Administrators in Higher Education
111 K Street, NE
10th Floor
Washington, DC 20002
www.naspa.org

No part of this publication may be reproduced, stored in a retrieval system, or transmitted in any form or by any means, now known or hereafter invented, including electronic, mechanical, photocopying, recording, scanning, information storage and retrieval, or otherwise, except as permitted under Section 107 of the 1976 United States Copyright Act, without the prior written permission of the Publisher.

Additional copies may be purchased by contacting the NASPA publications department at 202-265-7500 or visiting http://bookstore.naspa.org.

NASPA does not discriminate on the basis of race; color; national origin; religion; sex; age; gender identity or expression; affectional or sexual orientation; veteran status; disability; marital status; personal appearance; family responsibilities; genetic information; educational status; political affiliation; place of residence or business; source of income; caste; matriculation; credit information; status as a survivor or family member of a survivor of domestic violence, a sexual offense, or stalking; reproductive health decision making; or any other basis protected by law in any of its policies, programs, publications, and services. NASPA prohibits discrimination and harassment at any time, including during its events or within publications and online learning communities.

Library of Congress Cataloging-in-Publication Data

Names:	Pina, Jason B., editor.	Hecht, Amy, editor.
Title:	The next act : realigning your mindset, purpose, and career / Jason B. Pina, Amy Hecht, and associates.
Description:	Washington, DC : NASPA–Student Affairs Administrators in Higher Education, [2024]	Includes bibliographical references and index.
Identifiers:	ISBN: 978-1-948213-47-9 (paperback)	978-1-948213-48-6 (ebook)
Subjects:	LCSH: Student affairs administrators--Vocational guidance.	Student affairs services--Vocational guidance.
Classification:	LCC: LB2342.9 .N49 2024	DDC: 378.197023--dc23

Printed and bound in the United States of America

FIRST EDITION

Contents

Foreword ... vii
    Stephanie A. Gordon

Preface ... xi

1   Quiet Quitting and the Job Market ... 1
    Amy Hecht and Jason B. Pina

2   Changing Institution Type ... 15
    Martino Harmon With Jamie V. Sanchez

3   Shifting Roles Within the Same Institution ... 41
    Jeanna Mastrodicasa and Katie O'Dair

4   Serving as a Vice President for Student Affairs for the Long Term ... 55
    Michael N. Christakis, Pauline Burke, Shannon Ellis, and Patricia A. Whitely With Heather M. Stevens

5   Serving Higher Education Through Consulting ... 73
    Erin Hoffmann Harding and Ana Rossetti

6   Transitioning From Higher Education to New Industries ... 99
    Constanza Cabello and Sofia B. Pertuz

7   The Unexpected Return to Campus ... 123
    Gage E. Paine

8	The Call, Push, and Pull to Academia: Navigating to Faculty	143
	Michael S. Funk, Tamara Bertrand Jones, and Natasha N. Croom	
9	A Return to the Administrative Side	167
	David J. Nguyen	
10	Going Global: Student Affairs Practitioners Abroad	183
	Ainsley Carry, Baishakhi Taylor, and Raphael X. Moffett	
11	Transitioning From Higher Education to PK–12 Education	207
	Karen Warren Coleman	
12	Boundaries, Balance, and Moving Forward	237
	Darryl Lovett and Marcella Runell	
13	Presidential Perspectives on Student Affairs Careers and Preparation to Move On	253
	Kenneth Elmore, Thomas Gibson, Ajay Nair, Ellen J. Neufeldt, and Lori S. White	
14	Values as a Framework for Career Realignment	283
	Amie K. Hammond	
Appendix		305
Editors and Contributors		311
Index		327

Foreword

When I began my career in student affairs, nearly every new professional I met said their career aspiration was to someday serve as a vice president of student affairs. All of us appeared to have the same goal. There weren't many decisions to be made or pathways to pursue—it seemed reasonable to assume that if you wanted to be successful in student affairs, a vice president's job should be the objective. Yet, in a world that is constantly in flux, where the only certainty is change, the pursuit of a thriving career requires continual adaptation, innovation, and self-discovery. Nowhere is this more evident than in the current state of the student affairs profession. For today's student affairs educators, guiding students through their collegiate journeys while navigating their own career paths has been particularly challenging amid shifting landscapes and evolving priorities.

The Next Act: Realigning Your Mindset, Purpose, and Career, edited by Amy Hecht and Jason Pina, allows readers to reflect on, prepare for, and navigate the future of student affairs and beyond. It also serves as a testament to the resilience, creativity, and determination of professionals in the field. No more is the vice presidency the only way to lead change in higher education or affect student success. Even in my own career, transitioning to NASPA–Student Affairs Administrators in Higher Education as a full-time employee provided me with a way to stay connected to student affairs and influence student success at the global level. This change also challenged me, as I had to understand the nonprofit business, forge partnerships across the academy, and make the corporate connections that are key to higher education's success. So many more student affairs educators like me are finding ways to ensure that their impact is felt in multiple places and spaces. This book contains stories of the many ways our colleagues have reimagined careers that are beyond the traditional norms.

From changing institution types to transitioning to consulting and "student affairs–adjacent" careers, professionals are no longer required to simply choose from a set of institutionally defined roles. This book provides strategies for self-assessment and workplace evaluation; it also encourages readers to think about how skills can be transferred to PK–12 education, faculty positions, and academic affairs. The contributing authors, drawing from a rich set of experiences and expertise, discuss the ways personal fulfillment and professional growth intricately intersect.

Adaptability is the name of the game—whether it means shifting direction professionally or simply understanding the changing needs of students and the transitions required for success in the evolving higher education environment. From redefining leadership paradigms to embracing global perspectives, the authors share stories of accomplishments in unexpected places and address stereotypes that sometimes hinder our perceptions of success. Boasting diverse experiences and perspectives, the narratives also contain practical strategies and insights that will resonate with the aspirations of a new generation of professionals.

At its core, career exploration is not just about professional advancement or strategic planning; it's about finding meaning, purpose, and fulfillment in the work that we do. I have found my purpose and passion in helping student affairs educators learn and grow in the profession. I know that this text will help others see that many people navigate this change in myriad ways. The chapters in this publication provide a pathway for evaluating what brings you joy, how your passions can fuel inspiration, and when it's time to move or change direction in your career. The book takes a deeply human approach to career development and reminds us that our careers are not just about *what we accomplish*, but *who we become* in the process.

STEPHANIE A. GORDON
Vice President for Professional Development
NASPA–Student Affairs Administrators in Higher Education

Preface

In the early days of the COVID-19 pandemic, much of higher education was compelled to make significant financial decisions that affected the workforce. According to a 2021 *Inside Higher Ed* article, higher education shed 4% of its workforce in 2020; the reductions disproportionately affected community colleges as well as part-time and service workers (Lederman, 2021). One of this book's authors was forced to lay off more than 100 people during the pandemic's prevaccine period.

Although this reduction was not unusual during the early months of the pandemic—nor was it even the highest force reduction across industries—it served as a bellwether for the student affairs profession. A 2022 study conducted by Macmillan Learning sought to examine the state of professional satisfaction in student affairs. The study "found that 37% of student affairs professionals are actively looking for a new job. Ten percent of those surveyed were solely looking for a new role inside higher education, 19% were solely searching for roles outside of higher education, and 8% were searching both" (Macmillan Learning, 2022, para. 2).

The arrival of vaccines and the resumption of on-campus instruction across the country were met by empty student affairs offices and a slow, at times nonexistent, return to prepandemic workforce levels. Colleges and universities faced high percentages (in some cases, almost 40%) of open student affairs full-time equivalent positions—and the resultant gaps in student support services. This landscape inspired us, the coeditors, to create this book.

This text is a compilation of diverse narratives that provide guidance and inspiration to professionals and leaders alike. We have four goals: First, we aim to present the vast scope of directions in and out of higher education that professionals may pursue for a highly desirable career. Second, we want to deliver a dose of reality for those leaders who still hold outdated beliefs about employment. Third, we want to convey the viability of long-term student affairs careers. Fourth, we seek to provide some recent research and guidance to help those currently employed in student affairs evaluate their pathways.

The first six chapters address more traditional transitions promoted and explored in the field. From an overview of the current student affairs job landscape in Chapter 1 to examples of conventional long-term career navigation in Chapters 2 through 5, the contributing authors offer unique narratives and recommendations to support those individuals working in higher education. Chapter 6 contains examples of successful student affairs professionals' transitions out of higher education and adjacent industries. Chapter 7 presents returning to on-campus employment following a successful consulting stint. Chapters 8 and 9 focus on faculty transitions. Chapter 10 offers two examples of a growing need for student affairs professionals at higher education institutions outside the United States; in contrast, Chapter 11 focuses on transitioning to K–12 education.

The final section of the book addresses the personal work that is needed throughout a career (Chapter 12), offers sage advice from student affairs professionals who ascended to the presidency (Chapter 13), and concludes with recent research to help readers evaluate whether their own values align with those of their employers (Chapter 14).

Readers will find a rich blend of narratives, professional insights, and recent research to help them make more sense of their career paths. These 30 authors have only scratched the surface when it comes to the diverse directions a career may take. As coeditors, we hope you find this book enlightening and inspirational—and challenging to many traditional career notions.

JASON B. PINA
AMY HECHT
August 2024

References

Lederman, D. (2021, December 13). How the pandemic shrank the higher ed workforce. *Inside Higher Ed*. https://www.insidehighered.com/news/2021/12/14/higher-ed-workforce-shrank-4-fall-2020

Macmillan Learning. (2022, November 17). *Nearly one third of student affairs professionals seeking to leave higher education* [Press release]. https://www.businesswire.com/news/home/20221117005138/en/Nearly-One-Third-of-Student-Affairs-Professionals-Seeking-to-Leave-Higher-Education

Quiet Quitting and the Job Market

Amy Hecht and Jason B. Pina

A crucial pillar of academia, student affairs ensures that students have a well-rounded and enriching educational experience beyond the classroom. Professionals in the field play a pivotal role in shaping student development, fostering a sense of belonging, and providing essential support services. However, despite its significance, this career path has witnessed an excess of trained professionals opting out of graduate programs, a surge in dedicated employees being emotionally disengaged from their work, and many practitioners leaving the field due to burnout. Alongside this issue, the job market's ever-evolving landscape poses additional obstacles for those seeking to build lasting and successful careers in higher education and student affairs (HESA).

When the two of us discussed the content of this book, we were interested in the idea of what comes next in careers—not only for ourselves but also for those we coach and mentor. Both of us reached the role of vice president with at least 20 years to go before retirement. Achieving the "dream job" early on prompts you to rethink your goals; you realize there are still decades left for you to work. And given the tumultuous times in higher education, the question of how long you can sustain the work also becomes top of mind. We are getting more questions from mentees, peers, and supervisors about the next steps and, more than ever, hearing from colleagues who may not continue in the field of student affairs or even higher education. The rules of career progression we had learned from those who came before us were less and less relevant to the current moment.

Growing numbers of professionals are breaking the old rules of career progression and carving new paths. The chapters in this book highlight many of them. From assuming leadership positions in K–12 schools, consulting, or taking on faculty roles, roles outside of student affairs, or outside of the United States, to staying the course and leading at the same institution for decades and ascending to the presidency, there are many options for the "next act." By speaking openly about their journeys, the authors here are expanding the options for student affairs professionals to consider.

The idea of a next act is also relevant for higher education graduate programs and their recent graduates. What are the options for individuals obtaining these degrees, and how transferable are the skills acquired? Is there value in these degrees beyond working within a student affairs department or university? We believe there is, and the stories in this book will showcase the many directions a career can take and the variety of ways that passion and success can be found.

How Did the Field of Student Affairs Get Here?

The field of student affairs is constantly evolving. The issues that were at the forefront 25 years ago are seldom discussed anymore, and there are new challenges that were once unimaginable. Well before the wide-ranging impacts of COVID-19, higher education faced strong headwinds from declining public opinion, fewer high school graduates, and more demand on student affairs to serve students—all of which triggered a watershed moment seldom experienced in our profession. These pressures forced HESA professionals to reevaluate their career goals and professional intentions.

Institutions have faced a reduction in their workforces, whether through attrition, layoffs, hiring freezes, or position eliminations. During times of crisis and uncertainty, these decisions are usually viewed as prudent and broadly accepted; however, the challenges on campuses have remained the same, and the work has remained the same. Those who remain on campus have assumed more and more responsibilities. The pressures of staff shortages and more complex job roles have left many employees reassessing their work lives and the associated personal toll, such as new staff expectations, stagnant salaries, limited upward mobility, and the overall impact of the global pandemic.

Stagnant salaries and limited upward mobility—unfortunate aspects of positions in student affairs—have been accepted by many career professionals. These regrettable mainstays have an even more significant impact on a division's ability to fully staff and deliver on employees' articulated needs. Past generations of student affairs practitioners accepted the long hours required of assistantships as well as the entry-level pay for master's-educated professionals, which has been embarrassingly low for decades. Yet in recent years, it has become increasingly difficult to hire and retain entry- and mid-level staff. Historic numbers of failed searches or successful searches resulting in underqualified professionals have exacerbated the pressure many of us feel to deliver a level of student services required to support today's students.

Institutions across the country have faced challenges recruiting from limited talented pools. We've found that candidates are now behaving differently, often reaching the ends of searches successfully and then backing out once an offer is presented. Several search consultants have also confirmed this trend and shifted the advice to campus hiring managers to pursue multiple candidates, invite larger pools of candidates for on-campus interviews, or prepare multiple job offers, understanding that the turndown rate (not accepting a job after completing a lengthy hiring process) has risen. We have also had candidates accept job offers and change their minds before arriving on campus. We've reexamined qualifications for positions and even broadened the expertise we've traditionally sought in candidates.

A 2022 report by NASPA–Student Affairs Administrators in Higher Education examined vital issues and postpandemic trends in HESA. Nearly 9 in 10 respondents said that salaries and compensation packages needed to be more competitive given the level of experience and education required for the work; 8 in 10 said they felt undervalued by their institution. One dean of students noted, "When we look at the senior leaders in student affairs, they work 80-hour workweeks. They seem overwhelmed. They seem overtaxed, while at the same time, they seem undervalued and underappreciated at their home institutions. I don't think that's attractive to our early-career student affairs professionals" (NASPA, 2022, p. 22).

This report captured the current climate of higher education, and indeed it is overwhelming to think of succeeding in such a space. NASPA found inequities in completion rates for Black, Latinx/a/o, Indigenous, first-generation, and lower income students; a worsening mental health crisis among college-age students; a devaluing of higher education by the

American public; a worsening of college-degree affordability; challenges associated with pivoting to online and virtual instruction, addressing a national and international movement on violence and systemic racism, and maintaining enrollment numbers; a divisive political climate; and the use of some state higher education institutions as political pawns. All of these and more led to new levels of burnout and exhaustion.

It's no surprise that these issues have led many HESA professionals to seek other employment and demand more workplace flexibility. The current climate has also seen the rise of quiet quitting. *Quiet quitting* refers to a phenomenon where employees, despite physically remaining in their jobs, are mentally disengaged from their roles and responsibilities. Factors that contribute to quiet quitting may include burnout, lack of career advancement opportunities, toxic workplace culture, and the changing dynamics of student populations. This combination of employee responses has taken HESA by storm, resulting in mass employment gaps and a reckoning of work expectations.

Perhaps some of us, as a field, needed to quietly quit. Are we, as HESA professionals, so invested in our careers that we're sacrificing our health and other interests? Do individuals in careers that instill a sense of pride for going above and beyond need to examine the toll these jobs take? Is this part of why many are burned out and seeking what's next?

Some of us can reflect on our careers and remember when we learned the painful lesson that organizations don't care for us. All of us are replaceable—regardless of the hard work, dedication, and loyalty we've given. And as much as we love our institutions, they rarely love us back. But the implications of quiet quitting are extensive. This phenomenon affects student engagement, the overall campus climate, and the reputation of institutions as both communities of learning and workplaces.

The student population's diversity and evolving needs require HESA professionals to adapt and innovate continually. What it means to stay relevant has also changed: Although traditional professional development opportunities and graduate education remain critical for many student affairs roles, the field has changed faster than its curriculum, and the demands of HESA careers can affect the mental health of those professionals in them. Outcry over the reasonableness of job expectations has risen to a fever pitch in student affairs. Gone are the days when professionals were expected to sacrifice their well-being for the greater good of an institution. Thankfully, it has become more commonplace for professionals to question expectations and demand more appropriate benefits (financial and fringe).

Strategies for Building a Fulfilling and Impactful Career

The HESA profession needs individuals to remain in the field and build on their experiences. To do that, professionals must adapt to better prepare for inevitable career and life changes. The following sections offer four strategies that are key to fulfilling careers. Throughout this book are related examples that have supported the career development of all the authors.

Seeking Professional Development and Enhancing Skills

Continuously improving your skillset is essential for success in any career. You should seek various avenues for professional development, but this development and enhancement occurs mainly in three areas: formal education, on-the-job experience, and formal professional development opportunities. Although both of us authors are proponents of graduate programs in higher education administration, counseling, and related fields, the foundation of an undergraduate education and all the associated experiences help shape the professional foundation.

HESA professionals are also formed by their roles throughout their careers. Ideally, each successive job change should be guided by personal and professional needs. Whenever possible, focus on individual needs, such as location or a more flexible work schedule, that will evolve throughout your career. Secondarily, successive roles should not only be built on previous experiences but also focus on filling professional gaps in a high-quality manner. The third area relates to formal professional development. Purposefully choose what you read and which meetings you attend. Financial and time limitations may affect the breadth and depth of professional development options, but the profession offers a wealth of resources for little or no cost. These opportunities often lead to the next strategy.

Building Strong Networks and Mentorship

Developing meaningful professional networks and finding mentors can significantly influence career trajectories. Our profession is small when considering the personal interconnections we enjoy. These relationships often span institution types and position levels, especially after a long career. The benefits of networks and mentoring are numerous. Regardless of where a career eventually leads, evolving professional networks and mentoring increase chances for "future-proofing." Active engagement with peers not only exposes individuals to professional development and sounding boards for critical situations but also to rich personal relationships that go far beyond.

All the contributors to this book believe that solid networks and mentors help professionals deepen their knowledge of the field and, more importantly, help them ride the inevitable waves during career progression. The time-honored adage that the student affairs profession is small will serve you well. Nurtured networks and strong mentorship support development and, at times, survival during challenging moments. Active engagement in networking and mentorship results in many positive outcomes.

Cultivating Resilience and Adaptability

In a dynamic job market, resilience and adaptability are critical traits for career longevity. It is fascinating that many HESA professionals have spent their working lifetimes teaching and instilling resilience in students while only sometimes possessing it themselves. Traditionally, higher education, like other education fields, has attracted individuals who value job security and professional stability. Recent history has taught us that those aspects are in short supply in almost any field. The examples throughout this book testify to how resilience and adaptability can work for professionals who decide to remain in HESA and for those who transition to other fields. It is time to build these skill sets and use them for professional growth and career stability.

Empowering and Advocating

Empowering yourself and advocating for positive change within the field are crucial for a fulfilling career. These efforts, often viewed as a way to give to others, reach their fullest impact when they are implemented by those who hold positions of power and privilege within institutions and the higher education industry. Using your voice to bring about change and enhance the experience of others is often a selfless but powerful act. This book is a small attempt at just that type of advocacy and empowerment. Bringing forward an array of narratives incentivizes HESA professionals to reevaluate a career and offers insight into the positive aspects of staying the course.

The Only Thing Certain Is Change

All of us accept—cognitively—that change is constant, yet when we consider our careers, we often view change as a position with more and greater responsibilities than the previous one: an increased salary, a more senior title. That view limits our ability to consider alternative career paths and could result in missed opportunities that would provide greater fulfillment. Life has a way of forcing us to view things differently. Our careers can experience disruptions that cause us to reconsider our linear way of thinking about long-term career opportunities. Feiler (2020) categorized these disruptions into five categories: love, beliefs, work, identity, and body; see Figure 1.1.

Figure 1.1

Deck of Disruptors

DECK OF DISRUPTORS

LOVE
Getting married
Spouse beginning/ceasing work
Divorce/end of relationship
Reproductive difficulties
Gaining new family member
Illness of child
Child with special needs
Change in custody of children
Child leaving home
Childhood sexual trauma
Domestic violence
Divorce of parents
Death of partner
Death of close family member
Suicide of loved one
Caring for sick family member
Caring for aging parent

IDENTITY
Change in living situation
Moving between countries
Change in sexual practices
Change in gender identity
Major change in finances
Attempted suicide
Homelessness
Public humiliation
Victim of crime

BELIEFS
Beginning/ending school
Adult education
Political/social awakening
Personal calling
Change in religious observance
Change in religion/spirituality
Extended personal travel
Change in community service habits
Collective event (war, storm, protest)

WORK
Change in work responsibility
Changing jobs
Losing/quitting job
Changing careers
Starting company/nonprofit
Sexual harassment/discrimination
Public recognition (TED talk, award)
Retirement

BODY
Accident/personal injury
Chronic illness
Mental illness
Personal addiction
Recovery from addiction
Weight issues
Changing personal health habits

Note. "Deck of Disruptors" from LIFE IS IN THE TRANSITIONS: MASTERING CHANGE AT ANY AGE by Bruce Feiler, copyright © 2020 by Bruce Feiler. Used by permission of Penguin Press, an imprint of Penguin Publishing Group, a division of Penguin Random House LLC. All rights reserved.

Disruptors are events or experiences that cause a change in a person's daily life; they cause individuals to reprioritize areas of their life. Although the term *disruptor* may sound adverse, many events or experiences are positive. Life is full of positive and negative disruptors. As we as individuals grow and evolve, reassessing our lives, passions, and purpose is unavoidable.

A Collective Lifequake

Before 2020, many people had reassessed their work lives, but when the world, collectively, experienced a staggering series of pandemic-related disruptions, the result was a large-scale simultaneous reevaluation of careers, purpose, and meaning by professionals in all fields. A buildup of disruptors can create what Feiler (2020) termed a *lifequake*—"a forceful burst of change in one's life that leads to a period of upheaval, transition, and renewal" (p. 79).

HESA felt this quake acutely: The challenges of low salaries, long hours, and little appreciation and respect for the work, paired with the collective reckoning brought on by the COVID-19 pandemic, led to many HESA staff quitting or reevaluating their purpose. The lifequake initiated many periods of self-reflection and forced HESA professionals to ask, "What is it that I am passionate about? How does that align with my current life and career?" Ultimately, many professionals left the field. For many organizations, the turnover was unprecedented. No generation of student affairs leaders has faced more challenges in retaining and hiring staff as this one.

This pandemic (or postpandemic) moment feels overwhelming because of the sheer numbers of individuals who experienced a lifequake. However, as the world becomes increasingly complex, individuals will likely experience three to five lifequakes in their lifetime (Feiler, 2020). Lives play out differently, of course, and a lifequake can happen at any point, but nearly half of adult lives are spent in this type of transition. With this type of experience becoming commonplace, those who can best handle them will likely ultimately experience more life satisfaction.

Challenging a Career That Tracks Up and to the Right

For decades, most of us have been taught that our lives are linear; we know when to expect a midlife crisis or stages of maturation. We have been conditioned to think success always means that our career trajectory should appear up and to the right if it was charted, emphasizing growth in areas like prestige, titles, salaries, and responsibilities. However, we also know that change is constant and understand that the world is not linear. And we now have data that tell us that life disruptions will be something we navigate for roughly half our adult lives (Fieler, 2020). Careers can ebb and flow; the idea of a career that moves up and to the right until retirement isn't likely—nor should it be the model we use to define a successful career.

Over time, what brings a person meaning and purpose can change. Many of us in HESA jobs ask our students these questions and offer their answers as a map to their future. But rarely are we asking it of ourselves once we've set out on a path. Reevaluating that path should be a regular part of professional development and growth. It seems now more than ever, people are searching for meaning and prioritizing it as a necessary component of their work. It has been almost 80 years since Viktor Frankl (1946) published *Man's Search for Meaning*, which has sold more than 12 million copies. Frankl launched a wave of books on meaning and purpose in all disciplines. Human beings search for purpose, and it is a source of satisfaction when we find it.

All of us should take the time to reflect on the meaning of our lives, the way we spend our days, with whom we are spending them, and what we are working to create. HESA careers are diverse and purposeful, and there are many more opportunities for an impactful role than we may have previously been taught. There are opportunities for our skill sets and experience around the globe, within consulting firms, in K–12 schools, as faculty members, and at higher education institutions outside of the roles of student affairs and the presidency.

Navigating careers in HESA becomes more complex with each passing year. Finding moments to reflect and reevaluate is essential. And understanding what options you have for a next act can provide a renewed sense of energy and purpose. The two of us find continued satisfaction and purpose in our careers by embracing our resilience, empowerment, and advocacy. This book testifies to how high-performing professionals can navigate their careers—and flourish.

References

Feiler, B. (2020). *Life is in the transitions: Mastering change at any age*. Penguin Press.
Frankl, V. E. (2006). *Man's search for meaning*. Beacon Press. (Original work published 1946)
NASPA–Student Affairs Administrators in Higher Education. (2022). *Charting the future of student affairs*. https://5721802.fs1.hubspotusercontent-na1.net/hubfs/5721802/Download%20Files/The_Compass_Report_2022_Web.pdf

Changing Institution Type

Martino Harmon

With Jamie V. Sanchez

As I approach the twilight of my career, I increasingly reflect on my journey and how I got here. Although I have more mountains to climb and more lives to affect, I sometimes marvel at how fortunate I have been to reach this pinnacle given my background and strikingly unconventional career path. Over the past several decades, I have navigated significant changes in my trajectory between the private sector of sales and the immensely varied world of higher education as well as between institution types in higher education: 2-year community colleges and 4-year universities. My experiences have taught me many lessons about how to succeed in a nontraditional career path in higher education. In this chapter, I outline the nine most important lessons learned and discuss the context in which I learned them.

The Start of the Journey

Before all of this, I was a kid from Cleveland. As a solid B student who worked hard, I didn't believe that my grades would earn me a college acceptance, and even if they did, I did not honestly believe I would graduate. Despite a history of struggling on standardized tests, achievement tests, and even my high school entrance exam, I was admitted to Benedictine High School, a college preparatory high school, on probation. As I saw it, a probational student did not belong there—but the school had given me a chance.

Although my parents never graduated from high school, they always knew college was attainable for me. So they invested their hard-earned money to send me to private secondary schools and signed me up for several college tours before making their most important investment.

Amid the whirlwind of touring a dozen colleges within a few days, I fell in love with the University of Toledo (UToledo). The visit made it clear that it was the right college for me. Still, I never dreamed of earning my bachelor's, master's, and doctorate degrees there. I never dreamed I would have a fantastic career at UToledo, including becoming the first African American to lead the freshman admissions office. I never envisioned that I would eventually create an office focused on turning around low-persistence and graduation rates for African American students. I had no idea then that my bus visit would be so meaningful—that I would later use bus visits to recruit underrepresented students, many of whom looked like me. How could it be that, years later, I would welcome buses of students from Benedictine High School to UToledo and that those students would be proud that one of the men of Benedictine was the director of admissions?

My teenage self, who boarded those buses as a probational student, would have laughed at these ideas.

I entered UToledo as an education major, and today I am an educator with my organizational skills and love for helping others. Yet, when I was a young, impressionable first-year student concerned about passing the term, it took only one conversation with someone who told me I would never make any "good money" to rethink my major. Within a few weeks, I switched from education to business. I had leadership and organizational skills, and my parents were entrepreneurs. I decided to become a wealthy CEO if I made it into year 2 or even graduation. In June 1987, I became a first-generation college graduate, prepared for a successful career in corporate sales.

After a few years of bouncing among Fortune 500 companies—selling postage meters, Nabisco cookies, and paint—I realized that working in sales was not my passion. Exceeding sales goals offered me only monetary gain, and that simply did not motivate me. I was not bad at the work, but it was not in my heart. I began to consider returning to college. Unfortunately, no research was available from the UToledo career office about careers in higher education. The online search tools we take for granted today, like Handshake (https://joinhandshake.com) or the Pew Research Center (https://www.pewresearch.org), were not available. In fact, the web itself didn't even exist yet.

In 1989, I applied for entry-level admissions and alumni association positions, thinking I was a shoo-in. After all, I was Mr. University of Toledo. I had graduated only a few years prior as an accomplished campus leader, and I was young, talented, and ready to return. Although I was a finalist in both searches, I was not selected. Devastated, I focused on a successful sales career, even if my heart was not in it. I finally settled into a job with Michelin Tire Company in the New Jersey and Philadelphia area.

Several years into this role came a seminal moment that would forever alter my career trajectory. This was the early 1990s, and I spent Saturday mornings running an enrichment program for Black male youth. It was a volunteer program created by my fraternity, Alpha Phi Alpha. A fellow fraternity member and retired teacher named Bill Tyler pulled me aside one morning after watching me facilitate the weekly workshops. Bill asked a simple question: "What do you do for a living?" I responded proudly that I was a Michelin sales rep. With dismay, he said, "It looks like you missed your calling. I watch you every Saturday with these young men. You inspire them, and you are excited to inspire them. This is your calling. You missed your calling—you should be doing this every day."

The light bulb went on. Why had I changed my major? I was an educator, and it was apparent. I found joy in preparing for the Saturday program. I found purpose in helping younger generations. I became more determined than ever from that point forward to find a pathway to education. No matter what it took, I would need to make the change. By then, I had spent nearly 9 years in sales, so the time to pivot was now.

Lesson: *Follow your passion, not a title or a salary.*

Pivoting With Purpose: Back to UToledo

In 1996, I began to look for opportunities to return to UToledo, where several administrators still knew me. I was optimistic that I could capitalize on my reputation as a student leader to get my foot in the door. Yet my lack of master's degree seemed to limit my choices to entry-level positions in admissions, financial aid, or alumni affairs. Those options seemed plausible; I simply needed to get into the field.

Eventually, I was able to leverage a relationship with a former mentor. Joyce Mathis, a manager in career services, heard that I was looking to return and contacted me about a grant-funded position. It was guaranteed for only about 4 months, until the grant ended, but the university needed to fill the vacated position quickly. The interview process went well, and just like that, I was back home. My higher education career began as a job location and development coordinator, working to build the base of off-campus jobs for students. I took a 39% pay cut from what I was making in sales, but I was excited and happy to have a job where I felt a sense of purpose every day. After the grant-funded position ended, I landed a permanent one in admissions, taking the first real steps on my higher education career path.

I was excited to work in admissions because I could build on my sales experience. During my 9 years in sales, I sharpened my communication and presentation skills. I knew how to travel and was not intimidated by a quantitative goal–driven position. I was nonetheless disappointed that I was making far less than my salary in sales, but those days were over, and I was starting from an entry-level position. Finally, I had a job that enabled me to find passion and purpose. I introduced students to higher education while encouraging them to attend a university I loved. It was a lot easier than selling truck tires and travel guides. I provided many students access to a bright future through higher education. Also, my skills were far more advanced than those of many of my colleagues, who had only just completed their degrees, so I knew growth opportunities were possible.

I never lost sight of the need for a master's degree. If I wanted to apply for higher positions, especially roles that included supervision, I would need an additional degree. I made that assessment based on my review of job postings. Today, the United States Bureau of Labor Statistics projects "a 22% growth in jobs that require postgraduate training, [and] pursuing a master's degree in higher education and student services gives you solid career options" (Green, n.d., para. 1). Based on what I knew in 1996, I quickly enrolled in a student development theory class, thinking I would apply for the master's in the student affairs program. However, I had been out of college for 9 years, and I was not comfortable with the degree of scholarly writing required in that program. Still, I had my sights set on student affairs.

UToledo's College of Education had a program called Human Resource Development; it was focused on training and development, but the degree was in educational technology. The program fit my business background, and I was confident that this degree could help me get a job in student affairs. However, it was also clear that if I wanted to work my way into student affairs, I would need to do the extra things to gain the same experiences as other students in the program with assistantships.

As an admissions recruiter, I regularly added a star to the contact cards that prospective students filled out during my visits or college fairs if they showed particular interest, reminding me to follow-up with phone calls or emails to thank them. By the end of the travel season, I typically had around 100 unique contact cards. I tracked those students so I could follow their activity through the admissions process to see if they visited campus or applied. For those who registered for classes, which might total 30 to 50 students per year, I would meet with them during the fall welcome program or at least once per semester.

My admissions colleagues thought it was bizarre that these students would stop in the office to visit me. I would even take some of them to lunch. Some staff would ask me why I spent extra time meeting with students after they had enrolled. My response was simple: I had recruited them and cared about their success. Later, I would understand that I was already working on retention and student success.

I involved myself in student affairs work in my spare time, although I was not officially in student affairs. I was advising student organizations and developing a yearly connection with student government leaders. I often volunteered to assist at events, especially those supporting underrepresented students. It was not about finding a new career track; rather, I felt I had a responsibility to help students succeed, especially those who looked like me. I remembered people in my life who went the extra mile to show care and concern for me.

I actively sought opportunities to serve as a leader on campus projects, committees, and statewide and national enrollment organizations. I also assumed progressive leadership roles in admissions—first as the campus visit coordinator, a retention opportunity for which career services recruited me to assume a higher position, and then as the associate director of multicultural recruitment, a role that allowed me to develop an aggressive strategy to increase the enrollment of Latinx/a/o and African American students.

The role I did not pursue—but that unexpectedly catapulted me to a supervisory position—was associate director of admissions. The associate director had abruptly left for a leadership position at a community college (fatefully, I would eventually take a job in the same community college). Suddenly, a group of young admissions professionals needed a supervisor.

This was the single most crucial leadership moment of my career at that point. I stepped up on faith and voluntarily agreed to serve as acting associate director—without additional pay. The move would give me valuable experience in supervision. However, I had no idea how long this would last, and it was risky because if it went on too long, would I be able to return to my multicultural recruitment position? Moreover, I was still doing both jobs. What if I failed at them? I had leadership experience but no formal supervisory experience. Universities rarely offered supervisor training, and we were at the start of fall recruitment season, so there was no time to train.

But it was simply the right thing to do. I had great confidence in my leadership ability. Even if UToledo did not eventually do right by me—formalize my role with a commensurate title and pay—I could use this experience to find a job elsewhere. After several months, I was promoted to permanent associate director without a search. This step provided a pathway to becoming a director at UToledo or elsewhere. Another risk had paid off.

It was vital to extend my leadership skills outside the university. I assumed leadership positions with the Ohio Association of College Admissions Counselors (OACAC). I served on committees and eventually chaired an OACAC diversity, equity, and inclusion (DEI)–focused conference. I was asked to serve on the ACT (American College Testing) Ohio Council, eventually becoming the chair. My leadership role with Ohio ACT led to my appointment to the College Board's Regional Council.

In most cases, leaders in the organization recommended me or encouraged me to pursue these roles. Whether a position came about through a voting process or an ascension, I attained it only after someone believed in and encouraged me. All these progressive efforts working in key professional development organizations continued to strengthen my leadership skills.

In addition to professional development organizations, I served on many university committees, which required significant extra work outside my day job and sometimes took a personal toll. I was determined to lead and make a difference, but I often wondered if it was worth it. Meanwhile, I was cementing my reputation as a critical contributor who performed high-quality work. By 2000, 4 years after returning to my alma mater, I had gone from a temporary position in career services to an entry-level job there to the associate director of admissions.

Another significant change was coming that would affect my career trajectory. The university was rocked by a failed presidency that ended only 17 months after it started. Before President Vik Kapoor was fired, he appointed someone with no relevant experience to serve as admissions director. Because of my leadership experience, everyone saw me as the de facto director. In the aftermath of the shakeup, a former dean of enrollment, the legendary Dick Eastop, came out of retirement to lead all the enrollment departments. One of his first orders of business was assessing admissions leadership, which culminated in my appointment to the director position.

Ironically, Dick was the person who did not hire me back in 1989. But the risk and sacrifice had paid off: I was now the first African American director of first-year admissions in the university's history. And Dick Eastop would be my mentor for many years.

Lesson: *Be willing to take calculated risks, even when the path ahead is murky.*

The 4 years I spent as director were a period of profound professional growth. I learned how to provide visionary leadership for a department of 16 staff. The responsibility of bringing in the first-year class was intense and required me to support and hold a team of mostly young professionals accountable. The staff needed guidance and mentorship, and it took a strategic approach to help them grow. Although the pressure was immense, I was up for the challenge. Meanwhile, as the representative of my department, I used my expansive knowledge of the university, derived from years of involvement outside of my department, to lead crucial campus committees. I was acquiring UToledo experience and learning how the academy is run—and that combination would be necessary for future roles.

Becoming a dean or vice president of enrollment would have been an expected next step in my career track. I could have headed toward becoming a vice president or provost for student success, a position that public institutions were starting to create to increase retention and graduation rates. Then I had another pivotal conversation. Paula Compton, a well-known admissions director who had formerly led the Ohio State University admissions office, was serving in a senior leadership role in enrollment management at UToledo. She told me, "You are going to become a great vice president for enrollment management."

I thanked Paula and respectfully replied, "I don't think so. I want to be a vice president for enrollment who is also responsible for student affairs." She always had confidence in me, so her response was clear: "Martino, if anyone can do it, you can." I had no idea that a little more than a decade later, I would assume the position I had been dreaming of for years.

No Boundaries: From Admissions to Student Success at UToledo

My conversation with Paula was a moment of enlightenment that set me on a path of progressive experiences, some planned and some not. Because of my involvement and interest in student success, I developed a heightened awareness and understanding of persistence issues, particularly those affecting African American students' success at UToledo and similar public institutions.

I was still maintaining contact with students I had recruited. In admissions, we devoted time and resources to developing strategies to increase African American and Latinx/a/o enrollment. I was aware of the anecdotes about students flunking out, experiencing difficulties adjusting, or dropping out for financial reasons. I also started actively asking students why they did not return for their second year. I often heard that an alarming number of them returned to the cities where we had recruited them. They returned to Cleveland, Akron, Cincinnati, Columbus, and other urban areas where we had coordinated bus trips to bring them to campus visits. It was not just troubling but a tragedy. I took it as a failure—as if I had sold them a bill of goods. I had to do something to stop this disturbing trend.

African American student leaders also believed something had to be done to stop this drift. A coalition of these student leaders was at the forefront of bringing this issue to the attention of the university administration. Ultimately, senior university leadership invited faculty and staff members to present ideas for change. There was no promise that this effort would lead to funding, but it was an opportunity for me to bring forward recommendations to address this long-standing issue. In fact, as a student in the mid-1980s, I had worked with my fellow Alpha Phi Alpha members to create a mentorship program to keep new African American students in school. Here I was nearly 20 years later, trying to solve the same issue.

Shortly after presenting my ideas, I received a call to meet with Provost Alan Goodrich. He wanted me to partner with two faculty members—Angela Siner and Selina Griswold—to write a proposal as a white paper. We quickly worked together to write the African American Student Enrichment Initiative. The president and provost swiftly accepted the proposal with a funding commitment of $265,000. Even while writing the proposal, I had no idea who would lead this initiative. If asked, I knew I would consider it. After all, I believed no one was more passionate and committed than I was, but I was on a career track that did not include running a two-person office. I had a staff in admissions who counted on me. What if I had to apply for this role and someone else were hired?

In the end, Provost Goodrich asked me to serve as the director of this new office. It would be a lateral move, which some considered a downgrade because I would go from being a high-profile director supervising a staff of 16 to having a small office with a shrunken budget and a team of two—including me. I took a few days to consider this opportunity carefully. Several supportive mentors urged me to consider the potential ramifications of stepping off my career track. Others were more direct and warned me about being pigeonholed into a multicultural office that focused primarily on one race of students. I thought about how this office would help students like me. What was the possible impact on a first-generation student—on an African American student who lacked confidence? Suddenly, it was not a risk. It was a calling. It was a chance to make a significant difference and leave a legacy. I did not know what my next step would be, but I knew at that place and at that time, students needed me. It would end up being the best career decision I ever made.

The nearly 3 years I led the African American Student Enrichment Initiatives Office (AASEIO) brought me joy. Undoubtedly, it was the most impactful and rewarding position I held in my higher education career. The decision to make this monumental pivot was challenging, but it followed a consistent theme: I made a thoughtful, intentional choice to follow my passion.

Lesson: *Step up when your name is called to be a change agent.*

Community Colleges: A New Pathway to Growth

As I continued to grow AASEIO, this new and exciting program, I could not help thinking about the next step in my career. I had no regrets, but I never envisioned I would run a small office for the rest of my working life. I was about halfway through the coursework in my doctoral program. It would take only 3 to 4 years to put the AASEIO on firm ground so someone could succeed me, and I was preparing the young program coordinator in the office to be that person.

I had opportunities to grow at UToledo during this period. After the first successful year, the AASEIO moved from academic affairs to student affairs. I was excited because I was now a part of student affairs in a formal way. It differed from the results-focused world of enrollment management and the resource-rich world of academic affairs, where leaders could function independently as long as concrete assessment measures were in place to demonstrate impact. Yet I increasingly felt as if the senior leadership in student affairs and I did not see eye to eye. At times I felt like an odd duck who was respected but perhaps seen as a threat because of my strong institutional connections. I was popular with students. Many student leaders knew me. At times, colleagues acted as if it was my fault when the students were at odds with the administration. In reality, I was a buffer.

I was encouraged to apply to be the director of the Office of Multicultural Student Success (OMSS), which would have been a growth opportunity because OMSS had more staff than AASEIO. It also was a chance to align the two departments, which senior leadership wanted. But I was not selected, and I was devastated. Shortly after, I was asked to serve as co-interim associate dean of students while the dean of students ran housing. It felt like a recognition of my leadership role in the division and an opportunity to build trust. I knew it was a temporary arrangement, but I hoped to continue in that role. When only my colleague was invited to remain in the position, it was another gut punch.

Lesson: *Pay attention to signs that there is an opportunity to pivot.*

I started to consider taking my talents to a community college. I knew community colleges focused on access and student success, two objectives that were also passions of mine, and I had seen how excited my mother had been to become a college student when she finished her GED later in life. She enrolled in Cuyahoga Community College in Cleveland. If community college could be that influential to her at that stage in her life, then perhaps it could be a new venue where I could have a positive impact.

After reviewing various job postings at community colleges, I realized I could become a dean of students before completing my terminal degree. It was an opportunity to advance my career in a critical leadership role while continuing my progress toward a doctoral degree at UToledo. I applied for the dean of admissions, retention, and student success position at Washtenaw Community College (WCC). The interview process was rapid, and before I knew it I was a dean—a dean! The decision to leave UToledo was painful. I used the title to justify the move. As someone wrote in a farewell card, it was the end of an era. I was not just leaving a job; an important chapter in my professional life was closing.

The move to WCC was not successful. Truthfully, I made a critical error by not closely researching the institution. Had I done so, I would have discovered my skills were not a match for WCC and what they wanted at that time. It was a large institution with a strong enrollment, but they were years behind current practices in recruitment and retention. Enamored with the dean title, I ignored the characteristics of the college and my lack of fit. It was a lesson for future searches—a career mulligan, to use a golfing term.

Once it was clear that WCC was not right for me, I negotiated a paid leave that gave me time to job search and reflect. I knew to be more cautious about future opportunities to ensure a better fit. I learned that while employers were interviewing me, I should be interviewing the institution and the supervisor. In future interviews, I was transparent that I had not analyzed fit for the WCC job—and that it was essential for me to do so moving forward.

Lesson: A career mulligan is a crucial opportunity to reflect and humbly own what you could have done differently.

A Fresh State in a New Sector: 2-Year Colleges

Still, I wanted to continue my commitment to community colleges. After reflection, I became the dean of student development at Rhodes State College, a small 2-year college in Lima, Ohio. This time, I researched and used this lateral move to learn what it would take to be a successful dean.

The Rhodes position was another growth opportunity where I learned how to oversee some essential functions that would be critical for my career advancement. I managed student conduct for the first time. I was the only conduct officer at the college, which enrolled 4,300 students, and oversaw multiple offices whose directors reported to me. Supervising directors was very different from managing staff: I could not get in the weeds. I developed a much-needed counseling office and supervised directors from departments with which I was previously unfamiliar, such as academic advising and learning support. I was also responsible for familiar departments like career services and student activities.

More important, this position allowed me to take the required step back to learn the culture of an unfamiliar institution. I needed to learn and lead while fitting into my new environment. But the daily 186-mile round-trip commute between Toledo and Lima for nearly 4 years burned me—and the engine of my Nissan Altima—out. It was time to pursue an opportunity at a larger community college that paid better.

Lesson: *Be willing to gain experiences outside of your immediate expertise.*

In May 2012, I became the executive director of student success at Cincinnati State Community and Technical College (CSCTC). It was similar to my role of building a student success initiative at UToledo. At CSCTC, I was charged with assessing and developing a major student success initiative for the entire college, which enrolled more than 10,000 students. The position reported directly to President O'dell Owens, the first president to whom I ever directly reported, and he was an African American male—another first for me. I thought reporting to a president would be a valuable experience for becoming a vice president one day. I looked at this as a 3-year opportunity to create meaningful change. It was funded on soft money because President Owens wanted to see what progress could be made in 3 years before committing to a permanent position. I was completing the third chapter of my dissertation, so I viewed this job as a transitional move.

About a year later, I received a phone call that brought an unexpected opportunity. A prominent higher education search firm contacted me about an associate vice president position at Iowa State University. My first uninformed thought was *Why would I want to work and live in Iowa?* I was convinced that the state was no place for a person of color, although I knew nothing about it. Once I received information about the position, I started to weigh the potential advantages and disadvantages. If I believed I would want to return to a 4-year university, Iowa State was not a bad option. It was a comprehensive university with a reputable student affairs division. Several distinguished faculty in student affairs taught at Iowa State, including Nancy Evans, who co-authored the influential book *Student Development in College* (Evans et al., 1998). Tom Hill, the senior vice president for student affairs, was an African American who had been in the role for 13 years. If he could stay at Iowa State for 13 years, I could work as his associate vice president. Perhaps he could mentor me.

In crept the doubts. The WCC experience had scarred me. I had been away from 4-year institutions for 6 years; perhaps I was no longer a competitive candidate. Also, I had been in student affairs only briefly at UToledo. But the search firm had called *me*; I did not call them. I had nothing to lose by applying. If I did not get the job, I would continue creating systemic change at CSCTC while completing my dissertation and earning my doctorate. Then I would move on as initially planned.

In April 2013, Tom offered me the position. The interview process showed me that my unique background was an excellent fit for the job. A large portion of its duties was providing oversight to the enrollment units: admissions and financial aid. I discovered that 23% of Iowa State students at the time transferred from 2-year colleges (Iowa State University, 2013). Moreover, the position collaborated closely with the associate provost, who was leading student success initiatives.

Lesson: *Never discount having a variety of unique skills and experiences.*

Onward to Iowa State: Choosing Adventure in the Heartland

The opportunity to lead as associate vice president at Iowa State University was possible only with Tom Hill's mentorship. During the interview process he provided clear signals that I was a strong candidate and that, if I was hired, he would invest in me; indirectly, he was saying he was looking for his successor and would prepare me for that role. He crafted the job description to include high-level strategic oversight of the division budget and human resources. After he hired me, he assigned me to fix core deficiencies in a few departments.

Every day, I felt like he was preparing me for a vice president role, and he made it increasingly apparent as time went on. He eventually told me, "I can't guarantee that you will be the senior vice president when I retire because that is the president's call, but I can assure you that you will be ready to be a vice president, here or somewhere else."

It was April when I accepted the offer. I defended my proposal in March, so I had two chapters of my dissertation to go. I was close to a monumental accomplishment. Before I made the final decision, I considered how a new job, hours away from UToledo, would affect my ability to finish my degree. Tom asked me when I thought I would finish. I told him I hoped to finish in July but was unsure whether my dissertation chair would remain engaged over the summer.

It was clear Tom was fully invested in my success because he wanted me to start the job only after I successfully defended my dissertation. I was stunned but worried that my defense might not occur soon enough. "Don't worry—the job is yours," he reassured me. "I just need you to finish because once you start working this job, you will never finish." His motivation was twofold: He wanted me to focus on the job once I started, and he knew I could not be a vice president without a terminal degree.

I resigned from the job at CSCTC in June and became a full-time doctoral student. I went without a paycheck until my dissertation defense that September. Then, three days after I became Dr. Harmon, I drove 10 hours through the night to Ames, Iowa. By 8:00 a.m., I was at my desk.

Tom was delivering on his plan. He had positioned me as his number two by allowing me to lead key initiatives. In addition to campus leadership, he let me serve in leadership roles with national organizations such as the University Innovation Alliance, a consortium of 11 large public institutions, including Iowa State. In addition, I provided leadership with professional development organizations such as NASPA–Student Affairs Administrators in Higher Education and the Association of Public and Land-Grant Universities. In my earlier involvement with enrollment management organizations, I gained experience and national exposure. Because my portfolio and responsibilities were so diverse, there were no boundaries on the types of experiences I could pursue, all of which would allow me to attain a more diversified set of skills.

Tom gave me a few significant assignments that would define my leadership legacy at Iowa State, such as when he appointed me to lead the reformation of the Thielen Student Health Center (TSHC) after the director retired. I told him, "Doc, I have no experience in college health." He replied, "That is exactly why I am giving you this assignment, and I know you will do well as we transition." Tom also assigned me to be the hiring authority for the TSHC director position. Within a few years, I became known for my work addressing student health and well-being, which, ironically, was one of the areas where I had no prior experience. Tom, an astute leader, knew how to prepare me by giving me experiences that would make me more effective.

Rising Into Senior Leadership as an Iowa State Cyclone

In December 2015, Tom announced that he was stepping back from the senior vice president role to serve in a transitional position working directly with the president. I felt ready to apply for his position. I knew the division and its staff and believed the directors had confidence in me. This was a high-profile vice presidency, and the search would be competitive. Still, I knew I brought a diverse set of skills to my current role; in the more than 2 years in it, I had developed additional skills and experiences that would help me provide effective leadership.

During the search, I promoted my experience and knowledge of the division but clarified that I would bring new ideas. Everyone knew I had a different style than my mentor Tom Hill, and people were ready for a new direction. It was challenging to balance honoring a legend while at the same time promoting the opportunity for change. However, I felt comfortable after a conversation with him that I will never forget. He said, "Martino, you are far more prepared for this role than when I was appointed 16 years ago." Hearing him say that gave me a burst of confidence, and he gave me the license to feel comfortable saying I would be a new and different leader.

After nearly 3 days of interviewing, I was named the fourth vice president of student affairs at Iowa State University. I immediately reflected on my conversation with Paula Compton 13 years earlier, when I told her I wanted to be a vice president for student affairs with enrollment management in my portfolio. I had finally achieved that goal.

Lesson: Major career goals are achieved through countless decisions that either bring you closer to your destination or push you further away. Choose what brings you closer to that core goal or at least does not distance you more from it.

A recurring theme in my career story is how instrumental mentors were in helping me find ways to move toward my goals. Long before Tom Hill, there was Lancelot C.A. Thompson, vice president for student affairs at UToledo. As UToledo's first African American vice president and its first African American vice president for student affairs, he was a strong leader and a caring administrator who took the time to meet with students. He provided mentorship from my undergraduate days throughout my entire career, including motivating me to finish my dissertation. When I was appointed to the vice presidency, I called him, and both of us cried.

My mentor Dick Eastop also guided me through many career decisions. He gave me a chance by appointing me as the first African American director of first-year admissions. I never met a leader who cared more about his staff. People would run through a wall for him. If he was successful, you would be successful. I modeled my supervision and leadership style after him.

I was also mentored by Melvin C. Terrell, director of minority affairs and later vice president of student affairs at Northeastern Illinois University in Chicago, whom I first met when I was a student at UToledo. From my student employee career to my vice presidency at the University of Michigan, Terrell provided me with guidance and mentorship. Each of these leaders and mentors—and too many others to name here—shaped my experiences and supported me throughout my journey.

Lesson: *Develop a core group of trusted mentors, even if they might tell you things you don't want—but need—to hear.*

During my time at Iowa State, I used my unique experiences to reform and re-create the array of student mental health services and fortify the institution's DEI efforts. Simultaneously, I gained extensive experience managing various social justice issues brought forward by student activists, an experience that would prove valuable in future roles.

Although I had not publicly stated my intentions, I planned to remain at Iowa State for 8 to 10 years. I was generally happy, and I was becoming more proficient at running the division. But certain events began to set the stage for reevaluating my plans, starting when President Steven Leath abruptly resigned. After a period with Ben Allen, a great interim president, I was excited at the appointment of the new president, Wendy Wintersteen. She was a long-standing dean at Iowa State with whom I had occasional opportunities for collaboration. As president, she trusted and appreciated my leadership and relied on my expertise about student issues. Then, several months into her term, she made a shocking decision. She moved the key enrollment units of admissions, financial aid, and registrar to academic affairs, where they would report to the provost. The decision was made unilaterally, and I had no opportunity to make a case for why it was better for students and the institution that those departments remain in student affairs.

I did not consider this a move to push me out, and President Wintersteen made that very clear in a public way. However, losing three units and their staff made my portfolio look like that of many of my vice president peers at major public institutions. I had turned down numerous opportunities to apply for positions at larger institutions and similar universities in more desirable locations because I was committed to putting in more years at Iowa State. I knew my portfolio with enrollment departments was more extensive and diverse than traditional student affairs portfolios. I have a strong background in enrollment management, and my career goal was to use my unique background to have a broader impact on the entire student experience. In one fell swoop, those opportunities I previously declined were worth considering. When I was contacted about the vice president position at the University of Michigan (U-M), I thought, *Why not?* U-M was an extraordinary institution and only 45 minutes from Toledo.

A New Frontier as a Michigan Wolverine

By late February 2020, I was concluding my final interview with U-M President Mark Schlissel. I was optimistic because he made a soft offer, and only an extensive background check remained. I left campus thinking how amazing it would be—a first-generation college graduate who had doubted he would make it to his second year of college would likely become a vice president at the University of Michigan, one of the most prestigious public universities in the nation!

I was not concerned that the position did not include enrollment management because at U-M the division of student life alone was larger in budget and staff than student affairs at Iowa State. However, this was a new frontier—a new challenge. I was following another legend in E. Royster Harper, the recently retired vice president.

I will never forget President Schlissel's last words that February: "If everything works out, I will bring you back for the board of regents meeting next month. We will have a big reception where you will meet people from across campus." Little did we know COVID-19 would change the world only a few weeks later. The next thing I knew, I was on a video call informing my leadership team at Iowa State that I was leaving. They were stunned and confused; no one knew how to react on little video screens. I then began meeting my new leadership team members in a virtual format. It was a sad and bizarre way to leave a place I loved and people I cared for deeply.

Once the shock wore off, Iowa State held a car parade for me led by President Wintersteen. It was not how I envisioned nor planned to leave for the biggest job of my professional career, but the pandemic left few options.

Today I am in my late 50s, in what I consider the twilight of my career. My journey has been filled with many unexpected but amazing accomplishments. For the first couple of years at U-M, I was focused on the new job and trying to lead at an unfamiliar university during a global pandemic. I had to focus on learning a division and an institution—and moving the division forward—while in constant crisis management mode. Although I was leading a strong division, I still needed to think about how to lead systemic change designed to improve the impact of our work.

The pandemic has faded, and the work has primarily returned to the traditional in-person student experience. While I remain entirely focused on the task at hand, I have a 5-year contract and 10 to 12 good years left before retirement. I have to think about what I still want to accomplish.

The Cleveland Kid's Next Move

My career pathway is murky for the first time since I entered higher education. It still seems incredible to think that this kid from Cleveland would one day say, "I am a Wolverine now! Go Blue!" But have I reached my ceiling? Should I plan to retire at U-M? Do I want to pursue a presidency? I was fortunate to be selected to participate in the Association of Governing Board's Executive Leadership Institute. Despite the pandemic's disruptions, the experience was wonderfully informative, but it did not clarify my career track. Instead, it validated that I could become a president, but do I want to?

The choice to apply for a presidency depends on timing, location, institutional size, mission, and myriad other factors. I could finish my career in a higher education policy organization. Indeed, my diversity of experiences will be valuable in any role I pursue, including remaining at U-M until retirement. Though the road is not clear, it is evident that I need to let my path evolve as I have always done and remember everything I have learned along the way:

- Follow your passion, not a title or a salary.
- Be willing to take calculated risks, even when the path ahead is murky.
- Step up when your name is called to be a change agent.
- Pay attention to signs that there is an opportunity to pivot.
- A career mulligan is a crucial opportunity to reflect and humbly own what you could have done differently.
- Be willing to gain experiences outside of your immediate expertise.
- Never discount having a variety of unique skills and experiences.
- Major career goals are achieved through countless decisions that either bring you closer to your destination or push you further away. Choose what brings you closer to that core goal or at least does not distance you more from it.
- Develop a core group of trusted mentors, even if they might tell you things you don't want—but need—to hear.

These nine guideposts can provide clarity for those pursuing an unconventional career path. My unusual career path has taken me to new heights I would have never envisioned. I could have continued on an enrollment management track—but if I had, I never would have affected the many students who benefited from engagement with the African American Student Enrichment Initiatives Office. I would not have learned much about effective retention and student success strategies. If I never took the major risk of leaving U Toledo to pursue positions at 2-year colleges, I would not have quickly gained experiences in academic advising, learning support, and student conduct or developed a counseling program. These moments were vital in developing a comprehensive student success initiative at CSCTC. My experience developing student success initiatives made me more marketable when I applied for the associate vice president position at Iowa State. And all my accomplishments there positioned me for leadership at the University of Michigan.

Each unconventional but intentional move weaves a fascinating tapestry. Yet, no matter how my story ends or where my career path takes me, I am still a kid from Cleveland—with no regrets.

References

Green, A. (n.d.). *What can I do with a master's degree in higher education & student services?* CHRON. https://work.chron.com/can-masters-degree-higher-education-student-services-27442.html

Evans, N. J., Forney, D. S., & Guido-DiBrito, F. (1998). *Student development in college: Theory, research, and Practice.* Jossey-Bass.

Iowa State University. (2013). *Fact book 2012–2013.* Office of Institutional Research. https://www.ir.iastate.edu/sites/default/files/factbook/Archive/FB2013ALL.pdf

Shifting Roles Within the Same Institution

Jeanna Mastrodicasa and Katie O'Dair

As many student affairs professionals consider the next step in their career, the question that often comes up is *Should I stay or should I go?* This chapter highlights two long-term student affairs professionals who changed roles within the same institution, leaving the student affairs field to contribute in another way. The authors share their journeys in student affairs, describe what led them to consider other career fields, discuss what went into the decision to change roles, and outline some of the considerations for those thinking about making a change within their own organization. They identify key skills that student affairs professionals bring to their work that translate broadly to other areas.

This chapter is directed toward readers of all career levels—from early professionals to senior student affairs officers—who want to stay at their current institution while broadening the areas in which they can advance.

■ ■ ■

TO MOVE UP, MOVE OVER

Jeanna Mastrodicasa

A few times I considered national job searches to move to a new place, but I haven't found the right pull yet. My career has definitely not followed a typical student affairs professional path, but it all makes sense when I add up all my experiences.

My career certainly wasn't what I thought it would be. As a master's student in the mid-1990s at the University of Tennessee, Knoxville (UTK), I was pretty sure that I would eventually become a dean of students and then a vice president for student affairs, and my career would take me all over the nation to various universities. I was so excited that I had found this career path; I had just finished law school in 1995 and decided to stay enrolled in higher education to pursue this new direction that seemed to fit me better than the reality of post–*L.A. Law* legal work.

"One-institution wonders" was a common demeaning term for people who stayed at one institution. It implied that those professionals didn't have a good perspective or experience because of a lack of employment diversity. Good student affairs professionals moved around; they tried different areas of the country and myriad types of institutions, and they moved up directly within the division of student affairs. They found life partners who supported them and their work, and it would all work out to shuttle around to interesting places.

I am still employed at my first full-time institution of higher education, the University of Florida (UF) in Gainesville, after more than 26 years. I can always count on a good joke about my unwavering passion for the football team at the University of Georgia despite my working at the school's rival or about my four degrees from three large public, Southern, land-grant universities with great Southeastern Conference football. I also married later in life and now have two children in middle school as I enter the senior phase of my career.

I began in 1997 at UF, hired as a prelaw academic advisor in the college of liberal arts and sciences. As a practicum student, I had tried academic advising, volunteering my time and learning more about advising at UTK—and, of course, I had a law degree. In 1999, I moved to the dean of students' office at UF to become the director of orientation, applying my 2 years of advising experience to lead the broader annual summer program for more than 6,000 new freshmen. I also became the first liaison to the LGBTQIA+ community at UF, introducing me to a new community and its unique advocacy and student success issues.

It was around this time that I sought out some new opportunities. I became involved in the community by joining a political organization and volunteering on local campaigns. I met new people who didn't work at the university, and I worked to elect good people to local office. I also started pursuing a doctorate in 1999, taking classes in the evenings as I worked full time. I got involved with the state and regional levels of NASPA–Student Affairs Administrators in Higher Education in the beginning of my time at UF as well.

In 2000, I was recruited to become UF's associate director of the honors program, which was led by the associate provost of undergraduate education. I not only served as an academic advisor but also led several campuswide programs, such as undergraduate research and prestigious scholarship advising, and started a weekly email newsletter for students (*The Gator Times*), which has existed in some format for nearly 20 years.

I joined some community advisory boards during these years and ran for local office in 2006, getting elected to the Gainesville City Commission for two 3-year terms. In 2007, I became the assistant vice president for student affairs, and I held two jobs for 6 years: one at UF and one at the City of Gainesville. During this busy era, I also got married (2008) and had twins (2010). For my ability to prioritize family and life in my work, I credit former UF Vice Presidents for Student Affairs Patricia Telles-Irvin and Dave Kratzer as my role models. My job at this time included student affairs assessment, the division's $95 million budget, student government's $20 million budget, information technology, annual reporting, student legal services, and off-campus life.

It was a wild ride from 2006 to 2012, when I was in public office and working in student affairs at UF. In 2008, the city passed a local ordinance adding gender identity to its nondiscrimination clause, and a year later on my reelection ballot there was a referendum to remove both sexual orientation and gender identity from the nondiscrimination policy. I was reelected to my seat by 58% of the vote, beating four men who ran against LGBTQIA+ rights—and the nondiscrimination clause was retained. It bears noting that the current day rhetoric about LGBTQIA+ individuals is frighteningly similar to that during the 2009 campaign.

Some successes from that two-job era include focusing on student and nightlife safety in Gainesville; changing some city ordinances to incentivize bars to be better stewards of safety and to follow laws; updating campus policies and processes to include stronger medical amnesty for individuals and student organizations; supporting off-campus students with information about parties, code enforcement, and best practices; talking about town–gown collaborations and making them happen; and beginning structured assessment activities and communications in student affairs. I have good memories from that time when I collaborated with different people and departments.

A campus service activity that I began in 2016 was to try to surprise a friend who was earning her PhD at UF by reading her name at our commencement ceremony. I was successful, but I ended up being called in to work more ceremonies, and now it is a primary service activity where I stand in a marshal's robe and read a student's name every 4 seconds as graduates cross the stage in a giant arena with cheering supporters. It is an entirely frightening and thrilling unpaid assignment that I really enjoy. It turns out that I have some skills here—maybe from foreign language study years ago or from 20 years of working with a diverse student body.

In 2015, I switched jobs again to do operations for UF's Institute of Food and Agricultural Sciences (UF/IFAS), where I now serve as the senior associate vice president of agriculture and natural resources. UF/IFAS is a large organization spread out across Florida, with employees in all 67 counties and 4 million square feet of space. A recent reorganization moved finances directly to the chief financial officer, and I now manage human resources for 3,800 full-time employees. I'm the chief operating officer, and I also work with facilities, IT, business operations, administrative needs, and many operational systems to support the work of our faculty and staff. I don't really work with students anymore, so it's a true delight when I can spend time with some. UF/IFAS is a giant organization with the original land-grant mission of teaching, research, and service through extension—and there is always something happening.

Upon reflection, I see some themes of my career that bring it all together to make sense. None of the jobs from one to the next seem to be in a clear line; they go back and forth between academic units and student affairs. But each job prepared me for the next; for those aspects that I didn't already know much about, I took the time to learn, and I continue to do so. Each career change switched up my day-to-day involvement with different people, and the inability to move up in that specific job was why I could move to a different unit. The following are some themes that I see from my experience.

Operations Experience

My operational experience is quite varied. I've managed large campuswide events, communications with parents and students, protests on campus, study abroad in the Yucatan, community service trips, and more. All have helped me figure out how to solve problems and develop plans, processes, and policies. We learn something every time we help make a process improvement or resolve a challenge. I am an ally for our student affairs division, which is not always afforded a seat at the table.

Understanding Campus

Through the years I have developed strong relationships with campus and community partners, and that is a benefit I bring to our team. Many processes at UF are neither simple nor clear, and often it takes a bit of effort to understand how to resolve something. Similarly, I feel the need to educate about the successes of my units (both current and former) throughout the organization as appropriate. I see the role of commencement as a crucial milestone with a lot of pomp and circumstance—and it fills the arena for each ceremony with family and friends with smiling faces.

Community

I derive a whole sense of grounding from my community connections, and I am lucky that I am in a college town that I enjoy. I read the local newspaper, follow the actions of our local governments, and occasionally speak up as a citizen. I serve on community boards and participate in local activities, and I like my college town's downtown. I have written about town–gown relations and continue to do my best to connect the various entities I can. Also, I like being out in the community and seeing its vibrancy in person. My spouse owns part of a small business in Gainesville and works with local government and developers. My fondness for the community adds a great deal of satisfaction to my life. I have known people who are always looking for greener grass in a new place, but I am not one of them.

Lifelong Learner

In everything I have done, I have needed to continue to learn. I earned a doctorate and even a nondegree graduate certificate while working full-time, giving me academic credentials. Serving in public office taught me about running a 2,000-person municipal government staff, including managing a $100 million budget during a recession; leading a city-owned utility company; and working with public services such as police, fire, public works, parks, and buses. I understand and am comfortable with how local and state government works. I knew nothing about Florida agriculture before starting at UF/IFAS, and now I can have general conversations about current topics.

Politics

As a former elected official with a public voting record, I can never escape those positions. However, I don't discuss my opinions and often find myself in quite different political circles than I did when I worked as a city commissioner. I just listen a lot, engage in conversation, and find that many wonderful people out there see the world differently. I work to find a common ground to keep it friendly. It usually works out.

My career plans from my graduate student days did not pan out at all the way I anticipated at the time. However, each new step provided me with an opportunity to develop new skills, build new relationships, and learn about how things work in the real world—all as a one-institution wonder.

WHEN OPPORTUNITIES ARISE: ADAPTING YOUR SKILLS

Katie O'Dair

Student affairs professionals who transition to a different area within their institution can benefit from both personal and professional growth. Yet planning for such a transition takes time and attention. It is often your actions *before* you consider a job change that can set you up for an internal transition.

I frequently receive requests from both young and seasoned professionals about career opportunities. Typically, these "coffee conversations" are with people interested in a change. I have made a significant job transition within my own institution, each time moving into a field where my skills and experience in student affairs provided a solid foundation from which I could enter a new and exciting area of higher education.

I have more than 30 years of student affairs experience—all in private higher education in New England. My long career has involved various roles of increasing responsibility at several institutions in the region.

After receiving my BA in communications from Miami University in Oxford, Ohio, I moved to Boston and worked as a publications assistant at the National Bureau of Economic Research in Cambridge. After a year I went to graduate school at Northeastern University, where I received my MEd in student personnel and counseling. My first professional position in student affairs was as a program coordinator in the office of student activities at Tufts University; after 2 years there, I was promoted to assistant director of the campus center. After 5 years at Tufts, I joined the student life team at the Massachusetts Institute of Technology as assistant dean for student life programs and, 4 years later, worked as assistant dean for residential life programs. I moved to Boston College to serve as the associate dean for graduate student life and after 5 years was promoted first to executive director for the vice president for student affairs office and then to the role of associate vice president. In 2016, after 12 years at Boston College, I joined the office of student life (which I later reorganized to be the dean of students' office) at Harvard College as dean of students.

Ready for a Change

After 6 years as dean of students, I was ready for a change—but I did not know exactly what kind of change I wanted. I loved my job, my team, the students, and the institution, but it was time for something new. I knew when I came to Harvard that I would be in the role for 5 to 7 years, and after emerging from more than 2 years of the pandemic, the time was right to transition. Yet I could not envision a role that would provide as much personal and professional satisfaction as the one I was in, nor was I sure I could find an institution where my values so closely aligned with the mission.

As fortune would have it, a role came open that seemed perfect for my skill set: university marshal. This is not a role that anyone—including me—would have set their sights on as a child or young professional; it is unique even in higher education. In short, the university marshal is the chief protocol officer of the university, coordinating visits from foreign dignitaries and heads of state, working with faculty and administrators from across campus to organize high-level diplomatic and academic delegations, and overseeing special university events such as commencement. It was a perfect match for the skills I have honed over decades in student affairs—diplomacy, team and relationship building, structure, and organization. It helped that I knew the institution and senior leaders, had a good reputation for getting things done, and loved a rebuilding project, as the office had been largely dormant during the pandemic and needed revitalization.

Yet making a significant career move can be risky. Despite being at the peak of my career, I was making a turn to an entirely unfamiliar field. I knew I would experience the kind of discomfort that comes with being new and was fortunate that my experience in student affairs prepared me well. Since making my transition, many of my colleagues in student affairs who may not have considered other opportunities at their institution have reached out to talk, and I have welcomed them into conversation about their goals and career.

Coffee Conversations

I invite friends and colleagues into conversation about their career path and opportunities from a place of inquiry. Following are a few of the topics I weave into the conversations, though each one is different depending on the person and context. There are three general categories: awareness of competencies, professional reputation and relationships, and mindset and intrinsic motivation.

Awareness of Competencies

- **Know your strengths and at what you excel.** What evidence do you have that you are good at a specific thing? Do you have someone in your life—a colleague, friend, or family member—who can be honest with you about where you shine and your growth opportunities? Be adept at reading the situation at your institution. Have you been encouraged to apply for something? Have you been given additional tasks or a promotion?

- **Seek out every opportunity to get feedback.** Pay close attention to all available evidence. What did you hear in your annual review, both positive and constructive, that resonated? How did you respond? You should also note other data points. Do you get asked to join committees or to volunteer for campus programs? Are you known as a go-to person, even outside of your current role?
- **Know your transferable skills.** What are the skills and experiences you gained while working in student affairs? Take any prospective job description for a role in which you are interested and map your skills to the responsibilities. Highlight your strengths during the application process and emphasize how they can contribute to your success in your new role.

Professional Reputation and Relationships

- **Be good at your job.** It may seem self-explanatory that being good at your job is essential, but when you are good at what you do, people notice. Being good at your job also means you show professionalism and enthusiasm for your work.
- **Earn trust and hold it close.** Be the person people come to because they know you can keep a confidence and will be honest with them. Show them that you value the relationship. Being trustworthy matters, and earning a reputation as someone who can be trusted is one of the most valuable assets in a workplace.
- **Build and leverage your relationships.** Reach out to colleagues, mentors, and supervisors who may have connections in other departments or areas of the institution. Express your interest in exploring new opportunities and ask if they can provide any recommendations, introductions, or advice. Personal referrals

can carry significant weight during the application and selection process. By proactively letting people know about your interest in other opportunities within the institution, you increase your chances of discovering new pathways for growth and development while leveraging your existing knowledge and experience.

- **Proactively speak with your supervisor or manager.** You do not want to surprise your supervisor by having them hear from someone else that you are looking. This part can be challenging for some people, but if you want to stay at your institution, it can be helpful to bring your manager in early to support you. Not only will you continue to work with them if you move elsewhere at your institution, but they may also be able to offer insights and guidance as well as connect you with relevant contacts.

Mindset and Intrinsic Motivation

- **Listen to your inner voice.** What are you curious about yet have never explored because it did not fit with your career plan? What areas do you keep coming back to or wish you were doing more of in your daily work? Whatever has held you back, it is never too late to try something new.
- **Embrace a learning mindset.** You will very likely have a learning curve, so embrace it. While most of the skills that got you where you are will help you in your transition, showing an eagerness to learn is essential. Seek out opportunities for professional development in areas that go beyond student affairs, attend relevant workshops and conferences, and keep current with the latest research and trends in other areas. Embracing a learning mindset will not only help you adapt to your new role more effectively but also demonstrate your commitment to professional growth.

The student affairs field is the perfect training ground for so many possibilities within higher education. It is never too early or too late to explore these opportunities.

■ ■ ■

Serving as a Vice President for Student Affairs for the Long Term

Michael N. Christakis, Pauline Burke, Shannon Ellis, and Patricia A. Whitely

With Heather M. Stevens

Working long term for a single company or in one position was once commonplace, but this practice has become unique. We, the authors of this chapter—Michael Christakis, vice president for student affairs at the University at Albany; Pauline Burke, vice president for student affairs at Stonehill College; Shannon Ellis, vice president for student services at the University of Nevada, Reno; and Pat Whitely, senior vice president for student affairs at the University of Miami—all have careers marked by long-term service. Each of us has served as vice president for student affairs or services (VPSA) for at least 8 years; as of the time of this writing, Shannon and Pat have served in their roles for almost 3 decades.

Serving as a VPSA requires a vast set of skills. These skills are gained through education (such as communication, student development knowledge, and cultural competency) and experience (such as political savvy, crisis management, and budget management). The approach to this work has changed over time. New students with different needs, wants, and expectations have graced the authors' halls and inboxes. New technology has been incorporated into VPSA practice; new policies and procedures have been implemented easily. Although adaptability has been an essential skill in maintaining long-term service, relationships, transition management, and ongoing dedication to learning have enabled us to overcome our fair share of challenges and become influential colleagues, leaders, and student advocates.

Discovering a Vocation

Each of us followed different paths to find our vocation in student affairs. Michael began his career under the mentorship of another long-serving vice president, Jerry Brody, at Alfred University. Jerry, who had served as VPSA for 11 years, set a standard for Michael—one focused on presence by attending student meetings regularly and accessibility with a willingness to meet with and mentor undergraduate students. Michael reflects that his countless hours with Jerry provided a front-row seat to what being a successful long-term institutional leader looks like.

Pauline, conversely, was thrust into the mantle of leadership when responding to a fire as a head resident assistant. While she was assisting with the cleanup, a professional staff member inquired about her future career plans. Student affairs was not necessarily a set path for Pauline, a first-generation college student who later earned her master's degree in social work. However, the mentorship and encouragement she found kept her on the path to VPSA. Similarly, Pat was called to the profession through a mentor, and experiences serving in student leadership positions in student government and orientation, although her career home was housing. While Shannon started her career in Greek life and the dean of students office, she quickly discovered that leadership enabled her to advocate for those who need support.

Although we followed different paths, each of us had an experience in which a leader identified strengths within ourselves that would be essential for a successful student affairs career. Such introduction to the field via mentorship cemented a long-standing focus on mentoring others, which has been an integral part of our professional practice.

Establishing and Nurturing Connections

Relationships, therefore, became the foundation for long-term service. Michael compares such relationship-building to fundraising. Any fundraiser, whether they work in higher education or otherwise, will tell you that "cultivating a gift" is about building relationships with prospective donors. Further, securing a six- or seven-figure gift does not happen overnight; it often takes several years, even decades, to forge the type of relationship required to ultimately make the request for a significant financial contribution. Establishing and nurturing institutional relationships with internal and external stakeholders are the same: Much like the relationships fundraisers cultivate to finally make the request, the relationships that a long-term VPSA establishes and nurtures over time also often lead to a request for support or resources. Those same stakeholders may, in turn, return the request. This request is built on trust that is established over time.

Michael applied this philosophy to connect with his fellow senior leaders. Within his first week on the job, the then-chief financial officer approached Michael about biweekly meetings. He found that this was a time when he could address mutual interest, build rapport, and, surprisingly, establish trust. Michael then applied this strategy by setting up biweekly meetings with the provost, athletic director, and vice president for advancement. Michael connected with each person in a different yet personal way—the chief financial officer, a passion for musicals (*Hamilton,* specifically); the provost, a mutual love of the ocean; and the vice president for advancement, cultural customs, traditions, and cuisine. He relied on vulnerability, one of the most important yet often discarded skills in a VPSA's repertoire. Building relationships on trust enables leaders to connect as humans. This is critical to the core work of student affairs.

Shannon maintains connections by attending business meetings, legislative sessions, donor banquets, and sport events. These events provide the chance to chat casually and cultivate friendships with regents and trustees, elected officials, and other senior leaders. She has then extended invitations to the individuals and their families to student events to showcase the real work of student services and to hear from students themselves. In a recent legislative season, Shannon and her team hosted four first-generation state legislators in a roundtable discussion with more than 50 first-generation students. Their instant connection has resulted in proactive legislation to provide the wraparound services needed for student success. It is important not to assume that a regent, a public servant, or even senior leader colleagues understand student life and the work of student affairs, especially as a long-term VPSA. As such, it is critical to illuminate the student experience, highlighting the highs and the lows for those who can contribute to change.

As the individuals with fiduciary responsibility for the institution, developing a relationship with these critical constituents as a leader can assist in understanding their priorities and what resources they wish to allocate. In Pat's experience, trustees have helped provide some of the most important student resources. A trustee provided the financial support to create a new student center at Pat's institution. This project, though, took 10 years to accomplish. Other projects can come about quickly because of existing relationships. Pat accomplished a significant goal for her students of color—naming a campus building in honor of two outstanding Black alumni—through the support of trustees.

Collecting Your Chips and Managing Politics

Even with strong relationships, serving as a VPSA will require knowledge about managing organizational politics. If the concept of politics is unfamiliar, within every organization, leaders have varying degrees of access to resources that enable them to get the work they need or want done. Politics is the process through which leaders form coalitions, gain access to necessary resources, create and resolve conflict, and generally accomplish goals. The concepts of resources or power can also be considered "bargaining chips." The greater your political savvy, the greater your potential for collecting these chips. Managing politics has proven to be the most critical knowledge base any long-term VPSA should possess. How do you gain knowledge in this area outside of trial and error?

One way is mentorship and observation of someone who excels. University of Miami President Donna Shalala provided that background to Pat regarding how she works with trustees, community members, students, faculty, and staff. In some areas, Donna excelled, such as how she would go into the on-campus Starbucks and buy the students coffee. Students flocked to her when she was across the campus, searching for a photo opportunity. In many ways, her presence with the students was a form of political capital, as she always had their support for their actions. There are many varying interest groups to consider when making changes on a college campus. The time of day, loosely or tightly coupled interest groups, impact effects, customer service responses, and others can all play a role in how to approach the process of change. In essence, rollout requires a strategy. President Shalala taught Pat the value of a well-developed strategy to accomplish a goal. Additionally, strong strategy development requires political acumen, knowing who the players are, who has the power, what are the available resources, and how to navigate the issue.

Long-term VPSAs gain a unique form of political capital—institutional knowledge. Pauline has received requests to lead key strategic initiatives, both within and outside the division. The president has sought her out for ongoing guidance and wisdom, especially during challenging moments. Being afforded these responsibilities as VPSA allowed her to build a strong reputation within a senior-level position and helped create a collaborative and productive work environment. The trust built from being reliable, accessible, and generous with her time has afforded her benefits within her role. The unintended outcomes of autonomy and empowerment enable her to freely design and implement a dynamic student experience for an ever-changing population. Of most value, Pauline has found trust within herself and an appreciation for the strength and value of her voice.

Building Opportunities to Mentor

As student affairs professionals rise in the ranks, they can get further away from daily interactions with students. Serving as a VPSA at a small, faith-based institution provides Pauline with the ideal environment to meet the goal of student connection. As it was modeled early in her career, she constructs her days to include student contact and mentorship. Whether leading a first-year experience class (as her president does), attending student government meetings, cheering on teams during competitions, or meeting one on one with students to offer support and guidance, time spent with students inspires and energizes Pauline. These moments also allow her to do for others what so many have done for her, helping them uncover their "why" in this world and determine who they seek to be.

Pat annually hosts an annual 4-week seminar for graduating seniors in the spring semester. A reflection course inspired the seminar she participated in during her final semester of college, where her mentor requested everyone complete a reflection paper and share it with the class. Reflection provides many benefits to the students but similarly helps Pat understand the highs and lows many students experience while pursuing their degrees. With this knowledge, she can best understand how students develop resilience, what key events and experiences remain worth investing in, and how to stay relevant with the students. Typically, the seminar is a self-selected group of 10 to 15 students who have all served in at least one student leadership role. Some seminar cohorts develop strong relationships, while others are more transactional. However, no matter the group dynamic, seeing the institution from a student's perspective is always beneficial.

Navigating Leadership Transitions

Transition can be challenging; some leaders come into organizations and bring their established teams. Proving yourself as a gatekeeper to this new university community is essential. VPSAs must continue building relationships and not simply rest on their reputations.

A strong long-term VPSA should continue starting fresh when a new person joins the ranks. Michael, for example, sought to provide a new provost at his institution with insights to help her succeed by setting up in-person check-ins. Whenever a new colleague joins the cabinet, he welcomes them to the team via email and shares his cell phone number, directing the new person to call or text with any questions they might have as they transition into their role. Michael readily acknowledges that after 23 years in the area and on campus, he has insights to help these new staff members learn the other leaders' culture and values; he also became the requisite campus tour guide for each new team member. In addition, Michael is able to indicate to his new president which campus events are essential and most meaningful for students, what campus spaces are the student hangouts, and where to find various offices and staff. As new people join the organization, the VPSA can shed light on the student experience and the culture of leadership and collaboration at that institution.

As she came to know the new president at her institution, Pat was able to identify ways to support his leadership style. One was an idea that would have failed under the previous president. Specifically, she would now make connections herself rather than create opportunities for the president to engage with students. After visiting another college campus, Pat saw how a provost was trying to connect with students over food. It is universally known that college students love free food. She brought this idea back to her campus and established Pancakes With Pat, where she served students pancakes as a late-night study treat eight times a year in various locations across campus. This effort gave her face time, name recognition, and relationship-building opportunities with students, helping her stay connected to her motivation to serve them. This event also let students view her as someone to contact with concerns or assistance—something better suited to her current president's focus.

Aligning Institutional Values With Your Own

One value of bringing someone new into a position is often their ability to critically assess the environment without any attachment to the past. Long-term VPSAs have the opposite value—the ability to deeply understand the organization, who is in it, what it values, and how work gets done. Given her values, Shannon has grounded her practice in spreading kindness to her students. When students are protesting a campus policy, she goes out of her way to listen deeply and reflectively to their needs. In these situations, kindness in response to their demands—often delivered in anger—is simply unexpected. She recalled that a few days after a particularly contentious meeting with students about raising a fee, a few of the leaders came by Shannon's office to ask for a job, request a letter of support for a scholarship application, and share an appreciation for the smile and box of Kleenex she offered at the meeting where they were all so upset.

Examples often abound of toxic work environments, which can be demotivating and soul-crushing and precede a burnout. For a VPSA, the environment is as much a critical component of the work as the team, students, and colleagues. Pauline has found that identifying a climate that truly aligns with the mission, creates space for authentic relations, and presents opportunities to develop meaningful connections with students has been critical to her continuing to perform the high-stakes work. Further, she believes that working within an institution whose mission and values align with her own has been nonnegotiable throughout her career. It can be challenging to determine if the facade of the job interview matches the purpose, culture, and value in practice. One way to find out about institutional culture is to ask various groups of people about their own experiences there. Also, the institution's student newspaper will often reflect the student body's true feelings about campus leaders and resources.

Creating the Future Always

For long-term VPSAs, looking to the future with hope and excitement is as essential as having the resources to support overall student success. The field of student affairs experienced the reality-shaking effects of the COVID-19 pandemic, which is a reminder that even the most carefully laid plans can be disrupted. The crucial role of VPSAs, with their confidence, relationships, and trust, is to ask provocative questions that engage others in the thoughtful creation of a future—a future that recognizes that strategy is still relevant and necessary even if the exact outcome is not what was expected. Shannon and her team's experience involved, in the peak of unknown future pandemic choices, free laptops and Wi-Fi access and rent support, a book fund, and food assistance (in partnership with the city) for income-qualified students. These resources became permanent as society learned to live with and manage the virus. Over time, students came to find faculty more empathetic, flexible, and accommodating when learning was disrupted. As her team began to brainstorm big, hairy, audacious goals—BHAGs, as they call them—for a new 5-year strategic plan for student services, Shannon was not surprised to see a focus on creating a climate of access, inclusion, and support rather than one on expanding the campus footprint.

Because of his institutional knowledge and reputation as a reliable community member, Michael has co-led his institution's first-ever strategic enrollment plan. Pauline has been able to make informed decisions to align her institution's short- and long-term goals, including the creation of comprehensive divisional learning outcomes and assessments as well as a recent transition to Division I athletics membership. Leaders who seek to stay within a community for the long term must not only come up with a fruitful idea but also see it through and ensure its continuity.

For anyone working in higher education, the opportunity to help support a student along their path to adulthood simply sparks joy. Staying in place for the long term allows time to fall in love, gain confidence, cultivate trust, and earn the respect of others. Your presence as a reliable fixture inspires students and staff to want to work with and for you.

Witnessing the Results of Leadership Choices

The opportunity to see your leadership choices put into action, adjusted, and put into action again is ultimately the difference between long-term VPSAs and shorter-term ones. As nerve-wracking as it can be, the most influential leaders will live with their changes by committing to remain. After years of public debate and endless data gathering in Nevada, Shannon stayed the course as a leader at one of two universities that were allowed to make admissions standards more rigorous while also ensuring the shift would not diminish traditionally marginalized student populations from accessing education at the institutions. Two nail-biting years followed that immediate change; however, she and her fellow leaders knew the results would take time to accrue. Shannon was relieved and satisfied when the number of underserved students grew to record highs.

On the other hand, she also witnessed the implementation of an excess credit fee on students by her board of regents. The intention of this change was purely punitive, and although many efforts to overturn the decision took place, none were successful. Finally, after 7 years of the fee, she had the data to prove the fee was negatively impacting students rather than increasing their ability to achieve their degrees or create a profit as intended. Because Shannon had the ability to stay the course and relentlessly plan for a future, she was able to oversee the repeal of the fee with a unanimous board vote. Choices like these may be considered "playing the long game." They require constant adaptation and pivoting of tactics and strategies to achieve goals. Although a pivot may not change a long-term goal, it addresses short-term updates in areas of critical need.

Leading Through a Crisis

Pivots are also an essential part of crisis leadership. Institutions can conduct tabletop exercises to learn their roles in a crisis; crises can also be career-defining moments.

Consider Hurricane Andrew, which hit the University of Miami in 1992. Pat oversaw residence halls and rode out the storm on campus with more than 2,000 students who were there to attend new student orientation. There was significant recovery work to perform after the storm, including getting those students home. While the campus was closed for 2 weeks, Pat met daily with the president and a group of staff to review tasks. She learned about different areas across the institution—from facilities to information technology—that needed to coordinate work together by simply showing up and being present. With the catastrophic damage to Miami-Dade County, many faculty and staff had to dedicate their energy to their own families. So Pat had the unique opportunity to work directly with the president and many other leaders. Within the coming years, she handled two more crises: the double homicide of students Marlin Barnes and Timwanika Lumpkins and the ValuJet crash in 1996. These moments required her to coordinate multiple areas, activity that again brought her to the attention of institutional leadership.

Getting on the radar of institutional leadership is as much about chance as it is about intention. It involves volunteering for opportunities that may not show a clear professional benefit, such as helping with a large-scale campus visit, or those that do show a clear benefit, such as serving in on-call rotation. One valuable way to assess the need or capacity to volunteer is to evaluate long-term career goals. For example, a VPSA needs knowledge of many areas within a university, not only student affairs. As such, VPSAs should ask themselves, *What areas do I know less about? In which areas do I possess strong understanding?* From here, VPSAs should seek out opportunities to volunteer in those areas needing growth or cultivate relationships with other colleagues so that VPSAs are viewed by other staff as reliable. Through her service, Pat learned who was at the university, what they were assigned to do, what they actually did, and how that work had an impact on the entire institution. She then stood out to leadership as someone dependable. Responding to crises has become the hallmark of her long-term service as a VPSA.

Engaging in Lifelong Learning

Even while progressing within a career, higher education professionals must never lose sight of the core outcome of the field: education. Each experience we have in our careers grants us the opportunity to learn lessons from ourselves, our students, our supervisors, and our fellow leaders. Pat learned a valuable lesson in the first months of her vice presidency as she faced a student-focused challenge that resulted in a lawsuit against the university. Essentially, university leadership wanted quick action on the closure of a student organization, yet that quick action contradicted established policies. Following leadership's direction, Pat closed the group, and the group responded with a legal challenge. From that lawsuit, Pat learned that obeying established policies and procedures has been critical to combating legal issues, as, historically, courts have ruled in the institution's favor if an established policy was followed. Many of these early lessons about structure presented her with boundaries to lead within, resources to understand better, and people to move toward a goal.

For example, during the 2020 election cycle, one student organization made a reservation to post signs in public yet reservable space to support their preferred political candidate. This student group posted more than 200 signs in its reserved space, resulting in a significant outcry from other students who were upset about the signs. Although Pat received many requests to remove the signs, official policies stated no limit on the number of signs allowed. The students had followed the policy of having a reservation and the specific information required to be on the signs. So, it was not possible to simply remove the signs. Furthermore, Pat knew she could not change her policies during an incident or in the middle of an academic year, as students had already committed to specific rules or regulations for that year. Thus, she later collaborated with necessary areas to ensure that policy was amended to limit the physical number of signs permitted and to ensure only those that had actionable items or event-related descriptions were included.

Becoming Involved in Professional Networks

Professional networks are not formed by chance; rather, they require significant time and attention to cultivate and maintain. Even before becoming VPSAs, Michael, Pauline, Shannon, and Pat found involvement and leadership in professional associations to be a fundamental way to build vital connections while staying challenged and current within the field.

Pauline's professional home, as with Michael, Shannon, and Pat, became NASPA–Student Affairs Administrators in Higher Education. Pauline quickly learned that to maximize her knowledge base, broaden her perspective on our shared work, and build credibility as a professional both on and off campus, she needed to show up to professional development opportunities. As has been the pattern in her career, Pat was encouraged by a trusted mentor or colleague to step forward, reinforcing the value of these relationships and encouraging her mentorship of others. Having served in multiple leadership roles on the regional and national levels, she has strengthened her credibility as a long-serving VPSA at a single institution.

During significant moments of challenge, such as with the COVID-19 pandemic and ongoing racial unrest on college and university campuses, professional networks prove invaluable. Professionals often turn to colleagues for ongoing benchmarking, alternative perspectives, sound advice, and sanity checks. As such, those professionals working long term in VPSA roles must cultivate a diverse, talented, and trusted network.

Developing Confidence and Ease of Authenticity

Serving as a VPSA, especially a long-term one, requires a healthy dose of confidence. Nevertheless, there are still days when even long-serving VPSAs may need more self-assurance. They may lack self-confidence; they may feel simple doubt or have imposter syndrome (Clance & Imes, 1978; Langford & Clance, 1993). Nevertheless, long-term VPSAs often find comfort in their roles over time. Michael describes this as an "ease of authenticity," which addresses how he actively engages campus stakeholders, especially students. When new in any job, people often tend to be hyperaware of interactions, language, and social media presence, among other things. Early on, Michael responded to every email and attended every event. He would carefully curate his social media posts to look and sound just right. He asked a mentor who had served as a long-term VPSA if the breakneck pace ever slowed. The mentor responded, "Only if you make it slow down." This advice helped him to reflect on what he did and did not enjoy doing. He found that attending the student government meetings, visiting student organization executive board meetings, walking around campus, and sending out biweekly emails to his entire division, called "The Friday Letter," were activities he enjoyed doing *and* made him a stronger VPSA. He notes that the pace has not necessarily slowed with more time served, but he has become much more comfortable approaching and engaging in his work.

In the same regard, Pauline has paid attention to the unique aspects of her community—a small, private, Catholic, liberal arts institution in the Northeast—throughout her leadership. Pauline, the first female in the VPSA role traditionally held by male religious figures, has felt a profound responsibility and mounting pressure to prove herself. Her leadership choices have consistently demonstrated her unwavering commitment to living the mission and focusing on her students, as have the choices of her predecessors and mentors. The relationships she has formed with students, staff, faculty, fellow leaders, and trustees have boosted her confidence, like a foundational skill. Knowing that others believe in her has been helpful, yet she has also had to build trust in her experiences to lead effectively and be viewed as an authentic leader.

Receiving the Support to Lead

Service as a long-term VPSA includes phenomenal highs and earth-shattering lows. The role of support systems, such as partners or spouses, family, and mentors, must be considered. For the four of us, our families are more than just means of self-care; our families are fixtures within our campus communities. Our families understand the complex and time-consuming work of serving an ever-changing, ever-growing, and ever-graduating community, recognizing that this work becomes, as Pauline shared, a vocation.

Why become a VPSA? Pat sees serving as a VPSA as the opportunity to make an impact and be a role model in the lives of students as they journey through college careers. Shannon recommends serving as a VPSA to change people's lives, those of both students and their families, for the better. Michael notes he was driven by making a positive difference in a student's educational journey one student at a time in much the way that Jerry Brody, his mentor, made a positive, lasting impact in his educational journey. Pauline became a VPSA to give back to others in the same meaningful way others have given so much to her. Being a VPSA has allowed each of us to invest in and serve individuals at an institution while utilizing the gifts and talents we have been given to do what the world needs from us—empowering others to find their voices, to uncover their vocation, and to give back during their own journeys.

There is no clear-cut way to be an effective VPSA, especially not a long-term VPSA, but anyone who has found success in serving their community for the long term relies on some key elements. They include establishing and maintaining strong relationships with as many constituencies as possible: students, immediate staff, faculty, staff across institutional areas, fellow senior leaders, community members, legislators, alumni, professional association connections, and trustees or regents. These relationships require knowledge about your political capital (i.e., knowledge of the resources, such as space, money, and buy-in from constituents) and that of collaborators and competitors. Relationships can also have deeply altruistic aspects that allow you to mentor and be mentored. These relationships provide the foundation for you to manage even when leadership, resources, or policies and procedures change your campus. As leaders, long-term VPSAs must find ways to align their values with those of their institution, create intentional strategic visions for their teams, and commit to seeing their leadership decisions through to the end. They, too, must step up in times of crisis with enough knowledge of their institutional infrastructure to determine who can be relied on to get work done and return the organization to stability. Finally, long-term VPSAs must never stop learning—whether at their institution, in the field, or within themselves. Although they will become comfortable with and confident in their work, they must never become complacent.

References

Clance, P. R., & Imes, S. A. (1978). The imposter phenomenon in high achieving women: Dynamics and therapeutic intervention. *Psychotherapy: Theory, Research & Practice*, *15*(3), 241–247. https://doi.org/10.1037/h0086006

Langford, J., & Clance, P. R. (1993). The imposter phenomenon: Recent research findings regarding dynamics, personality and family patterns and their implications for treatment. *Psychotherapy: Theory, Research, Practice, Training*, *30*(3), 495–501. https://doi.org/10.1037/0033-3204.30.3.495

Serving Higher Education Through Consulting

Erin Hoffmann Harding and Ana Rossetti

Student affairs is mission-oriented work, with all the associated rewards, risks, and challenges of helping young people grow and develop. It is also a profession with a variety of defined career paths, such as an assistant director role through a graduate program, a senior student affairs officer, or even a college president. With a noble calling and a recognized playbook for success, what happens if you are considering a detour or life circumstances require that you take a break? Can you have a meaningful professional life on the other side of higher education? This chapter offers lessons learned about successfully transitioning out of higher education and highlights the stories of two former student affairs leaders who now work as consultants within firms.

Reasons to Move

The reasons and timing for leaving student affairs differ for every individual. Student-facing roles in higher education have historically been demanding in terms of time, credentials and training, and emotional labor. Conversely, average compensation for these roles, particularly at early to midcareer levels, is often lower than commensurate roles and education levels in other industries. The intensity of serving students can cause burnout or trauma. Serving in a role for a long time may increase your desire to try something new. An institution's priorities or policies may change in ways that are incompatible with your values or with your view of student development or equity. For some, navigating the demands of a dual-career partnership can be exacerbated by evening, weekend, and on-call work. Welcoming a child or becoming a caretaker can alter your priorities and financial realities. Declining enrollment trends may result in a reduction in roles or institutional closure. Post-pandemic changes in workplace norms or personal priorities may give rise to new considerations. In other words, as a student affairs professional, a career transition can happen after much discernment, at different points in your life or career, through no choice of your own, or as a result of changes in your life circumstances or priorities.

Where to Move

Leaving higher education can be both unsettling and invigorating. It also need not be permanent. In fact, serving in an environment outside of higher education could make you a more desirable candidate if you choose to return to a university environment at a later time. On the other hand, it may allow you to build an entirely different career path that leverages your experiences and transferable skills. If you are considering a transition out of student affairs, several questions could help you determine your next best employment fit.

What Type of Organization Do You Want to Be a Part Of?

If you would like to remain in a mission-oriented environment like higher education, you will find many organizations, from health care to social service agencies, that serve different topics or constituent groups. Nonprofits, philanthropic entities, and foundations are mission-oriented organizations driven to demonstrate results and impact. However, for-profit corporations can also provide a sense of purpose, and some may provide the opportunity to have a positive impact on students and communities. Corporations can offer greater clarity and alignment on tangible objectives, higher compensation, and more defined career growth pathways, which can be appealing if the environment, culture, and work are the right fit for you. Startup opportunities may allow you to experiment with new technology, innovate a business model, or become part of a smaller dynamic team that boldly seeks to drive change. You will need to consider how the purpose, objectives, culture, and overall benefits and drawbacks of an organization align with your own professional values, interests, and needs.

What Type of Work Invigorates You?

Student affairs roles vary in terms of their interface with people, pace of change, and degree of certainty. Residential life or case manager roles typically require unconventional hours and adeptness in identifying and responding to crisis situations. Career services roles must respond to industry dynamics that are always shifting in the market for talent, requiring an openness to adapt to technology and comfort with analysis and management of metrics. Recreational sports and student activities roles work directly with students to support their leadership and skills development, challenging professionals to respond to shifts in student populations. These types of roles and many other student affairs functions can be found outside of higher education. It is important to determine which elements of your current student affairs work best leverage your strengths, which you find most exciting, which drain your energy, whether certainty and routine are important to you, and whether seeing the direct impact of your work on others is important.

In What Type of Work Environment Will You Thrive?

Just as the culture of colleges and universities can vary, you should carefully consider the culture of the organizations you explore outside of higher education. Is decision-making collaborative, centralized, or hierarchical? How much flexibility in work location or hours is provided to employees, and is hybrid work embraced or feasible? Do career mobility options exist for roles within the organization or across locations? What are the organizational norms around typical hours, evening or weekend work, and protection of vacation time? What information about the organization's operations is shared transparently, and which elements are more closely held? How are performance evaluations handled, and are employee training and development a priority? How diverse and inclusive is the workforce? Does the organization have specific diversity, equity, and inclusion goals and metrics? Do the organization's policies and practices reflect those objectives? What progress has been made toward equity goals?

Student affairs professionals have diverse skills that can be readily transferred to roles in other organizations. The creativity required in programming roles could serve you well in a hospitality environment or event planning. The networking skills you honed through professional organizations can be a good fit for sales, business development, or fundraising roles. Crisis management skills can be deployed in health care or public service. Individual counseling skills can be effectively deployed in human resources. Building management experience can be adapted to many operational and facilities responsibilities. In other words, student affairs professionals develop varied skill sets that are valuable within and beyond educational organizations.

How to Move

Once you have decided to move out of a higher education role and even if you have an idea of where you would like to go next, the process of finding your next opportunity can take time and may involve stops and starts. The search may be different from your path to student affairs, which, especially for entry-level hiring, likely involved a posted position and a series of formal interviews. Keep in mind that the seniority and responsibilities associated with similar titles can vary greatly across industries. A "director" or "vice president" title is typically not comparable between a university and a corporation. Familiarize yourself with structures, levels, and career progression within each organization or industry you consider. For experienced hiring, networking is crucial. Reaching out to former colleagues, professional association members, former classmates, friends, and family members helps you learn about different types of roles or new industries. It can also give you early insight into roles that are not yet posted. Taking the time to conduct informational interviews with a broad range of people can help you discern what may be a good fit for you and will sometimes alert you to options you may not have known about or considered otherwise.

The materials you need for a successful search outside of higher education may also differ. For higher education–adjacent roles, a multipage academic résumé, filled with publications, administrative and teaching responsibilities, committee service, and education credentials, could be well received. In contrast, most corporate résumés are one or two pages and are more likely to highlight skills, capabilities, and impact. Many search firms also recommend preparing a networking résumé, which is a one-page summary of your professional experience. These types of résumés can be valuable if you are in the process of switching industries or engaging in informational interviews. Finally, ensure that your LinkedIn profile is up to date and includes a professional summary of your capabilities and qualifications.

The role and use of referrals also vary widely across hiring organizations. Before using someone's name, be sure to request their permission or notify them if they have previously agreed. Ensure in advance that these contacts are willing to speak positively and knowledgeably about your work. Provide details about your interests and qualifications for the role with your referrer in case they have an opportunity to share them. Some firms encourage referrals and offer financial compensation for the referrer. In other firms, recruiters note referrals but keep this information hidden from interviewers to ensure objectivity in their assessment.

Once you land an interview, ask about the hiring process. Larger organizations could have formal processes that involve personality tests, screening interviews, skills-based exams or situational interviews, and group interactions. At the other extreme, you could be offered a job after an informal set of conversations that might not have even felt like interviews. In some cases, you might interview for one role and be offered a different position if the prospective employer thought you would be a better fit elsewhere in the organization. The role of multiple interviewers also differs. In some companies and organizations, the hiring manager is the decisive factor. In others, each interviewer could carry substantial weight in the decision to make an offer. In some interview processes, the decision about whether you move forward to the next step is made after one or more rounds of interviews, each of which may evaluate you in different ways. You should also assume that any prospective employer is likely to examine your social media presence to assess your professionalism. In total, the process for hiring can give you important insight into the organization's formality and whether its culture will be a good fit with your own preferences and priorities.

Do your best to stay positive and have patience if the search process takes a while or if you feel that you are interviewing at many places without success. Like the new students you welcome to campus, it often takes time to find the people, organization, or positions that integrate best with your own talents and aspirations. Ask for feedback about your materials, your interview performance, and additional places where you might seek professional opportunities.

Finally, once you receive an offer, carefully examine the compensation package. Some organizations offer both base salary and bonuses, and it is important to understand your eligibility for bonuses, the metrics on which they are based, and how this differs from annual salary increases, which may also be determined by your contribution rating relative to expectations for your role or level. Beyond salary, policies for paid time off can vary widely, and work location flexibility has become more important for many professionals. Benefits, for example, may be robust at established companies and less extensive at startups or smaller organizations. Retirement program contributions and plans are another important area to consider. Many organizations expect candidates to negotiate their offer package. Companies that do not offer significant flexibility in the base salary or bonus structure may be willing to provide a signing bonus or other one-time sums, such as a home office stipend. Make sure you understand any provisions that require you to pay back the full original sum if you leave before a certain length of time. Finally, in considering the total compensation package, both monetary and nonmonetary, you should carefully discern which elements are most important to you as you evaluate an offer.

After the Move

Although new experiences can be exciting, they also come with uncertainty and disruption. Even if you are fully committed to the change, leaving a field with which you are familiar to enter a different one can be daunting. People often say it takes a full year in a new role—especially in a new industry—to find your footing and start to feel like you know what you are doing. Within that first year, there is typically an intense 3- to 6-month period that can feel like a rollercoaster of paradoxical emotions. The excitement of a new beginning, meeting new people, and imagining new possibilities is mixed with the discomfort and stress of profound adjustment, much new learning, and having to perform and make first impressions while lacking confidence and second-guessing yourself. Preexisting anxieties, lingering stressors from past experiences, and the degree to which these interactions feed or diminish your energy can all add to the stress of this transition.

Higher Education Consulting

Consultants who work with colleges and universities provide guidance and support in various aspects of institutional strategy, performance, planning, and organizational effectiveness. The work of higher education consultants encompasses a wide range of services aimed at helping academic institutions navigate various challenges, innovate and realize new opportunities, and enhance their organizational performance. Consulting projects, which may also be referred to as engagements, in academia can include strategic planning; assessments of departments, programs, and administrative or academic portfolios; financial aspects; and readiness for organizational or technological change. Projects can involve support with accreditation matters, enrollment strategy, or aspects of the student experience. They can also involve financial or human resources management; technology implementation or integration; facilities planning; management of an institution's research endeavors; diversity, equity, and inclusion strategy; leadership coaching and development; risk management; and organizational change strategy. This list is not exhaustive of the work done in higher education consulting, and firms vary widely as to their areas of specialization or reputation.

Engagements are conducted by teams of different sizes depending on the scope of the project. The statement of work for the engagement determines the activities and outcomes the client expects to be provided and the associated timelines and work products to be generated. Every field has its specialized jargon, acronyms, and working norms. Although these will vary among organizations and industries, the following elements stand out as some of the most significant shifts from the world of higher education to the consulting profession.

Outcomes

In consulting, work products produced for clients are generally referred to as deliverables. They can be slide decks, spreadsheets, reports, or any other kind of document or asset. Major deliverables for a project are typically outlined in the statement of work and constitute contractual obligations on the firm's part. Changes to agreed-upon deliverables may require a written change to avoid breach of contract, particularly in instances where you serve a public institution. Engagements typically include the production of various smaller-scale deliverables not explicitly mentioned in the scope of work that are still within the scope of the project. Depending on your level and role expectations, you may need to deepen your skills in

Word, Excel, PowerPoint, content management software, and other tools to produce high-quality deliverables for client projects. This expectation may differ radically from the world of student affairs, where so much of a professional's work is centered on being present and engaging with students. At the same time, relationship building with clients, with colleagues in your network, and within your firm is highly valued and essential to a successful consulting career.

Time Allocation

Consultants spend time with different clients, especially as they progress in their careers. Tracking your time for billable hours that need to be recorded and are invoiced to clients can be an adjustment. It is an ethical responsibility to be productive with one's time and to demonstrate value for time billed to clients. You must accurately track and report your billable time, which can be challenging when you are staffed on more than one project and work is dynamic across projects throughout the day. It takes time to become more efficient and to learn to streamline your effort to deliver excellent results to clients while not spending more time than necessary on one aspect of a project.

In addition to time spent on client work, consultants spend time on general administrative tasks, required training, internal meetings, internal initiatives, client development, and other nonbillable activities. Consultants at different levels will balance these responsibilities differently. For example, junior analysts and associates more typically maintain at or near 100% client service. Those in leadership roles spend more time counseling clients, pushing the analysis of the full-time team, pursuing client development, and fulfilling functions of evaluation within the consulting firm. Balancing client and nonbillable time can be challenging at first and will require new habits and approaches.

Organizational Structure

Consultants, like other professional service professionals, do not have a single supervisor and can be entrepreneurial about pursuing the type of work they do. They often report to a project manager for one client and to another manager for their next project. Consultants are also usually assigned partners or senior consultant "coaches" who support their professional development across projects, understand their trajectory, and assess their readiness for more senior roles. Every project team member gives performance feedback across all professional levels during the project. Consultants receive feedback from their coaches across their projects and meet regularly to discuss feedback, track progress against their goals, and discuss career trajectory and promotion planning, which can occur at set times each year.

Having a coach who is separate from the person who directly evaluates your work can be beneficial. Their role is to actively provide guidance on how you can progress to the next level of responsibility and compensation at the firm and to serve as an advocate during reviews and promotion discussions. Although answering to more than one person can have its pitfalls, having multiple voices at various levels and across multiple contexts throughout the year informing the evaluation of your performance can help mitigate potential bias. Within a coaching model, consultants serve as coaches to junior colleagues and champion the career trajectory of others. Former higher education professionals often find it rewarding to apply their past supervisory skills and experience in advising and mentoring undergraduate and graduate students in a new context.

The Advisor's Role

Transitioning from higher education to consulting also involves reorienting the way you think about your work in ways that may seem contradictory at times. As a consultant, you are an outsider coming in to learn about your client and to support their success. You may be welcomed as a helpful resource and partner, or you may be met with skepticism and resistance as an agent of change and disruption. You may bring extensive knowledge and relevant expertise, but you must approach each project with fresh eyes and you must demonstrate to your client that you respect and understand their uniqueness. You are highly invested in the project's progress and outcomes, but you will eventually step away from the project and may not always see the final outcomes. Your impact is often more indirect or behind the scenes; rather than having decision-making authority, you cultivate trust to influence decision-makers. You may provide brilliant analysis, insights, and recommendations, but the institution may not implement them. You may be leading a project, but your goal is to make your project sponsor and other institutional partners shine and not to focus the attention on yourself. Former higher education professionals may find that consulting lacks the rhythm and rewards of an academic calendar, including campus traditions, ceremonies, and celebrations. Depending on the types of projects you work on, you may have few if any opportunities to interact directly with students, family members, or the broader campus community. On the other hand, many types of engagements involve interviews or facilitation of sessions with members of the university community.

Professional Development

Consulting work involves constant learning and development, which involves a combination of self-directed learning, formal training programs, and on-the-job apprenticeship. Many firms invest internal resources and have their own learning and development professionals. As a result, engagement in professional associations and conferences differs. Many higher education professionals are members of professional associations, attend conferences, and volunteer their time to plan events or give presentations. In contrast, as a consultant, your role at a professional association or conference is more akin to that of a vendor. Attending a conference paid for by the firm could carry an expectation of business development. This could involve representing the firm at the vendor exhibition area, speaking and presenting, building relationships with prospective and existing clients, identifying new business opportunities, and learning about trends in the industry and how they may affect the firm's offerings.

In the following sections, we recount our decisions and experiences in transitioning from careers on campus to consulting roles in the field. Our experiences in academia, as well as our commitment, resilience, and adaptability, proved beneficial in our consulting work and prepared us for challenges in our new roles.

■ ■ ■

A PIVOT INTO CONSULTING

Ana Rossetti

Throughout my 18 years working in campus-based roles in higher education, I have sought out new challenges every few years. Each time I became relatively comfortable in a role, I felt an urge for variety and sought a new opportunity, whether at a different institution or a different role at the same institution. Later in my career, as I approached 10 years at an institution where I had enjoyed several growth opportunities, I once again had an urge for a new challenge. I was finally ready to pursue the doctoral degree to which I had long aspired. Although it was reasonable to expect that a doctorate would positively affect my job prospects, as an immigrant woman from a low socioeconomic background, my true motivation was to challenge myself, to prove to myself that I could do it, and to grow through the process as a researcher, learner, and person.

When I was accepted to my target doctoral program, I planned to stay at my institution, where I had a strong team and network. As it turned out, a few months later, I was unexpectedly recruited to lead a fellowship program at a prestigious international nonprofit. This role was an exciting challenge in a new field that allowed me to apply my higher education experience and my commitment to educational equity to help college students from intergenerationally marginalized communities across the country graduate from college and transition to the workforce. Although I would not recommend entering a new industry to run a startup program while pursuing an accelerated executive doctoral program while having a family with young children, I certainly would not recommend doing so during a global pandemic.

Those 2 years were challenging and filled with both expected and unexpected transitions. In addition to a demanding full-time job, a full-time accelerated doctoral program, and dissertation writing, because of the pandemic, our then 2-year-old daughter was home from daycare for 10 months, and our son started kindergarten on an iPad at our kitchen table, attending school either fully remote or hybrid for 7 months. During this time, my spouse temporarily transitioned from an executive campus role to a stay-at-home father and household manager. Despite the many challenges of this time, those 2 years were also fulfilling and revelatory. I had challenged myself as a learner and researcher, and not only did I succeed under difficult circumstances, but I also grew immensely, forged new meaningful relationships, and had a renewed sense of my potential and aspirations. I emerged from that experience knowing that I was more committed than ever to remaining engaged in the higher education sector. However, I did not see myself working on campus at a single institution. My doctoral studies broadened my perspective and knowledge across varied institution types and geographic contexts, and I was eager to keep learning and gaining experience with a variety of institutions, contexts, and leaders. Additionally, the flexibility and time savings of being able to work from home became essential to our household as my husband returned to a campus role and as our children became more engaged in activities and formed their own social networks.

When I considered my next transition, rather than target a particular industry, role, or title, I focused on how I wanted to use my skills and how I wanted to spend my time. I started reaching out to people in my network for exploratory conversations to help me discern what kind of work, role, and organization might be the next best fit for me. During one such conversation with a long-time colleague, friend, and mentor, she remarked that my skill set, experience, and interests were well suited for higher education consulting. She explained why she thought consulting would be a good fit for me: I crave variety, I relish constantly learning new things, and I am adept at managing multiple work streams and projects at once. I have strong relational skills, and I enjoy navigating interpersonal and institutional dynamics and politics. I enjoy being immersed in the challenges and obstacles that higher education leaders face, I am energized by problem solving, and I enjoy finding solutions. These qualities describe many of my student affairs colleagues as well.

I learned that in higher education consulting, I would be valued as an asset just as I was. I did not have to translate my résumé into different jargon or try to explain my prior work to a new industry. As an "experienced hire," my understanding and familiarity with the higher education context would bring added credibility to project teams. I would be seen not just as a consultant but as a subject matter expert and as someone to whom clients could relate and trust. I would be able to immediately contribute higher education–specific insights that might take a career consultant longer to develop. I would be learning about the consulting industry, but I would arrive with the ability to add significant value right away.

I had never considered consulting, and I quickly realized that I did not know what it entailed. My colleague connected me to several of her contacts in higher education consulting, and through these conversations, I discovered what an ideal fit this could be for me in this chapter of my career. Consulting has changed significantly since the COVID-19 pandemic. Travel has diminished greatly—the weekly grind of traveling to work at a client site Monday through Thursday is no longer standard at most firms—and various firms now have fully remote workforces with optional access to an office environment. For me as a parent with young children and a dual-career partnership to navigate, the opportunity to balance occasional travel, in-office camaraderie, and work-from-home flexibility was ideal. Having never envisioned transitioning into consulting, I feel fortunate to have been welcomed at Huron Consulting Group, a firm with a supportive, collaborative culture where I get to work with smart, resourceful, and motivated people in the Higher Education Strategy and Operations practice who care deeply about higher education and each other.

Coming into higher education consulting as an "experienced hire" with 20 years of work and management experience and a doctorate had many advantages. I came in at a more senior level and was quickly brought into business development as a subject matter expert, where I had the opportunity to learn about this important aspect of consulting. I was recruited into internal initiatives and leadership roles where I could contribute my knowledge and experience while building broader relationships at the firm. On client engagements, it quickly became apparent how much I could contribute based on my experience and education and how much this was valued by clients and colleagues.

My pivot into consulting has felt more like an evolution of my work in higher education. As a consultant, I approach many of the same challenges from a different vantage point, applying my years of campus-based work and the collective wisdom of my consulting colleagues to support the work of higher education leaders in whose success I am invested. On a personal level, I am thrilled to have found new, exciting dimensions to my vocation and to be able to pursue them in a format that is a great fit for my strengths and for my current life circumstances.

A FULL CIRCLE RETURN TO CONSULTING

Erin Hoffmann Harding

During the latter several years of a meaningful 9-year tenure as vice president of student affairs (VPSA) at the University of Notre Dame, I actively considered the possibility of transition—at some times more seriously than at others. My discernment also had both internal and external motivations. For example, by the end of my fifth year, I had held my role at Notre Dame longer than any other role in my career, and I am a person who thrives in an environment of change. I also realized I was approaching a tenure that matched several of my long-serving vice president predecessors, and whether it was the toll of student tragedy or ramifications from controversial strategic decisions, longevity in the role was not guaranteed. On the other hand, I continued to be passionate about our division's work, cared deeply about the colleagues I worked with and the students I served, and was excited about possibilities for the future.

As a result of these competing forces, my exploration of additional roles was sometimes opportunistic and only occasionally planned. Over several years, I explored small college presidencies, other roles at Notre Dame, roles outside of higher education, and even other Research 1 (R1) VPSA roles. In every case, my involvement in the search process was extremely helpful. I learned a great deal from talking with colleagues in the interview process about the qualities they were seeking in a new leader, why they were excited about the new role or the new institution, and whether I connected well with the mission and people of other places. And each time, the exploration process ended differently. In one case, there was an amazing match of people and mission, but pursuing the role would have made my husband's commute infinitely more complex, and we would have had to move our three young boys away from our extended family. The personal sacrifices simply were not worth the professional excitement. In another case, I learned quickly from a targeted search committee question that coming from Notre Dame would not have been viewed as an asset to some leaders at the other institution. I was not surprised when I did not advance as a finalist. In yet another case, I was honored to be invited to become a finalist but withdrew from the search after an agonizing reflection process when I realized I was not passionate enough about the institution's mission. My transition process had many twists and turns, and, during each experience, I learned more about myself and how I next wanted to serve.

After a grueling year of COVID-19 on campus and losing my mother to an aggressive leukemia, I was delighted to return to my original professional home at McKinsey & Company in the summer of 2021. Yet, despite all my other exploration, this opportunity arose unexpectedly. I began my career at McKinsey after receiving my undergraduate degree. The opportunity to work in consulting arose by chance after I completed my junior year internship at a major accounting firm. A Notre Dame alumnus contacted me after seeing my résumé and invited me to interview for a business analyst position, which is typically a 2- to 3-year role. I found McKinsey's standard case interview process both challenging and intellectually interesting. I was excited about a position that would provide exposure to strategic, organizational, and operational work, all while allowing me to travel the world. Taking the chance to explore an entirely different profession at the beginning of my career truly paid off. I loved the people, the institution's values, and the complex questions we tackled on behalf of our clients. I went to law school with the full intention of returning to McKinsey (although I took and passed the bar exam just in case!) and enjoyed a wonderful few years working in health care and the social sector before an unexpected call came my way from Notre Dame. In 2005, I left McKinsey to help support my alma mater at a time when a new president, provost, and executive vice president were taking office. It was a tremendously exciting time for Notre Dame, yet I sincerely believed I would return to consulting after 2 or perhaps 3 years. Instead, I stayed at Notre Dame in various roles for 16 years! However, in February 2020, I traveled to Indianapolis for a statewide conference hosted by the Lilly Endowment, and I learned that McKinsey had started a thriving education practice several years after I left. I distinctly remember missing several of the presentations while I was on the phone talking with our vice president for internationalization about whether we should discontinue our Rome study abroad program because of COVID-19, although I did manage to introduce myself as a proud McKinsey alumna to several of the partners at the conference.

I kept in touch with McKinsey's education practice from 2020 to 2021, learned that McKinsey now hires both new college graduates and experienced professionals, ended up interviewing with six partners for a role to return, and accepted an offer in early 2021. (Given my public role, I did not announce my departure until late in the spring 2021 semester.) I was motivated by the chance to work with a wider variety of education institutions, especially at a time of great change within our sector. The people I met in the education practice were extremely smart and passionate about making a difference, and our practice's explicit purpose is to have a significant impact on students. The post-pandemic change in work norms allowed me to work with colleagues and clients remotely part time so I could transition professionally without having to relocate my young family.

My work at McKinsey has provided me an opportunity to stretch in new ways. Although I often have the opportunity to help highly selective R1 institutions analyze growth plans, redesign aspects of their student experience, or consider where and how they might advance their research, it has been an exciting challenge to learn more about how to creatively deploy resources at tuition-driven institutions or to serve a group of employers who need higher education to produce more graduates with various skill sets. Through the project teams I lead, I still can mentor newer professionals or counsel clients in the next steps of their own careers.

Now, almost 3 years into my return to consulting, I feel lucky to be serving education in a new way. My experience on campus has been invaluable in establishing credibility with clients, especially given the breadth of departments I led at Notre Dame, from student affairs to institutional research to involvement in the onboarding of new campus executives. When we are asked about the impact of a new strategy on campus, I have an informed perspective about how students, faculty, donors, or alumni might react. My children are now of an age where traveling with some frequency is feasible, and I am lucky to continue to be surrounded by a wonderful support structure where my husband and I can pursue our dual careers.

I still, however, do not know what the future holds. I continue to nurture relationships of those serving directly in higher education and try to remain abreast of evolving campus issues. When the time is right for my family and the professional match is right, I could imagine returning to a campus role where I can have a direct impact on one institution. In the meantime, I am extremely energized about the variety of client work, the opportunity to perform and publish research, and the systemwide impact that I can have through a more indirect counseling role.

■ ■ ■

Authors' Similarities

As our stories illustrate, despite varied trajectories and motivations, we both arrived in higher education consulting from student affairs work. Following are some key similarities in our experiences.

Purpose-Driven Work

We are committed to the opportunities that higher education can unlock for learners and their communities. Despite having transitioned to for-profit corporations, we continue to do impactful work that contributes to the success of higher education institutions. Both of us derive fulfillment in being able to support campus colleagues in doing their work more efficiently, shoring up an institution's operations and finances, designing strategies to help maximize students' outcomes, or facilitating thoughtful, data-informed planning for the future. We feel a strong calling to higher education, and our consulting roles provide another avenue to remain engaged with that vocation.

Education and Credentials

Both of us had earned graduate degrees that played an important role in our career trajectory and discernment. Our goal was to pursue a career path where we could apply our education and where our credentials would still be valued.

A Burden Lifted

Although consulting has its own stresses and pressures, nothing in this work compares to the magnitude of stress and responsibility that can accompany student affairs work. The specter of student harm or death was a constant concern, including middle-of-the-night phone calls, crisis intervention, crisis planning, and various high-sensitivity interactions, including phone calls we dreaded making to students' loved ones. In addition to the personal toll this takes, there was the added responsibility of supporting our staff and colleagues as they dealt with the burden of their stress and trauma. After student affairs work, the stresses of consulting pale in comparison.

Missing Campus Life

As professionals devoted to higher education who spent decades of our careers on college and university campuses, we agree there is no substitute for the rituals and traditions of academia. The rhythm of the academic calendar, opportunities to connect directly with students, and the joy and emotion of commencement simply cannot be replaced. We are enthusiastic for the chance to deeply understand and visit a variety of institutions through our consulting work, but we carry nostalgia for truly being a part of a campus community and all its unique facets.

Experienced Hires

Our higher education careers were not something we had to translate or explain when transitioning to consulting. Our prior experience working in practices focused on the higher education market was immediately valued as an asset. Experienced hires bring added credibility and relatability for clients. They also provide nuanced insights as well as technical and political knowledge unique to the academic context that is helpful to their project teams. Former higher education professionals turned consultants are often able to drive business development more organically through their existing networks and credibility. Our prior work experience was considered a key asset, and it made our transitions to consulting roles much smoother.

Authors' Differences

Despite the many throughlines and similarities in our transitions from higher education to consulting, some differences are important to note.

Transitions and Learning Curve

Erin had prior experience in consulting and "boomeranged" back. Ana had pivoted out of higher education and the nonprofit sector before coming to consulting. In each case, the learning curve of consulting and the significance of the transition were different.

Student and Staff Interactions

We differ on the degree to which we centered and felt the loss of a direct connection to students and early career staff. For Erin, the opportunity to mentor and supervise was a meaningful and rewarding part of her roles. For Ana, although this aspect was a meaningful part of the work, the big-picture, systems-level aspects of strategy consulting, which have broad-based impact on students, staff, and the entire university community, were even more compelling. While student interactions are not common in consulting projects, we do mentor and supervise staff and there are opportunities to mentor aspiring college or graduate students interested in consulting careers.

Returning to Higher Education

We have different perspectives about our likelihood to return to higher education. For Ana, the key would be weighing the overall value proposition between professional and familial factors. However, she would consider it for the right role at the right institution, with the right challenges, at the right time—all of which may require significant cosmic alignment. Erin remains open to returning and believes consulting for many higher education institutions could provide a valuable and wider perspective upon returning to a campus-based role.

Conclusion

As you consider your own potential transition out of higher education and reflect on both the similarities and differences of our stories, some advice might be useful no matter what you decide.

- **Meaningful impact is still possible**. You may find an organization whose cause ignites a passion. You may transition to a place where you are still able to work directly with the individuals you serve. You could find yourself advancing the thinking on a topic or making a systemic change within a sector. Give yourself permission to define how you can make a difference.
- **Both personal and professional factors deserve consideration**. Student affairs professionals are gifted, giving, and selfless people. However, it is important to prioritize your own well-being and that of your own community or family. Practice the same balance and integration that students are encouraged to apply to their experiences on campus.
- **Your skills are valuable in the market**. We now live in a world where artificial intelligence can rapidly synthesize information. However, interpersonal skills, the ability to adapt to quickly changing circumstances, and a deep commitment to the development of others are talents that have staying power. Student affairs professionals exude those traits and can leverage them effectively in other environments.
- **Nurture and leverage your network**. Calling on those who know you and serve in all capacities can be invaluable in deciding whether to transition, exploring what you could do next, and helping you land the next position. Spend real time in conversations with colleagues from all walks of your career.

- **Nothing is forever**. It is natural to feel that stepping away from higher education means that you can never return, and maybe at this time, you have no interest in doing so. But it is important to remember that careers are seldom straight lines and may include several unexpected twists and turns. These days, several university presidents have been hired from industry or other nonprofit leadership roles. If you feel the time is right for a transition out of student affairs or out of academia altogether, trust your gut and consider how you can manage your transition in a thoughtful and strategic manner. Consider giving yourself the option to return if you later decide that is what you want. Or maintain relationships and connections that you may be able to leverage in new ways.

There was likely a time when you could not envision yourself working anywhere but on a college campus or doing anything else but student affairs. But you can use your valuable skills and experiences in new ways and in other industries. So keep an open mind, stay curious, and never say never. The next act of your career may surprise you.

Transitioning From Higher Education to New Industries

Constanza Cabello and Sofia B. Pertuz

Leaving the field of higher education can be an option for student affairs professionals with skills, experiences, degrees, and credentials that transfer to other professions. This chapter challenges higher education leaders to normalize career shifts for their staff, as well as higher education professionals to explore transitions that reflect their values and capitalize on their career foundations, expertise, and skills.

Authors' Professional Journeys

In the following sections, we offer personal accounts as professionals with notable campus-based careers who decided to pivot from higher education to other industries. We have taken diversity, equity, and inclusion (DEI) roles in the nonprofit and corporate sectors. These unique journeys can serve as potential guideposts for current student affairs professionals interested in using their career foundations, expertise, and skills in new work environments and industries.

Having made difficult decisions to leave an industry where we had imagined ourselves making lifelong careers, we engaged in critical self-reflection to consider our next steps and share what we learned. We reflect on transferring the skills, experiences, and degrees gained as student affairs and higher education professionals to other industries; this effort brought some challenging reflection points, highlighting the issues and challenges we experienced within higher education that prompted us to look for opportunities elsewhere. Finally, we focus on the decision-making process of leaving higher education after building connected and respected careers. For both of us, the decision to pursue roles outside of higher education came only after careful consideration and weighing the risks and potential benefits. Ultimately, we realized that professionals with advanced degrees and training in higher education bring tremendous value to other industries. We took risks as we turned to nonprofit and corporate sectors.

■ ■ ■

NO RISK, NO REWARD

Constanza Cabello

My personal and professional journey shaped how I view my career and life's work. My passion for DEI comes from my identity as a first-generation American, the child of Chilean immigrants. I remember learning early in life about the haves and have-nots, but my curiosity to understand this circumstance came later in life when I began to learn how systems of power and privilege sustain these dynamics. I grew up in a racially diverse community. Although I understood what diversity and inclusion could be like, it wasn't until I got to college that I unpacked how equity was central to advancing justice work. I thought I would go to law school and become a family attorney, but realized I enjoyed working on campus and with students through my work-study job in student activities. So, I pursued a master's degree in counseling with a focus on student development.

After graduate school, I began my career in student engagement. Though I enjoyed the work, something was missing. I realized my passion was working with and for minoritized communities. I then spent the next 10 years in multicultural affairs, institutional diversity, and community engagement. Advancing DEI for students by working with groups across campus (e.g., human resources, academic affairs, community affairs) was where I found my niche. Direct student contact remained a central pillar of my success; however, I realized that to have even more impact, I needed to work with more stakeholders to create the conditions for students to thrive. I recognized that students did not need to be fixed; institutions and systems needed to be fixed to facilitate student success. This shift in mindset was an actual "ah-ha" moment—the switch flipped in my head, and I knew my work needed to go beyond direct student contact.

I found success relatively quickly. In my early 30s, shortly after completing my doctorate, I became a vice president for diversity, inclusion, and community engagement at a midsized public institution. I possessed the credentials and experience to advance. Simultaneously, I launched a consulting company to support this work with other educational institutions, nonprofits, and mission-driven organizations. I also volunteered and led professional associations.

However, in 2020 I felt the field changing and the work becoming "heavier" than ever (contextualized in the section "The Higher Education

Landscape During the Transitions"). I participated in several professional development experiences that gave me the tools and skills for success, but something was misaligned. I enjoyed working as a senior diversity officer, but I worried I might become stagnant and increasingly frustrated. During this time, I also attended a program to develop the pipeline for BIPOC (Black, Indigenous, People of Color) talent for college presidencies. This program confirmed that I did not want to pursue a presidency at this time in my career and that I would consider it later.

Left with this realization, I began to consider what I needed and wanted from my career. I always knew that my identity as a DEI professional was central; however, at this time, I felt my identity as a student affairs and higher education professional was less core to my mission. In the wake of George Floyd's murder, many influential and impactful organizations made commitments to racial justice. The boom of obligations was energizing, and I realized my skill set was highly valuable to organizations outside of higher education. Simultaneously, the pandemic led to some vital personal insights: I enjoyed the hybrid work schedule and having more time for things like family, friends, exercise, sleep, and rest. For example, with no commute, I began a dedicated workout time. This shift gave me better mental clarity, physical well-being, and mood. Although 2020 was a challenging year for many reasons, it gave me the necessary time to stop, reflect, and recenter.

The process could have been smoother at times. It was challenging to negotiate what it would mean to leave higher education. It felt like everything I worked for was in question. I feared that leaving higher education would result in failure, lost relationships, and judgment from others. I also felt a bit of shame for considering leaving the field, but the support of mentors, coaches, family, and friends helped me realize that career transitions are normal and exciting. That's when it became clear that taking a risk might be worth it. I thought about the risks my family made to come to the United States, start over, and bet on themselves—and it worked out. I began to ask myself, *What if I do try something else, and what if it works out?*

Spoiler: It worked out. I landed a corporate role as the vice president for equity on a global DEI team. The organization serves as an asset manager that provides investment services for clients around the globe. Although the firm differs significantly from higher education, the work focuses on my passion and mission to advance justice. The scale is more significant, and the work remains challenging. The shift tapped into an intellectual curiosity that is energizing. I remain connected to student affairs and higher education through teaching, consulting, and volunteer roles. For the first time in a while, I feel excited about the rest of my career.

CAPITALIZING ON TRANSFERABLE SKILLS

Sofia B. Pertuz

My professional journey began with the strong influence of my experiences as a first-generation immigrant born in the Dominican Republic and raised in the Bronx in a low-income household. While growing up, my siblings and I had to figure out many unfamiliar things, and our parents could not provide direction beyond being supportive and believing that education would unlock a bright future. Despite the challenges early in life, I thrived in my academic pursuits and became a first-generation college student, determined to make a difference in the world.

During my time as an undergraduate student, I followed a typical student affairs career path. I served as a resident assistant, immersing myself in the residential college community and developing invaluable leadership skills. I also became heavily involved in various student organizations, using my experiences to help others as they worked to attain college degrees. The idea of supporting students' personal and leadership development resonated deeply with me. Driven by this passion, I pursued a career in academia and earned a master's degree and PhD in higher education management, leadership, and policy. These academic pursuits allowed me to delve deeper into the field and comprehensively understand the higher education landscape as I gained professional work experience in student affairs roles.

Initially, I had never considered leaving the realm of higher education; I aspired to become a vice president or a president, driven by a desire to create meaningful change within the higher education system to ensure first-generation and underrepresented students like me could thrive. However, my path took an unexpected turn when I encountered a challenging time as an associate vice president and dean of students. The role was both fulfilling in terms of its campuswide impact, but also emotionally draining being on call 24 hours and handling major critical incidents while, at times, feeling isolated and unsupported. I also felt that as a woman of color, I had to straddle the role of student advocate and institutional representative, which often conflicted with my need to show up authentically in all spaces. During this period, I received a recruitment offer from a nonprofit organization whose mission closely aligned with my values. Intrigued by the opportunity to contribute to a cause I sincerely cared about, I decided to explore a different path. Deviating from my original plan was challenging, but such open-mindedness presented new possibilities.

As I embarked on a self-discovery and empowerment journey, my eyes were opened to the vast array of opportunities outside of higher education. While getting involved in professional organizations that included leaders from various industries, I realized that my talents, skills, and educational training could be put to work to make a difference in multiple sectors.

The "real world" beckoned, offering the chance to contribute to other causes while ensuring a more secure financial future for my family.

The transition away from higher education proved to be fruitful. Not only was the compensation much higher outside of academia, but I also seized the opportunity to become an entrepreneur and start my own business. I discovered that my expertise and experience were highly valued in the consulting world, allowing me to pursue a fulfilling career that offered financial stability and professional growth. I even ventured into executive coaching, leveraging my leadership skills to support others in their personal and professional development and transitions—especially their journeys of discernment as they consider career pivots of their own. Consulting and coaching has been very fulfilling, and I never would have realized how much this work was a calling had I not bet on myself and left the safety of higher education to explore the wider working world.

Although deciding to leave was difficult, stepping away from higher education and into a new sector proved to be easy. My first role outside academia was at a nonprofit organization doing mission-driven work closely connected to higher education. This nonprofit organization was focused on protecting the emotional health of and preventing suicide for teens and young adults within higher education, so I could stay connected to the academic world. During this transition period, my higher education training truly paid off, as part of the role was to visit and consult with multiple higher education institutions in person and online. As a result, I was able to apply my knowledge and expertise to help greater numbers of students and make an impact on many more lives, which had always been my goal. I was still teaching as an adjunct faculty member. I maintained a close connection to higher education through mentoring, coaching, consulting, and teaching, so this new role turned out not to be a complete step away but rather a redefined relationship with my first career love: higher education.

My professional journey is a testament to my resilience, adaptability, and unwavering commitment to creating change. My experiences as a first-generation immigrant and college student shaped my perspective and fueled my drive to help others navigate unfamiliar territories. Through the pursuit of education, self-discovery, and entrepreneurship, I forged a path uniquely my own, one that embraced both my passion for higher education and a desire to contribute to broader causes, including mental health, life and career planning, and organizational development.

■ ■ ■

The Higher Education Landscape During the Transitions

To understand the transitions detailed in our narratives, it is essential to understand some of the tensions occurring in the world and, ultimately, in higher education at the time. Sofia left higher education in 2018, and Connie left in 2021. This period was complex; the world faced ongoing racial reckonings, a global pandemic, and an economic downturn. It was a perfect storm that brought moments of personal and professional reckoning for Connie and Sofia; we reflect on our values, priorities, and preferences.

Racial and Social Justice Reckoning

The highly publicized murders of Black men and women, including George Floyd, Breonna Taylor, and Ahmaud Arbery, ignited a racial reckoning that shed light on how much work remained in the areas of racial and social justice. There is much to say about how these lives changed the world, and there are so many more individuals to name. We simply cannot do justice to the topic in this chapter, but we put forth these names to show that these lives mattered—they, and the countless Black and Brown people who have lost their lives at the hands of law enforcement officials and other individuals who uphold racial hierarchy, mattered. They made people face the realities of racism that are as pervasive as ever, and we found ourselves rising to the occasion of this reckoning by expanding our work beyond academia. The world, inclusive of colleges and universities, had to face racism head on.

As women of color in academia, we had to hold space for so much of this work to be explored with colleagues, students, and the community—while working through our own instances of oppression while holding various campus-based roles. The pressure higher education institutions put on leaders from underrepresented and marginalized identities and on DEI professionals to carry the racial and social justice work and mental load had damaging impacts. We knew this work was hard but necessary, and it came at a personal expense. Still, as we assumed DEI roles in the nonprofit and private sectors, we could take our original passion for racial and social justice and leave academia to make much broader impacts.

Impact of the Global Pandemic

The COVID-19 pandemic exacerbated many of the challenges colleges and universities were already facing and greatly impacted other industries as well. No one was prepared to navigate the ever-evolving environments that came with managing the pandemic. Senior leaders in higher education often take on multiple roles on their respective campuses, and the pandemic pushed many of these leaders beyond their limits. Having to make rapid decisions to keep students engaged in different modes of education forced colleges and universities to think about their roles in students' lives.

Questions that higher education administrators were only beginning to address emerged in more pronounced and immediate ways. How were students going to learn remotely when home was not safe? How will students in need get access to food, laptops, Wi-Fi, and other necessities needed to complete coursework? How will remote learning expose students' personal lives to campus administrations and professors in ways neither were prepared for? In trying to address these genuine concerns, senior leaders and especially DEI professionals were forced to navigate increasingly complex, sometimes controversial, and quite emotional issues.

Economic Downturn and the Great Reshuffle

One can track how the previously mentioned issues would affect the economy, but some institutions felt it uniquely. Empty residence halls and academic buildings, canceled in-person events, and other disruptions strained already-tight budgets. Administrators were expected to do more with fewer resources. The negative financial impacts were felt across institutions and by individuals working in academia who were doing their best to keep up while managing their own struggles. Many administrators began questioning their roles and the institutional support for their professional and personal well-being. They started searching for jobs outside of academia; some left with no immediate position lined up.

As stated in the *Forbes* article "The Great Resignation Becomes The Great Reshuffle," "While 4.4 million Americans quit their jobs in February [2022], more than half of the workers who quit are switching their occupation or field of work, rather than leaving the labor force altogether" (Meister, 2022, para. 1). Higher education leaders also had to face how they manage talent in this changing world (McClure, 2022). Higher education can be a gratifying career; however, it can also be where people experience harm, dead-end jobs, and inequities, leading many employees to leave as we did.

The Decision to Leave Higher Education

In this section, we delve into the decision-making and career-mapping processes that led us to leave higher education and take roles in the non-profit and private sectors. We practiced self-reflection and found everyday experiences in our moments of discernment. Finally, we share what leaving higher education looked like for each of us.

Leaving higher education proved to be a challenging process. Earlier in our careers, we found many aspects of higher education, particularly in student affairs, to align with our values; both of us faced pivotal decisions about where we wanted our professional journeys to lead and what risks we were willing to take. We share some challenges and opportunities we faced in considering our original career goals and the realities of our career paths.

Challenging Aspects of the Process

We encountered several challenges while deciding to leave higher education. The following are a few common themes that emerged within our experiences.

Feeling a Sense of Loss

As we contemplated leaving an industry and field in which we had envisioned building lifelong careers, this emotional journey mirrored the stages of grief and loss. We went through denial, anger, bargaining, and, eventually, acceptance. Realizing our paths were taking a different direction required a period of emotional processing and adjustment.

Contending With the Grinding Aspects of Higher Education

Although higher education presented valuable opportunities for personal growth, it also entailed challenges. Limited work–life balance, emotional strain, lack of flexibility, and inequities in financial and advancement opportunities took a toll. Recognizing our priorities as well as these negative aspects significantly influenced the decision to explore other industries.

Shifting One's Mindset to Transition out of Higher Education

Transitioning from higher education to other sectors demanded a change in our career-search mindsets. First, we had to identify and articulate our transferable skills using language that nonprofit and corporate organizations could understand and appreciate. This process involved reflecting on our experiences and expertise, examining how our strengths could be translated into other contexts, and highlighting the value we could bring to new environments.

Rejecting the Norms of Advancement in Higher Education

Leaving higher education also meant stepping away from the prescribed norms of career advancement, which often seemed subjective and arbitrary. We worked hard, attained the right advanced degrees, and spent countless hours volunteering for professional associations focused on student affairs and higher education. We had hoped the payoff would be advancement to senior-level positions that would make full use of our skill sets. Professional role models and the visibility of individuals within professional associations influenced these norms. Still, we could not help but notice that some people would quickly advance while others remained in mid-level jobs for the bulk of their careers despite applying for senior-level positions. The system did not seem to work equitably for everyone, and the norms of advancement did not work out.

Learning That Work Relationships Changed

Transitioning from one industry to another also meant that work relationships would change. We had established a network within student affairs and higher education—one deeply rooted in the field and its professional associations. However, moving into nonprofit or corporate environments necessitated developing new relationships and adjusting to different dynamics. Work relationships and expectations can differ significantly between higher education and other sectors, including professional development and association involvements.

Positive Aspects of the Process

Despite the challenges, we came to recognize and appreciate the value of our work in higher education and student affairs as well as the relationships we had fostered through professional development. These experiences provided a solid foundation that proved invaluable in our new roles outside academia.

Having Transferable Skills

We found that several skills from our higher education backgrounds greatly benefited our work outside of it. These skills encompassed emotional intelligence, crisis navigation, program development, budgeting, project management, networking, building relationships, influencing, public speaking, conducting assessments, analyzing data, and writing reports. Our strong foundation in higher education equipped us with a diverse skill set that proved adaptable and valuable in various industries. We also found that our advanced degrees and passion for lifelong learning gave us an edge in the corporate and entrepreneurial worlds and added value to what we have to offer in terms of respect and compensation.

Fostering Curiosity for New Opportunities

Leaving higher education allowed us to explore new industries and different applications of skill sets, areas of interest, and expertise. It opened up opportunities to venture beyond academia, stemming from a desire to satisfy our curiosity and embrace new challenges. We also gained the confidence to become entrepreneurs and start businesses to share our expertise with organizations looking to make a difference. We could do this by setting paths on our own terms.

Increasing Self-Efficacy and Compensation

By pursuing roles outside of higher education, we gained a sense of self-efficacy and compensation that felt more commensurate with our experience and expertise. This recognition of our worth and the impact we could have in different environments further validated our decision to leave higher education. Both of us have prospered and secured our financial futures in ways that may not have been possible had we stayed in student affairs and higher education.

What Leaving Higher Education Looked Like

We noticed similarities and differences when shifting from higher education to other industries. While certain aspects, such as the importance of building relationships, remained significant, the expectations and nuances of these relationships varied across sectors. In addition, we had to adapt to new communication styles, organizational structures, and professional norms. Recognizing these similarities and differences proved crucial in navigating the transition effectively.

Lifestyle Upgrades

Leaving higher education affected our lifestyles for the better. It meant a shift in work hours, as nonprofit and corporate environments have different expectations and demands. It also opened possibilities for a better work–life balance, allowing us to prioritize personal time and well-being. Lifestyle changes varied based on the specific industry and position each of us entered. Overall, leaving higher education brought positive changes to our daily lives.

Reconciling Past Connections With Current Realities

Each of us had built meaningful relationships within the field, and transitioning away from higher education meant finding ways to maintain and honor those connections while embracing new professional networks. This process involved open communication, explaining our decisions, and acknowledging that our career paths were evolving. It also required empathy and support from colleagues and friends in higher education while we embraced new connections that emerged in our unique endeavors. Finally, involvement in work events and professional associations beyond higher education brought opportunities to expand our social and professional networks.

By embarking on this journey outside higher education, we discovered new perspectives, found fulfillment in new ways, and leveraged our skills and experiences to make an impact beyond the confines of academia. The decision to leave higher education was challenging, but it allowed us to embrace personal growth, explore diverse industries, and pursue career paths aligned with our evolving aspirations. Leaving higher education also gave us self-efficacy and self-confidence by knowing we could use our skills more widely and could be compensated for our expertise, so financial stability became attainable.

Thoughts for Higher Education Leaders on Career Shifts

Leaders in student affairs and higher education can play an essential role in assisting employees with career transitions. With more openness on this topic, educators and employers can continue to develop talent for the field, adjacent industries, and the broader public. The main goal would be to create environments where student affairs and higher education professionals can use their transferable skills in exploring other industries when they feel stuck or devalued in their roles.

Call to Action 1: Normalize Career Shifts

As noted previously, exploring a career shift out of student affairs and higher education can be riddled with anxiety, shame, guilt, and fear. Part of this stems from a lack of normalization of career shifts in these fields. Leaders should create space for more explicit and realistic career mapping, including exploring various options within and outside academia. Not everyone will be a vice president or president at a higher education institution, so academia should foster and normalize a professional culture that supports and encourages career shifts.

Recognizing the Changing Professional Landscape

As professionals progress through their careers, positions that offer advancement opportunities for the skills gained along the way become less and less available. When employees have "outgrown" their current roles, and budget constraints or other institutional challenges limit the opportunities for growth, they need to be able to seek opportunities elsewhere. That might mean leaving their current institution or leaving higher education altogether. Leaders can aid in this process by providing professional development opportunities that help employees understand their unique skills and how they translate to other industries.

Providing Career Development Support

Higher education leaders are pivotal in guiding and supporting their staff members through career transitions. Leaders should proactively offer career development that helps individuals improve their skills and explore alternative career paths. In addition, leaders can bridge the gap between academia and other sectors by partnering with career services, organizing networking events, and hosting workshops that demonstrate how skills can transfer to other industries.

Celebrating Professionals Who Use Transferable Skills Beyond Higher Education

Leaving student affairs and higher education should not be considered a betrayal. We have had positive reactions to our pivots from student affairs. However, we also have heard negative comments about having "given up" on higher education or leaving others behind while we explored opportunities in the nonprofit, corporate, and entrepreneurial realms. Leaders should be open, realistic, and supportive of alternative career plans, especially when they don't have opportunities for shifts or advancement within their own institutions.

Cultivating Entrepreneurial Mindsets

Aside from finding positions outside of higher education, we were able to leverage our skills and professional relationships to start our businesses as consultants and coaches. Higher education leaders should foster an environment that nurtures an entrepreneurial mindset among their staff members to help the institution and professionals stay ready for any layoffs or other personnel shifts that may take place. By promoting innovation, creativity, and problem-solving, academia can equip employees with the skills to identify and seize opportunities beyond the traditional academic career path.

Call to Action 2: Address Challenges and Inequities in Higher Education Careers

Although we chose to leave student affairs and higher education on our own accord, it would be inauthentic to claim we were unaffected by institutional and organizational inequities, spoken and unspoken norms, ongoing challenges that cause burnout, and an unwillingness to address these issues. The following are growing concerns we believe need to be addressed by higher education leaders if they would like to retain their high-potential staff members.

Addressing Work-Life Balance

Student affairs and higher education professionals often need support with attaining work–life balance, or synergy between their professional and personal lives. The increasing challenges that campuses and students face call for many professionals to work exorbitant hours per week, especially those who have on call responsibilities as part of their roles. These professionals are often tasked with administrative work during "normal" business hours and then expected to attend events or respond to student issues at night and on weekends. This work norm is not sustainable, especially for professionals who are trying to balance their work responsibilities with personal and family obligations.

Addressing the Emotional Tax of Student Affairs Work

Student affairs professionals are often at the center of mitigating complex issues involving student and staff mental health challenges, social justice movements, campus morale, and general crises. Carrying this load can lead to burnout, emotional strain, and overall decreased quality of life. We made personal sacrifices to advance our careers in higher education. Yet, at the time, we felt we were doing what was expected to advance, and we ultimately did get promoted along the way, but not without experiencing the burnout and other issues described previously. Looking back, we share some of the fault for allowing this burnout to happen; we decided ultimately to mitigate the burnout by shifting to careers outside of higher education.

Addressing Total Compensation and Financial Security

Student affairs and higher education professionals should be paid equitably. Although many practitioners are drawn to these careers because the missions of the institutions they selected to work for were closely aligned with their values, these employees must also provide for their families and futures. For many, the compensation is insufficient, and they find themselves taking on part-time work or having to leave their positions for jobs that better compensate them. Student affairs professionals should not need to find additional sources of income to make ends meet. This is a real issue for many people from low-income and working-class families who are trying to change the trajectory of their social class. The disparity between senior-level compensation and that of entry- and mid-level administrators can be so immense that senior leaders lose sight of the gap and its impact on their teams.

Deconstructing the Unwritten Rules of Advancement

Many higher education institutions and professional associations are profitable and thriving because of the donated time, talent, labor, and money they receive from professionals. This volunteerism is often positioned as a way to give back to the student affairs and higher education profession and to provide opportunities to network for possible advancement. However, there seem to be unwritten rules about how volunteering actually contributes to advancement opportunities. Higher education leaders must analyze these tacit rules and consider how volunteerism may contribute to inequities. At a certain point, some employees realize that giving their free time to the profession through associations may feel like exploitation, especially when they don't see a return on their volunteer investment. Higher education leaders need to examine this norm and understand how additional time-consuming volunteer efforts may cause harm, especially for vulnerable populations. Clearer paths to advancement would help student affairs and higher education professionals gain an understanding of how their work and potential will be recognized and rewarded.

Reflection Questions for Student Affairs Professionals Contemplating Transitions

In reflecting on our journeys through and out of higher education, many questions came up that helped with decision-making. The following is a set of questions to guide readers who are considering shifting to careers outside of academia.

Values and Passion

If you have a good sense of values and passion, you will know how to decide if a particular move or position is right for you.

- What are your values?
- What's important to you?
- What guides your work?
- What do you enjoy about your work?
- What makes you excited to come to work?
- What are you passionate about at work?
- Does your work give you fulfillment?

Skills

- What skills have you gained and upgraded over time?
- How do you obtain feedback so that you continually work on developing your skills and gaining new ones?
- What are your greatest transferable skills that you can bring to other industries?
- What must you learn to qualify for the role(s) you are considering?

Lifestyle

- How do you want to spend your time in and out of work?
- What are your personal and professional priorities, and how do they intersect?

- What kind of work environment do you prefer (e.g., fast-paced, large or small organizations)?
- Is there a work schedule you prefer (e.g., more 9 to 5, flexible schedule)?
- Do you prefer a working modality (in person, hybrid, remote)?

Role

- What kind of work would you like to spend your time doing?
- Do you want to be an individual contributor?
- Would you prefer to be a manager who is responsible for the work of others as part of your team?
- Does the title matter to you?
- What kind of team would you like to be on?
- What kind of supervision would you like to receive?

Big Picture

- How important is it for your job to be mission driven and/or values based?
- What are your non-negotiables?
- What trade-offs are you willing to accept?
- What is your geographic flexibility if you cannot obtain a remote or hybrid role?

Finances

- What are your financial goals, and what does a secure future look like for you and your family?
- What do you need from your career or job to provide you with financial stability?
- Is money a motivator, or are you willing to sacrifice pay for other perks or benefits?

Conclusion

By sharing our own journeys, lessons, and insights, we aim to support professionals in their career exploration. Although the decisions to shift careers were deeply personal, we also maintain that higher education institutions must normalize career shifts. Professionals can consider the key reflection questions provided in this chapter while pondering whether to remain in student affairs and higher education or explore roles in other industries.

References

McClure, K. (2022, December 2). Higher ed is a land of dead-end jobs. *The Chronicle of Higher Education*. https://www.chronicle.com/article/higher-ed-is-a-land-of-dead-end-jobs

Meister, J. (2022, April 19). The great resignation becomes the great reshuffle: What employers can do to retain workers. *Forbes*. https://www.forbes.com/sites/jeannemeister/2022/04/19/the-great-re-shuffle-of-talent-what-can-employers-do-to-retain-workers/?sh=7dbd2c334cf3

The Unexpected Return to Campus

Gage E. Paine

There seems to be a nearly infinite number of myths or so-called rules about what professionals must or must not do to have a successful career in student affairs. Each requirement presupposes one version of a successful career. Most of the time, this successful career path seems linear, proceeding in an orderly fashion toward a specific goal. That goal is usually at the top of a career ladder or a particular organization. Reaching that final achievement seems to require spending the "right" amount of time in the "right" types of positions; it also seems to require looking, dressing, and acting in certain ways as well as maintaining a single-minded focus on the result. But a successful career progression does not always mean an upward trajectory to a senior-level position. Rather, that is one of many definitions of success; although it is not universal, it is often a presumption in conversations about careers in student affairs.

None of that conventional wisdom about a career path accounts for the reality that a career takes place over an extended period. And during multiple decades, considerable change will occur. Changes in personal life, interests and motivations, and organizations; changes across the landscape of higher education; and significant societal changes are to be expected during the course of any extended career. The conditions at the start of a journey and those at each decision point are often very different. The decision-making calculus used by any professional at the start of their career will have changed in several ways by the time that person begins to consider retirement.

In this chapter I cite my own experiences as a case study to explore how I made decisions over the course of my career. A review of my résumé might lead you to believe that my more than 40-year career in student affairs had followed a carefully planned, linear path. In fact, my career, like most, resulted from a mix of actions and decisions based on the variety of circumstances in place at the time of each decision. Although some decisions might seem unexpected, such as a return to campus work after 6 years of consulting, each decision was grounded in my deep belief in the overall value of higher education and my set of personal values, needs, and motivations.

This case study can be understood as an example of the concept of a *protean career,* defined as

> a process in which the person, not the organization, is managing. It consists of all of the person's varied experiences in education, training, work in several organizations, changes in occupational field, etc. The protean person's own personal career choices and search for self-fulfillment are the unifying or integrative elements in his or her

life. The criterion of success is internal (psychological success), not external. (Hall & Moss, 1998, p. 25)

Each of my decisions has an internal consistency that has led to a career both externally respected and, more important, internally rewarding. When viewed through this lens, the choices to leave campus-based work for consulting and then to return to campus in a position not in student affairs but in a college of nursing form part of a continuing pattern rather than exist as completely unexpected steps. This case study presents one model of the fluidity and change experienced throughout a sustained career and encourages student affairs professionals, at any point in their careers, to explore their history as they continue to navigate the bumps, curves, and surprises of their own careers.

How It Started: Know What

It is no more accurate to say that my career in higher education began as an undergraduate resident assistant (RA) than it is to claim my role as secretary-general of the Oklahoma Model United Nations (OMUN) was the start of a role in international politics. In retrospect, both the RA job and the student leadership position offered clues to my future; however, at the time, neither role was a step onto a path to some future employment. The RA position was merely a job, a very fun and rewarding job, but still understood as only a college job. Serving as secretary-general of the OMUN was an extraordinary opportunity to work on a team and then lead that team, but there was no expectation that this moment was practice for a leadership role. They couldn't be part of a career plan; I still had no idea what job I wanted after college, let alone what I'd choose for a lifetime career.

The careers website for Minnesota State Colleges and Universities (n.d.) has a simple set of definitions that clarify the difference between a *job* and a *career*: "The real difference between a job and a career is your attitude. People who want a career are always thinking about their long-term goals. They are thinking about what they can do now to make those goals happen in the future" (para. 3). The first mindset pivot an individual must make is to go from thinking in terms of *jobs* to thinking in terms of *careers*. Over the past few decades, researchers have chronicled another important change: Workers have moved from a career orientation based within an organization to careers that they themselves manage.

In a 2004 article, Yehuda Baruch quoted two other papers that describe the elements of such individually managed careers using the term *intelligent careers*:

> Arthur et al. (1995) suggested the phrase "intelligent careers" to manifest the elements necessitated for effective career management on the individual side. The "intelligence" meant the "know why" (values, attitudes, internal needs, identity, and lifestyle); "know how" (career competencies, skills, expertise, capabilities, tacit and explicit knowledge); and "know whom" (networking, relationships, how to find the right people). To these Jones and DeFillippi (1996) added the "know what" (opportunities, threats, and requirements); "know where" (entering, training, and advancing), and "know when" (timing of choices and activities). (p. 61)

This concept of intelligent careers—and the self-knowledge and abilities embedded in its elements—provide a way to analyze my career as a whole and as a set of individual actions and decisions.

For example, at the start of my second year in law school, I made my first true career decision. By then, I knew that I did not want to practice law, but I was no clearer about the kind of work I wanted to do than I was when starting college. I had taken a half-time job as a hall director in the campus residence halls for the coming year. Back on campus early for orientation and planning for the RAs to arrive, I realized there were many jobs on college and university campuses that could be a good match for me—jobs I would like and that I might be good at. My first true career decisions were made right then. This was a rudimentary version of knowing what—that is, the opportunities, threats, and requirements. This moment of realizing a variety of jobs on a college campus could be interesting was a recognition of opportunities for the first time. I didn't know much about threats and had only a minimal idea of what the requirements might be, but, at that moment, coming to understand those opportunities was a revelation and was the first step toward a path. Ultimately, I would decide to stay in law school and work in the residence halls while completing degree, but it was clear that after law school, I would look for work in higher education.

I took one other career-focused action while in law school that had unexpected results. Already thinking about the jobs I might qualify for and wanting to gain some experience outside of residence life, I asked to meet with the vice president of student affairs to discuss the possibility of an internship in his office. I presented my résumé to him and discussed my interest in a career in student affairs. It turned out that the internships were reserved for doctoral students, so that plan didn't work. However, three months later, when the vice president received a letter about a position at McMurry College (now McMurry University), a small school in Abilene, Texas, he forwarded the position announcement to me. And that was how I learned of the position that became my first full-time job in student affairs.

My willingness to reach out to the vice president even though I was a half-time hall director was an example of three elements of intelligent careers: (1) know whom—reaching out to a senior leader for guidance; (2) know how—knowing I needed to seek out additional experiences to develop skills and competencies; and (3) know when—waiting to reach out until I had worked in the division for more than a year. Though it wasn't clear at the time, I was already developing the mindset necessary to create an intelligent career: a willingness to take steps to seek out opportunities and skills I might need in the future. The first important career action was not the action of taking a job; it was the decision to ask a senior leader for help.

> ***Know What.*** *Has your answer to what you want from your career changed? Have the opportunities, threats, or requirements shifted over time? What, if anything, do you need to change in your career if any of these things have shifted?*

I Want Your Job: Know Why

Often when someone reaches the levels of mid-level manager and senior leader, they face questions from colleagues, students, and staff members. One question is often phrased like this section title: "I want your job someday. What do I do to get there?" Here is another way it's phrased: "What was your path to your job?" Both iterations tend to be based in the mindset of one path, one rule to follow.

It's tempting, usual even, to simply answer the question with details about decisions made, jobs taken, and degrees completed. However, the framework of an intelligent career offers another way to engage in this discussion. Rather than answering with specific details from the past, it might be more beneficial to respond by asking why. Why is the person interested in the job? Encouraging inquirers to consider why they want a particular job and to reflect on their values, needs, and desired lifestyle is at least as important as learning specifically how one person secured the position.

One issue that I have been asked about is whether it is possible to move between kinds of institutions. People in higher education have often been told that once they have "too much" (whatever that is) experience at one type of institution, they're locked into that type. In other words, a few years in a private college means it's impossible to move to a Research 1 (R1) university, or vice versa. Or if someone has worked in a faith-based institution, they won't be able to move to a public university or one of a different faith, or vice versa.

This is not a hard and fast rule. I have moved from a very small, private, faith-based college to a very large R1 university, back to a midsized faith-based institution, to independent private, to large regional public, and back to a very large R1 university. One reason I was able to move among types of institutions is that I have developed skills in understanding colleges and universities as *organizations*. I often tell new staff members that it's important to become a student of organizations: Understanding one university well makes it possible to learn other universities. Navigating organizational cultures well is a critical skill that makes moving between universities smoother and more possible.

Someone once told me that my movement between such different types of institutions meant I didn't know myself—in other words, I wasn't clear about knowing my why. In fact, there is consistency about the choices made based on something other than the type of institution. The common thread linking all my choices about positions, about becoming a consultant and returning to campus, was simple: I was looking for places where good people who want to make a difference were doing good work because those places best match my fundamental why, or purpose.

Understanding personal values matters in every choice, but most particularly when higher education professionals are considering a faith-based institution. The expectations can vary widely—based in both the faith or denomination and the way each individual campus interprets that faith or denomination. Some institutions prefer people to be of the same faith; others don't care about the religious beliefs of staff, asking only that they live within any constraints expected by the school. For example, the small faith-based institution where I first worked had no faith requirement, but there was a preference that faculty and staff not drink in public and be comfortable with the tenets of the Judeo-Christian traditions. Faculty regularly ignored the drinking-in-public concept. However, most were careful about their *decorum* in public. There was a very clear expectation that the dean and associate dean of students wouldn't drink in public. Such protocol wasn't a problem for me, but some people would have bristled under such constraint—meaning this school would not be a good match. It's important to understand the way each community lives their faith and what behaviors and beliefs are expected of the people who join that community.

If you want to move to a different type of institution, can you articulate your values, professional identity, and lifestyle in a way that helps interviewers understand that you will be a good match for the mission and values of that organization? Will you be able to illustrate that you understand the differences between a previous institution and the one for which you are applying? It is expected that interviewers will cover many topics, but at some point, often multiple points, during an interview, candidates will need to show they understand the institution and its values. In my experience, this level of familiarity helps interviewers understand that candidates can make the transition between institution types.

> ***Know Why.*** *Have you compared recently your why (e.g., values, attitudes, internal needs, identity, lifestyle) to your current circumstances? Are they still in alignment? If not, what do you need to change for them to be a closer match? If you are moving, is your purpose compatible with the new job and new institution?*

Changing Roles: Know How

The concept of knowing how may be the most familiar. It's often the first thing employers seek when hiring a new staff member, and it's a critical question for applicants to ask themselves: Do my competencies, skills, expertise, and so on align with the position description? Wanting to learn new skills and competencies is often a good reason to change jobs, and this is often the case early in a career, when it is important to develop new skills and have new professional experiences.

My first position after graduation from law school was at McMurry, an institution of approximately 1,600 students, about half of whom were part-time. I was associate dean of students. It was a wonderful job, in part due to the variety of responsibilities I had and, therefore, the variety of skills I could develop. For example, I served as director of housing, managing the four residence halls housing about 450 students and supervising four hall directors, coadvisor to student government, advisor to the governing council for women's social clubs (local sororities), and student activities programmer.

After serving in that role for 3 years, I made an unusual career decision: I applied and was selected for the position of director of alumni services/assistant director of development at McMurry. I took the position for two reasons. First, I was ready for a change after 3 years in the associate dean role. A fourth year would have been more of the same, and I was beginning to understand my need to be challenged and have opportunities to learn in my work (know why). Second, a faculty member had asked me if I had ever thought about becoming a president. That question forced me to consider the skills needed in a college president. One of them is fundraising, and though I didn't think I would enjoy that aspect of being president, the alumni and development position would allow me to learn about the actual work.

This is an example of the "know how" component (competencies, skills, expertise, capabilities, tacit, and explicit knowledge). I identified a skills and experience gap if the presidency became a career goal and decided to explore the field and close that gap. Although I remained in the position for only a year, that time did exactly what I had hoped: It gave me experiences and opportunities to develop skills that were useful later—not as a president but in every one of the senior-level positions I would assume. For example, that 1 year of learning how development worked, asking people for donations, and working with alumni gave me credibility with every development officer I would work with in the future. Later, as development became more important for every type of institution, senior leaders across campus began to have specific fundraising responsibilities. This meant that in searches for dean of students and vice president positions, 1 year of development was no longer an oddity but an asset.

Do you need to change positions or institutions to develop the skills and competencies necessary to progress in your career? I am an example of someone whose career included several moves, but many student affairs professionals have rewarding careers in one position or on one institution. Regardless of goals, continuing professional development is important in sustaining a long-term career. Knowing how to work in changing environments over time is a critical component of any career—no matter how it develops.

> **Know How.** *Have you been keeping up with the changes in your professional area? Are you continuing to develop your skills, expertise, capabilities, and tacit and explicit knowledge? Are you paying attention to developing the how you will need for a future position?*

Making Moves: Know When

Although I learned a lot in the alumni and development job, much of what I learned was why that position was not a good fit. Halfway through that year, I decided that I missed working directly with students and that I had been right—I wasn't very good at fundraising. I began an active job search, willing to move anywhere in the country. I had two basic criteria for the role: It needed to be somewhere I could begin to work on a PhD, and it needed to be at a different institution. It was time to move.

That second criterion, needing to change institutions, nearly led to the poor decision of taking any job to leave my current environment rather than waiting for a good position. Midyear, I interviewed for a residence hall director role. Most people would consider going back to a live-in position in the residence halls to be a step back, but in some circumstances, it could have been a step forward. The position was on a larger campus in a metropolitan area with a sophisticated student affairs division, meaning there would be new challenges and opportunities. If the institution had offered a PhD in a relevant program, this could easily have been a positive step.

I was offered the job and, up until the point of the official offer, I fully expected to accept it. But I asked for time to consider it and called back at the end of the day to decline the offer. That day of reflection led me to realize this job was not the right position. Although it would provide some learning opportunities, I would mostly be doing more of the same work at a different campus. Most important, the institution didn't have a PhD program in education or related subjects. What I came to understand that day was an important fact about my motivation: I was moving *away* from my current situation, not *toward* a new one. The position in alumni and development had not worked out as I had hoped, and I knew I needed to leave (timing of choices and activities), but it would be a better decision in both the near and long term if I could stay where I was long enough to find a *good* next position, not merely a *next* position.

Knowing when to make a career move is difficult. It involves having a healthy understanding of your needs, values, and motivations (knowing why). If a work environment is truly toxic, the need to leave may be urgent. But as long as the need is not critical, you should take the time to get clarity about why you are leaving and what you are seeking. This perspective is essential to making decisions about a change.

My plans and reality have often been at odds in terms of knowing when. My second institution was the University of Texas at Austin (UT Austin). It met the criteria of a positive move, a different campus, and a possible PhD, and it was a new and interesting position: assistant dean of student judicial services (conduct) in the office of the dean of students. I thought I might work there for 5 or 6 years, finish the PhD, and see what came next. I went on to work in the office of the dean of students for nearly 11 years. By that point, I had held roles in multiple areas, finished my PhD, and felt prepared to be a dean of students. Because that position at UT Austin was unlikely to become vacant on my timeline, I sought another position. The question of when resolved itself easily.

The next experience turned out to be an example of moving more quickly than expected. I accepted the position of associate vice president and dean of student life at Southern Methodist University (SMU) with every expectation that I would be there for several years. Instead, I said yes to a call from a search firm and found myself involved in a search for a vice presidency after only 2.5 years. The search consultant told me, "The president is new and building his team. He thinks their academics are in good shape, but the student experience needs some attention, and he's willing to put resources into that effort." These words connected to my values and represented an exciting opportunity.

This is where the "know when" comes into play. The lore surrounding rules such as "Don't stay in one position too long or you won't be able to move" or its variant "I should be in [position] by [age] to be able to do [something else]" is not useful. Conversely, it is true that many employers are concerned about candidates who move often or stay in a position for a short time period. Leaving this senior leadership position within 3 years could have resulted in some colleagues, including the vice president, having hard feelings. It was a risk. But opportunities for vice presidencies that are a good match for any candidate are rare. By this point, I knew I wanted to be a vice president, so I decided to apply. It was a tougher decision to leave SMU after 3 years than leaving UT Austin after 11, but I accepted when the position was offered.

As you try to determine when the time is right to move, what elements are critical to you? The timing of a move brings together various elements, many of which are out of your control. A spouse or partner may want or need to move. Family obligations may make it difficult to move, or they may make a move necessary. It can take longer than expected to complete a degree. A great position becomes available unexpectedly. All these factors can affect decisions about making a move or choosing not to go. It's also important to consider the rhythm of the academic year, since there are times that are better for searching and better for leaving or starting a position. It is often helpful to consider those patterns, without thinking of them as rules, when considering a job change.

__Know When.__ Are you staying alert to the timing of your choices and activities? Are you paying attention to the changes in your field and in your organizational experiences to be able to identify opportunities and threats?

Dream Jobs: Know Where

The element of knowing where is described as entering, training, and advancing; it is particularly relevant in student affairs given the various roles available in the field. This component of entering a field, training, and advancing has changed significantly throughout my career. For example, when looking for my first job, I read a paper copy of *The Chronicle of Higher Education*. After finding a likely possibility, I typed (on a typewriter) a letter and mailed it with a copy of my résumé, which had been typeset and printed. And then I waited to hear. It was a slow process. And this process is only one of the many procedures and systems that have changed significantly over a 40-year career. Technology has also brought change in other ways, but it's certainly not the only change.

A bit of wisdom shared by student affairs professionals with parents of incoming students is "Don't worry about students changing majors. They will likely have jobs that haven't even been imagined yet." And it's true. The world is changing that quickly. That wisdom is just as true for student affairs professionals.

The types of positions available in student affairs have changed over the years. At the beginning of my career, what is now known as student conduct work was merely a portion of the responsibilities of an associate dean. By the time I started at UT Austin, it was the primary part of my job, plus I supervised two people, though all three of us had additional responsibilities. It was in my second year in conduct work that the Association for Student Judicial Affairs (now Association for Student Conduct Administration) was created. Conduct is now a full-time position at many colleges and universities and a career path in itself for growing numbers of professionals.

With the implementation of the Americans with Disabilities Act (ADA), another career field was created. As more and more veterans returned from deployment in Afghanistan and Iraq, colleges and universities responded by creating new programs and services, and new career opportunities in veterans services were developed. Over the course of my career, society's understanding of individual identities deepened. In response, the profession shifted its ways of providing services from multicultural services to diversity, equity, and inclusion programs. Education and training for supporting LGBTQIA+ students, various gender identities, and undocumented students are now available at colleges and universities across the country. These changes have opened doors for professionals to find new career paths, none of which existed when I began my career.

Increasing legal and regulatory requirements have also brought new career possibilities. The ADA has been one catalyst, but new expectations of campus responsibilities regarding safety, Title IX, and compliance have also created new ways to work, sometimes in student affairs and sometimes in adjacent fields. The possibilities of where one might create a career while connected to an actual campus location now include this variety of specialty areas.

Student affairs staff often fear being pigeonholed in specialty areas, particularly if those employees share an identity or characteristic with the population they are serving. I have two examples from the same job search to illustrate this concern. For one institution, my experience in conduct and disabilities was not what the school needed for the new vice president; that institution wanted someone with significant student activities experience. However, in the same search, a different institution looking for a dean of students viewed my work in conduct and disabilities as just the experience they needed. In that case, my specialty work was an asset. Most of the time, it is not about being labeled or pigeonholed but about whether a candidate's experiences match that institution's needs.

What do you understand about the true match of your experiences, education, training, and such with the needs of the institution or position for which you are applying? Can you articulate why and how your specialty training and experiences support your work more generally and how they will be a match for the position and institution to which you are applying?

Know Where. *Is your current organization or field still the right place for you? Do you need to consider other opportunities for entering, training, and advancing?*

Personal Decisions: Know Whom

Effective career management drives individual career choices. Yet every career is connected to a wide number of other people. Family, friends, and colleagues all play a part in the day-to-day work and decision-making. Colleagues and supervisors, current and prospective, are critical to any career experience. Additionally, an individual's professional and personal networks can influence both opportunities and decisions. The element of "know whom" includes that network, relationships, and the ability to connect across a professional career.

Such connections played an important part in my career. At McMurry, where I held my first position, the dean of students, my supervisor, was tied to the campus's location. But he knew that I, his new associate dean, was not. It was only about 2 months after I arrived that the dean handed me a brochure for the annual conference of the Texas Association of College and University Student Personnel Administrators (TACUSPA) to be held that fall. At that event, I volunteered for the conference committee for the summer law conference. The chair was the dean of students from my law school campus. He, knowing something of my history, instead asked me to present at that conference. Attending that conference and presenting introduced me to people who continued to be friends and colleagues throughout my career.

One of the attendees at my presentation was not yet the dean of students at UT Austin. When I applied to UT Austin, the now-dean of students had seen my presentation skills and ability to handle some mild heckling from audience members. That knowledge played a part in the dean's decision to hire me. My involvement in TACUSPA, presentations in Texas and across the country, and participation in national organizations all helped open doors. Some of these opportunities were the next job; others were leadership positions in professional organizations.

It's important to realize that a career is made up of more than the jobs one holds. Engagement with others, sharing of knowledge (whether through a presentation or a phone call), and leadership work over time all constitute a vibrant career. All have to do with a professional's willingness and ability to do all the work connected to the concept of knowing whom. Understanding this component and engaging in networking in an openhearted, not a manipulative, way for a path to a rich and rewarding career.

What does your network look like? Whom have you helped and connected with over the years? Who has helped you? Where have you served your profession? Like a career, a rich network should grow naturally from the good work done and service provided. Still, when seeking career changes, a willingness to reach out to that network to ask questions, seek advice, or solicit support can be critical to success. From the chutzpah I showed as a part-time hall director contacting a vice president for advice at the start of my career to asking colleagues for guidance and introductions later in my career, I practiced the "know whom" component and found it to be an important part of developing my career over the years.

__Know Whom.__ With whom are you having lunch? (It's still a useful question.) Are you taking actions that expand your network and your reach? Are there other groups, committees, or organizations with which you would enjoy engaging? If so, what is stopping you?

Putting All the Elements Together

I held three vice presidencies over the course of 15 years. When search firms contacted me during my second position at the University of Texas at San Antonio (UTSA), I told them I wasn't interested in a third vice presidency. And then, I contradicted myself by taking the position of vice president at UT Austin. Four years later, I knew it was time to leave, but to what? And that, more than any other time, was when my network proved crucial. I contacted a variety of friends and colleagues to ask about other opportunities. I considered the idea of serving a range of institutions via interim positions. I had always wondered about consulting. It was while talking with the founder of a respected consulting firm about interim work that he suggested I think about consulting with his team. After several conversations, I left campus-based work to join that consulting firm and then, after 3 years, reached a mutual agreement to step away from that work to start my own agency with a different focus.

My work with one of my clients, the College of Nursing at the Health Sciences Center at the University of Oklahoma, began as individual coaching, moved into a review of the college's student services, and then shifted into ongoing support of both student services and policy review and development. The dean of the college twice asked me to come on full-time to help after a staff member left unexpectedly. Both times I declined, but the third time, when the dean asked me to serve as associate dean for academic affairs and interim executive director for student affairs, I accepted.

This position, even more than the earlier foray into alumni and development, could be seen as unexpected. An associate dean position in an academic college doesn't usually follow a vice presidency, particularly in this case: I have no experience or training in nursing. However, this college had many good nurses. What it needed was an experienced senior administrator who could help develop a solid foundation during a time of significant change in the college. I had that knowledge and, after a year and a half of working with the college as a consultant, I had also developed relationships with faculty and staff across campus. Yet again, the role met my criteria—good people who want to make a difference doing good work, plus a chance to use my skills to help make a difference. And it would be very different work. It met several elements of the intelligent career model, and the job was just an attractive opportunity in itself. A return to campus was unexpected—taking a position in a college of nursing was not part of the long-term plan, but neither was it an aberration.

Conclusion

Careers are not linear. Quite the opposite. Opportunities do not present themselves on a perfect timetable. In fact, they often seem to come at inopportune times. The rules of a career often need to be broken for a person to lead a rewarding life. While these elements of the intelligent career are new to me, discovered in the work of writing this chapter, they provided a good framework for an analysis of my career. They may be useful to professionals in making complex decisions about what comes next. These elements may also be a tool for understanding past decisions, good and bad, thereby functioning as a guide to the future.

Over a 40-plus-year career in student affairs, I wondered at various points whether it was time to leave the field of higher education. But I never did. I often said that even on the worst days, I always believed in the highest purpose of the institution of higher education, of student affairs. That deep belief in higher education kept me working in and around colleges and universities. Understanding my individual needs and values helped me make day-to-day decisions that supported my ongoing work. Making choices that made sense to me in my life, regardless of whether they made sense to others, gave me confidence to make other decisions. Each decision made sense in the context of the time; as a result, the choices have added up to a fulfilling career across decades.

References

Arthur, M. B., Clam, P. H., & DeFillippi, R. J. (1995). Intelligent enterprise, intelligent careers. *Academy of Management Executive, 9*(4), 7–22. http://dx.doi.org/10.5465/ame.1995.9512032185

Baruch, Y. (2004). Transforming careers: From linear to multidirectional career paths; Organizational and individual perspectives. *Career Development International, 9*(1), 58–73. https://doi.org/10.1108/13620430410518147

Hall, D. T., & Moss, J. E. (1998). The new protean career contract: Helping organizations and employees adapt. *Organizational Science, 26*(3), 22–37. https://doi.org/10.1016/S0090-2616(98)90012-2

Jones, C. & DeFillippi, R. J. (1996). Back to the future in film: Combining industry and self-knowledge to meet career challenges of the 21st century. *Academy of Management Executive, 10*(4), 89–103. https://doi.org/10.5465/ame.1996.3145322

Minnesota State Colleges and Universities. (n.d.). *Is a job the same as a career?* MyMnCareers. https://careerwise.minnstate.edu/mymncareers/finish-school/job-vs-career.html

The Call, Push, and Pull to Academia
Navigating to Faculty

Michael S. Funk, Tamara Bertrand Jones, and Natasha N. Croom

The faculty role in graduate preparation programs is critical to the student affairs profession. Program faculty educate future and current professionals who will ideally apply what they have learned in these programs, thus creating more thoughtful and informed professionals and practices across higher education institutions. Moreover, graduate preparation program faculty serve as the intellectual backbone and curators of the field's knowledge through their research, scholarly activities, and curricular decisions, which germinate and inform practice and culture across the profession.

Kniess (2019) outlined several considerations for student affairs educators who transition to the faculty role. Her advice includes understanding one's "why," or purpose for the transition (Austin, 2002; McCluskey-Titus & Cawthon, 2004), the differing cultures of student affairs and the professoriate (Boettcher et al., 2019; Kniess et al., 2017), the types of faculty appointments (i.e., contingent [adjunct, clinical, or visiting] and tenure stream), faculty work expectations (i.e., teaching, research, and service), and the support systems one needs for a smooth transition. Before getting to the transition stage, one must aspire to and experience some level of socialization toward the role. As Austin (2002) noted, graduate programs (particularly master's programs and some doctoral programs) do not situate the professoriate as an aspirational route. As a result, many students do not understand the importance of faculty's work in the profession. Eddy and Gaston-Gayles (2008) found that their participants had divergent socialization experiences depending on whether the faculty identified them as potential faculty colleagues, they self-identified as aspiring to the role, or they attended an institution and doctoral program known for preparing future faculty (Freeman & DiRamio, 2016).

More information is needed about how faculty in graduate preparation programs find their way to the professoriate. In this chapter, we offer our narratives of navigation to full-time faculty roles in professional preparation programs. Each of us offers aspects of our socialization experiences and recalls our entry into full-time faculty positions. Through our individual stories, we highlight how student affairs educators may be called, pushed, or pulled into the professoriate to demystify this critical career route in student affairs.

■ ■ ■

THE CALL

Michael S. Funk

Growing up in the church, I often heard the biblical passage "Many are called, but few are chosen." It typically denotes a unique charge or gift bestowed on an individual based on a predetermined fate from God. In the case of higher education and student affairs, countless students have been called to practice in the field of higher education based on rewarding experiences they may have received because of positive engagement with student affairs practitioners. Even with student affairs' positive impact on their experiences on campus, only some students choose to pursue the field as a career or as a path to advance one's education. Individuals following the road less traveled by transitioning from a full-time practitioner to a full-time faculty member are *called to* and chosen for the work.

hooks (2014) shared that education is the practice of freedom. Higher education proved to be a pathway toward liberation despite the obstacles I had to overcome to attain a career and life that bring joy and continually cultivate growth. Many students of color in K–16 systems are embattled by and required to move through what Love (2020) described as the "educational survival complex" because of the historical legacy of durable inequalities that induce trauma, self-doubt, and a process of internalization that generate fear and doubt in one's self-efficacy and self-esteem. As a self-identified Black-multiracial male, my experience was no exception. I attended a private Catholic grade school, and in second grade, I was tracked into the B group after a short reading assessment of my learning ability. I believed the "B" in B group stood for Black because every Black student in the school was tracked into B-level remedial education. Subsequently, I transferred to a public school where I feverishly played catch-up academically and achieved mediocre grades despite my best efforts.

After applying for one undergraduate degree and taking the SAT twice, I was admitted to Edinboro University, a comprehensive state school in Pennsylvania. I achieved a 2.1 GPA after my first year, and I was pleased with my status because I could avoid the stigma surrounding probation. Thankfully, because I was a hyper-involved student during my undergraduate stint, the director of the program with which I had been most involved, the Minority Student United Program, made an offer that would subsequently change the trajectory of my life. The director proposed that if I made the dean's list, he would fully subsidize a summer study abroad trip to Morocco in Northern Africa. I was in full-blown immersion mode during my sophomore year, so I seized the opportunity to lay foot on the Motherland. I held my end of the verbal contract by making the dean's list that semester and each semester after that until graduation. That one conversation at that moment helped me fully understand how every conversation or interaction a student has with a higher education administrator or faculty member deeply matters.

An Introduction to Higher Education and Student Affairs

A misconception about graduate school is the assumption that college graduates have figured out how to negotiate academia and its responsibilities. First-generation undergraduates emerge as first-generation graduate students and, in my case, first-generation professors. At each level of educational and professional mobility, I had to work hard to overcome the internalization of imposter syndrome, stereotype threat, microaggressions, and racial battle fatigue (Cokley et al., 2013; Smith et al., 2007; Solórzano, 2000; Steele, 1997). Despite these challenges, fate or fortune prevailed, and the call became more pronounced when I met a recruiter from the New York University (NYU) Higher Education and Student

Affairs program through a mutual friend. I was stunned that a person could earn a degree in everything I loved to do in college, which would mean earning an education in my favorite city. My lack of cultural and social capital influenced my application process when searching for a master's and doctoral program. Similar to my undergraduate application process, I applied to only one institution for both degrees.

The NYU Higher Education and Student Affairs program requires applicants to secure a 20-hour paid assistantship for full-time admittance. The program's built-in placement process allowed me to secure an internship and to obtain a position with the NYU College of Arts and Science Academic Advising Center. It was also responsible for advising a caseload of students from the general population and was charged with building a specialized portfolio by working with the school's Academic Achievement Program (AAP). This promising practice program serves as an academic enrichment and leadership development program for self-identified Black, Latinx/a/o, and Indigenous students. My role as an advisor to the general population and the thriving students in AAP encouraged bolstering academic and student affairs skills. After completing my first year, I was hired by my internship as a full-time academic advisor and soon after was promoted to AAP director. These generative roles allowed me to develop the skill of balancing a prescriptive and developmental approach to advising. They augmented my ability to support students through tough decisions, such as choosing an appropriate major and course selections, or by helping them maximize campus resources. It pushed me as a professional to embrace the notion of advising as teaching (Kramer, 2003), and I learned to accept that advisors are cultural navigators for our students (Strayhorn, 2019). Academic and faculty advisors often endure the same process as students when attempting to break through red tape and bureaucratic setbacks.

Directing AAP propelled me to begin leading with my ears as a supervisor, manager, and servant leader to students. By applying intentional and strategic practice (Harper & Quaye, 2009), I understood that students flourish if leaders provide a particular set of expectations and context. My students permitted me to shatter the single-story (Adichie, n.d.) approaches when working with minoritized students. I learned that if we are to meet our students where they are, we must be able to hold the historical and contemporary structures that often "other" and alienate them while simultaneously treating them as individuals with intersecting identities that make them distinct from any other student. I incorporated an equity-minded lens that shifted the onus for student success away from my students and instead turned the lens back on me and the institution I represented. Evidence-based practice served as my North Star. I borrowed many concepts surrounding student involvement, engagement, and development and infused supporting theories as I worked to exhibit reflective practice.

An Educator and a Student

My work as a practitioner coaching and cheerleading underrepresented groups that were overwhelmingly successful academically and socially on campus motivated me to apply to the University of Massachusetts Amherst Social Justice Education program. The combination of my roles as a student, practitioner, and aspiring scholar paved the way for my research, which was greatly influenced by the inconsistencies between what I witnessed from working directly with students of color, particularly Black males, and what the literature stated. In literature reviews in the program, I found that the bulk of what was written about Black males was overly focused on pitfalls, hardship, and futility, such as the deficit model. Freeman Hrabowski III, Sharon Fries-Britt, and the then-emerging scholar Shaun Harper were practitioners and researchers who offered a strength-based, antideficit analysis of Black males in higher education.

Building off the broader research agenda I developed in my master's degree program, I narrowed my inquiry to how "promising" Black males at predominately White institutions define *academic success* and what factors affected their academic success. Informed by my practice, the study explored the various influences that positively assist this population of men toward graduation and how colleges and universities can create sustainable strategies that contribute to their academic success. My work aimed to redirect research that focuses on futility and failure to a focus on high expectations, resilience, and proven achievement.

I remained a part-time practitioner as a doctoral student at the University of Massachusetts Amherst. During my doctoral studies, I codirected a special interest residence hall called Nuance, which is dedicated to undergraduates interested in multiculturalism and diversity. As teaching opportunities arose, I positioned myself to procure as many as possible, enacting what I call the "grad school hustle." Unlike many teaching assistant and graduate assistant positions where the graduate student accompanies a full-time professor who leads the classroom lectures and discussions, the program created pathways for its doctoral students to solely lead courses and evaluate students. After teaching my first general education course anchored in diversity in education, I obtained adjunct positions in the Smith College School for Social Work's master's degree program and at Holyoke Community College and a Hispanic-serving institution. I also taught at Westfield State University. Teaching at these types of institutions helped develop my faculty acumen and supported my future as a full-time faculty member.

Scholar-Practitioner Extraordinaire

After I received my doctorate and served as an adjunct professor at various types of institutions, the pull of the moon left me wanting to enter the cocurricular realm of higher education as a scholar-practitioner. Equipped with years of scholarship and affirmation from my classroom experience, I hoped to combine the two worlds. My relationship with New York City and NYU is nothing short of storybook extraordinary, so I applied to an enhanced version of my former position at AAP. Serendipitously (or perhaps divinely), a vacancy was available. However, it now required a terminal degree, which was helpful for my process. During my 2-year stint, I was reminded that we "never arrive" doing this work, and it is almost impossible to "get good" or, perhaps more appropriately, "stay good" at the work because students are constantly in flux. Their needs are as fluid as water that engulfs the earth.

My long-term commitment to higher education crystallized my commitment to leadership that aims to develop cocurricular education. I knew this demanded curriculum and pedagogies that foster critical engagement, encourage civic responsibility, contribute to current research, and connect with communities within and beyond campus parameters. This is what attracted me to the clinical faculty position I currently hold. My role as a faculty member is a unicorn (probably more appropriate than extraordinaire). I am not bound to the rigid expectation of publishing or perishing. However, my scope of scholarship enables me to write on accessible platforms that honor the social justice passions I pursue. The role is the best of both worlds, a position that bridges the evergreen dichotomies between academic and student affairs. I am rewarded for my work as a teacher, service to the university, contribution to the field, and administrative expertise. The clinical contract promotes a mutual courting process between the faculty member and the institution. This agreement poises both stakeholders to grow and to be their best.

My current role as a full-time faculty member and director of the master of arts in the Higher Education and Student Affairs program places me at the nexus of theory and practice. Each course I teach offers practice-based competencies that are requisites for any aspiring or current practitioner. I am guided by the frequently recited African proverb "It takes a village to raise a child." However, through my comprehensive experiences as a clinical administrator coupled with my role as faculty fellow in residence in a first-year residence hall, I have come to understand that it takes an entire campus community to graduate a student.

What I appreciate about my current position is that it enables me to combine faculty and administrative responsibilities to help develop curriculum and pedagogies that foster critical engagement, mentor and guide students, and complement functional areas within my home school and universitywide. The scope of this work extends beyond campus, as I am charged with supporting full-time graduate students at their internship sites. This includes more than 14 New York and New Jersey institutions, comprising more than 80 positions across higher education and student affairs.

As an educator and leader, I have demonstrated a commitment to critical, authentic leadership (Brown et al., 2020) and understand the importance of creating a community of learners. Higher education is a microcosm for our world, which demands that we be at the forefront of inclusive and promising practices in the field. Much as I have learned from second wave feminism, the personal is political, and the professional is equally political. Integrity entails an integrated self that refuses to compartmentalize my work and personal life. My position as a faculty member *pushes* me to be my best personal and professional self—inspiring students to become invested in a lifelong reflective process of learning about themselves and others as they continue their work as educators inside and outside the classroom.

THE PUSH

Tamara Bertrand Jones

Throughout my career in education, people have encouraged me to do my best and reach higher. Being the people-pleasing oldest child, I always followed their advice and knew they saw something I did not. As I reflect on my journey from administrator to faculty member, I see the influence my parents and mentors had on me fulfilling my life's calling in higher education.

Ready for the Perfect Position

My journey as a student affairs administrator started like many in the field. I was an involved undergraduate student who later learned about the field as a viable career and an option for advanced studies. Student affairs combined my love of programming, planning, and administration. When I learned I could get a graduate degree and a job, I said, "Sign me up!" A mentor told me all about Florida State University (FSU) and, admittedly, FSU was the only program I applied to. Once I secured a graduate assistantship, I moved from Texas to Florida for what I thought would be 2 years. Unfortunately, the divine had other plans!

During my master's degree program, I developed influential mentoring and professional relationships, connections I maintain today. As a result of a yearlong internship, I started my first position at Tallahassee Community College (TCC). The vice president for student affairs at that time was my supervisor and knew I wanted to continue my education by enrolling in a doctoral program at FSU. Given these plans, I was offered a position that would continue the work I started in my internship. Excitedly, I jumped at the chance to remain at the college and implement new ideas for my work with students. I tell my students that I grew up professionally at TCC.

I learned how to communicate with others, supervise and advise students, and work with and within institutional bureaucracies. I was allowed to be creative, work independently while still being supported, try new things, and experience different functional areas. Together, my time at TCC and my doctoral studies influenced my career trajectory.

After working at TCC for 5 years, I transitioned to FSU as the director of assessment and evaluation in the Division of Student Affairs. The position combined my higher education and student affairs training with my research and evaluation doctoral training to create a perfect position. After several years in the position, I became interested in professional development and teaching. Although I had taught classes at TCC, I first cotaught a graduate class on assessment in higher education with my mentor. After that experience, I taught as a co-instructor or instructor of record annually. Teaching and supporting other staff to design and implement their projects fueled me in ways I could not describe.

Around my third year in the position, I received a job posting that seemed perfect for me. The position combined my interest in research development for people of color and program management, so I applied for the position and received an offer. Unfortunately, the position was located in New Jersey, and personal reasons and my partner's professional circumstances did not allow us to relocate, so I turned down the offer. Although disappointed, I changed the focus of my search and honored the pull I felt toward a faculty position. I solicited feedback from mentors on transitioning my résumé to a curriculum vitae and even found a position in a town nearby that fit my experiences. I excitedly told my supervisor at the time about the position. (I had been transparent with her about the next step in my trajectory.) She burst my happy bubble. She told me I was diminishing my talents by choosing a small regional school. She suggested I look for positions at schools like FSU.

A year later at a conference, I saw the woman I would have reported to in the position I turned down. In catching up, she asked about my job search, and I told her I was still looking. She suggested I look at FSU for an opening. I admitted that there was an open search in the higher education program. She encouraged me to apply. "Oh, no," I replied. "FSU does not hire its graduates unless they have 10 years of experience post-FSU." She gave me the most profound advice: "You let them tell you no; do not tell yourself no." After I left her, I went home to apply for the position.

I applied, and they told me no. I met with the search committee chair and developed a list of tasks to tackle to improve my future applications. A few months later, I received a note from the department chair informing me that an additional position was available, and the faculty recommended me. Without my mentors' push and their confidence in my skills and abilities, I would not have put myself in a position to be considered. I later learned that their push was just one of many that would nudge me along in my faculty trajectory.

Black Women's Influence on My Trajectory

Throughout my graduate studies, I developed and maintained connection to other Black women graduate students and professionals through significant relationships that sustained me during challenging times, provided accountability for moments I wanted to give up, and gave me a safe spot to land emotionally and spiritually. Given the challenging graduate education environment for Black women graduate students, my relationships with other Black women served as a site of resistance, resilience, hope, and sisterhood. The counterspaces, professional and personal, resulted in our creating the Sisters of the Academy (SOTA) Institute so that other Black women could access community and the resources they needed for their success.

Creating SOTA was a pivotal moment in my professional journey, and the organization would help solidify my research agenda as a faculty member. Focusing on the experiences of Black women in the academy came naturally to me. After being surrounded by positive role models, mentors, and sponsors, I knew the importance of a supportive community but realized this was not part of every Black woman's experience. That saddened me, and I desired to learn more about our experiences in higher education and the ways in which individuals and institutions could better support our success. With SOTA's focus on creating professional development tailored to the needs of Black women, I saw the power of how equipping women with tools could positively shape their self-concept and, in turn, their career trajectories.

However, as I transitioned to faculty, I hesitated to explore Black women solely and felt out of place in my department as a qualitative scholar. So, I committed to refining my quantitative skills and fitting in with my colleagues. After the pre-tenure third-year review, I sought out one of the tenure and promotion committee members for her feedback. She admitted her surprise as she read my draft statements. She acknowledged the lack of congruence between my stated interests and what I wrote in my research statement. Admittedly, she was right. In my statement, I tried to portray the broader implications of my work for all graduate students and articulated how I contributed to understanding socialization, with Black women as a subpopulation, not the main focus. She told me that my work on Black women was *my* unique contribution and not to downplay it. Her permission released me from trying to morph into someone I was not. After that encounter, I no longer disguised my focus on Black women. Her push for me to be myself has sharpened my focus and solidified my advice to others. I encourage them to pursue work with which they identify and that allows them to contribute to our field in ways they deem meaningful.

As I continue my work on Black women's experiences, I learned that only focusing on the (minoritized) individuals and not the system ignored the reality that even the most knowledgeable, well-prepared, and savvy

Black woman encounters racism, sexism, and other oppressions that can negate all the work she has accomplished. Developing this understanding has resulted in a slight shift to my agenda. Now, I examine socialization and its contributors (e.g., mentoring, professional development) as both a process and an outcome. The experiences of countless Black and other women of color I have encountered through my work with SOTA and my research have only reinforced the push I feel in doing the work I do. That push encourages a commitment to interrogating the system and actively creating environments where Black women, and other people of color, can and do thrive in academia.

THE PULL

Natasha N. Croom

I never imagined myself as a professor. Veterinarian, yes. Career military. Physical therapist. College graduate. However, professor was never a part of my self-concept. I was completing my doctoral program and job searching when I was pulled toward the professoriate because I was *definitely* running away from faculty life. I remember the day vividly. I was beginning to work on job applications and knew I would need to secure references. I went to my dissertation advisor excited to share with her all the postdoc and academic administrative positions I was considering. When I finished, I asked her if she would be comfortable writing me a letter of recommendation for any of these positions. Now, my advisor has an uncanny ability to deliver unexpected news with a bit of a comforting smile, as if to reassure while also getting the other person together. With that comforting smile, she looked at me and said, "I'm not writing any letters of recommendation for anything other than faculty positions!" At that moment, despite my best Allyson Felix impersonation, I was forced to unpack narratives that informed the imposter syndrome I carried into her office that day and through the early stages of my job search.

Early Socialization Narratives

As an undergraduate student, I had the opportunity to participate in the Ronald E. McNair Scholars program, which supports first-generation college students in attaining terminal degrees in their respective fields and disciplines. During that time, I also participated in the Minority Undergraduate Fellows program of NASPA–Student Affairs Administrators in Higher Education. As an overachieving first-generation Black woman, I was ready to take graduate education and my chosen profession of student affairs by storm. NASPA's program helped me understand the student affairs profession. In contrast, my student leadership opportunities gave me an on-the-ground-level perspective. Entering the master's program at Texas A&M University, I fully intended to go "straight through."[1] As a direct result of my participation in McNair, I began looking at doctoral programs as a first-year master's student. Despite seeking doctoral programs at that point, becoming a faculty member was never on my radar. I assumed I would acquire a degree and enter an administrative position. Although the role of faculty in the field was never discussed in my early days as a master's student, an early narrative suggested that earning the doctorate straight out of the master's program was frowned on in our applied field. I believe some element of this narrative is wrapped up in adultism, which, in this case, suggests younger people lack experience and thus lack helpful knowledge and wisdom. This discouraged conversations

---

[1] A colloquial term used to describe people who earn their terminal degree without having worked in the field and an often-unappreciated positionality due to a perceived lack of experience in student affairs work.

about the doctorate and had a limiting effect on surfacing additional critical roles in the field, such as pursuing faculty appointments.

Doctoral Socialization

Despite the goal of entering a doctoral program directly after completing my master's degree, I chose not to go "straight through." I worked full-time for a few years and focused on the goal of pursuing a doctorate. While working in housing at the University of Maryland, College Park, I continued researching PhD programs. I eventually chose to pursue the degree at Iowa State University (ISU). After entering the doctoral program, I was still unsure what to do upon completion. However, building off my previous experiences, I was interested in diversity and equity and thought I would go into assessment work. A naïve me hypothesized then that people were not making good decisions about diversity and equity work because they did not have good data and information. I had several teachers and professors in my education journey, but it was not until the doctoral program that I had a model in Lori Patton. She was the first Black woman professor I ever had in college. I went to ISU to study with and learn from her. She became my dissertation advisor and my assistantship supervisor. I did not understand then that I was being socialized toward the professoriate. I cotaught or served as a teaching assistant (TA) for all courses in the student affairs master's program. I engaged in various stages of research with multiple faculty. I was engaged in service across campus, including in the department. Despite *doing* research, teaching, and service (the trifecta of faculty work), I still did not consider the faculty route.

The curriculum featured a class about the professoriate and the role of faculty in the institution. This class taught me about the various ranks, promotion, tenure, and faculty work. The class sparked my interest in studying faculty. It provided a more substantive filter by which to think about what I observed in the experiences of the faculty around me. Specifically, in working with Patton, I could observe her research, teaching, and service life up close. In doing TA work in her classes, I witnessed White students' microaggressions and her level of overpreparation for each class. I remember thinking I did not want to experience those things (Patton & Catching, 2009). I built relationships with Black women full professors in the field for my dissertation work. Although I was excited to learn from and with them, their collective experiences reinforced my suspicion that faculty was not for me. I did not feel resilient enough to combat misogynoir[2] and gendered racism.

Making the Decision

As I got closer to finishing up and began thinking about what would come next, these two narratives returned to the forefront: You are too young to have this doctorate. And as a Black woman, you will likely experience misogynoir. Either way, no one will hire you to do anything serious. Other narratives were creeping in toward the completion of the PhD as well. Namely, my cohort mates, students ahead of us, and those at other schools began regurgitating the notion that "no one gets tenure-track positions straight out of their program. It is too competitive." The narrative created an even smaller field of vision for what I would do. Were they suggesting that I would not be a competitive candidate? Would tenure-track positions be open? Would I have publications upon graduating? Would I be good enough to get a position at another research-intensive, Association of American Universities member institution, like Iowa State, Texas A&M,

---

[2] *Misogynoir* (Bailey & Trudy, 2018) refers to misogyny directed toward Black women, where racism and patriarchy/sexism intersects to create unique perspectives and expectations that inform their experiences.

or Maryland? I had resolved that I might be Dr. Hall Director by the end. Moreover, I never even considered contingent roles.

After my advisor declared that I would not get a letter of recommendation for nonfaculty positions, I set my sights on faculty jobs. It might seem odd that I would simply pivot given her comment; however, she engaged me in a conversation about my choice. In this discussion, the imposter syndrome I had felt reemerged. I shared with her that I did not feel ready to be a professor and did not want to experience misogynoir in the ways I witnessed and heard from other Black women faculty. Even the Black women full professors in my dissertation could name how gendered racism showed up in their experiences despite earning the highest, supposedly most respected rank in the profession. Never mind the narratives about publish or perish; with this knowledge, who would choose such a life? Patton gently reminded me of my preparation for the role and of the reality that I would be a Black woman anywhere and everywhere I went, regardless of the job. Therefore, the experiences I feared might, nevertheless, exist. It was the pull I needed.

Getting the Job

During my last year and job search, many of the faculty in my department departed ISU. Thus, a few faculty searches emerged. I remember being told by several people that departments do not, under any circumstances, hire their students, and especially not right out of the program. I did not even consider applying for the assistant professor position. One of my faculty members contacted me and asked why I had not applied. I shared with him what I was told. Although he agreed with the sentiment, he encouraged me to apply. He, too, reminded me of my experiences and reinforced my preparedness for this role and what I would need to grapple with if I got the job—transitioning from student to colleague with the remaining faculty. I applied for the job. I had one publication, a significant amount of teaching, and institutional and national service. Given what I had heard about publications, I was nervous about my chances—faculty needed multiple publications to get a tenure-track job at a Research 1 institution. It would not be until later in my faculty career that reality would disrupt these two narratives. Mainly, departments hire their students straight out of the program, although, in my experience, this pipeline seems to be primarily accessible by White women. Additionally, in searching for tenure-track assistant professors, having multiple, if any, publications is not always necessary. It is about the potential, especially if one expands the search beyond research-intensive institutions.

I ended up accepting the tenure-track assistant professor position at ISU. This news, of course, was accompanied by one of my program peers who shared that I had received the offer only because I am Black. As it may, haters gonna hate! Thankfully, I had mentors, sponsors, and a peer network that helped me unpack the narratives that served to deter me from the path of the professoriate. Moreover, my journey to the faculty role has helped me guide others who may deal with the same narratives. More than a decade later, I ask what is next as I consider the many doors that open by being a tenured professor. I recognize the value of being a student affairs educator, specifically, a scholar-practitioner, in academic administrative roles such as department chairs, deans, provosts, and beyond. Although the professoriate has many challenges, I am forever grateful that my network pulled me toward academia.

■ ■ ■

Conclusion

No one-size-fits-all path exists toward securing a full-time faculty position. Whether feeling called to the work, gently pushed and supported into applying for a faculty position, or pulled to apply for a faculty position by colleagues and mentors, each of us encountered a unique set of circumstances that ultimately brought us in front of the classroom. Although we had varied faculty titles and subsequent roles within the faculty realm, common threads we share span experiences in academia focused on educating, researching, mentoring, program coordinating, leading, event planning, and advising diverse populations of students at both the graduate and the undergraduate levels. Our combined experiences weave through an array of institution types throughout the United States.

There is a shared understanding about how the multicomponents of campus life should work in accord to form the student experience and help students grow holistically, academically, professionally, and personally. Higher education and student affairs preparation programs offer a rare platform that primes midcareer professionals for departmental and institutional leadership and prepares entry-level professionals for faculty roles. A path toward a rewarding faculty career is more achievable with deliberate planning when choosing an institution to pursue doctoral work.

Unlike selecting an undergraduate degree where the institution's prestige or the larger campus environment becomes a deciding factor, enrolling in a doctoral program encourages a mutual investment with the faculty members who will work with you throughout your process. In addition to financial support, these are questions to ask when exploring doctoral programs:

- Do any faculty members share my research interest?
- Do the faculty copublish with their graduate students?

- What are the formal and informal levers of support?
- Do teaching opportunities exist for graduate students?

Customized faculty advising, coupled with departmental support that guides students with intention and transparency, is a recipe for graduate student persistence and paves more apparent paths for faculty career development (Strayhorn, 2019).

Undoubtedly, the path toward attaining a faculty position in higher education and student affairs is narrow. Each of us has detailed how this narrow road is often filled with side steps, setbacks, and perhaps some backsliding. It is also true that it is almost impossible to do this work alone. The power and magic of relationship building in higher education and student affairs practice parallel the dynamic community-building components that help practitioners become faculty members. Identifying mentors is paramount for the trek. As Patton and Harper (2003) suggested, "Mentoring is a cornerstone in the success of graduate education and depends highly on student-faculty relationships propelled by trust, integrity, opportunity, and understanding" (p. 68). At all levels, finding faculty, peer and professional sponsors, and consultants who nurture you and advance your aspirations will allow you to fulfill your mission and complete the work you are *called, pushed,* or *pulled* to do as an educator.

References

Adichie, C. N. (n.d.). *The danger of a single story* [Video]. TED Talk. https://www.ted.com/talks/chimamanda_ngozi_adichie_the_danger_of_a_single_story

Austin, A. E. (2002). Preparing the next generation of faculty: Graduate school as socialization to the academic career. *The Journal of Higher Education, 73*(1), 94–122. https://doi.org/10.1080/00221546.2002.11777132

Bailey, M., & Trudy. (2018). On misogynoir: Citation, erasure, and plagiarism. *Feminist Media Studies, 18*(4), 762–768. https://doi.org/https://doi.org/10.1080/14680777.2018.1447395

Boettcher, M. L., Kniess, D., & Benjamin, M. (2019). From collaborative to collegial communities: Transitioning from student affairs practitioner to faculty. *Georgia Journal of College Student Affairs, 35*(1), 5–22. https://digitalcommons.georgiasouthern.edu/gcpa/vol35/iss1

Brown, R., Desai, S., & Elliott, C. (2020). *Identity-conscious supervision in student affairs: Building relationships and transforming systems*. Routledge.

Cokley, K., McClain, S., Enciso, A., & Martinez, M. (2013). An examination of the impact of minority status stress and impostor feelings on the mental health of diverse ethnic minority college students. *Journal of Multicultural Counseling and Development, 41*(2), 82–95. https://doi.org/10.1002/j.2161-1912.2013.00029.x

Eddy, P. L., & Gaston-Gayles, J. L. (2008). New faculty on the block: Issues of stress and support. *Journal of Human Behavior in the Social Environment, 17*(1–2), 89–106. https://doi.org/10.1080/10911350802168878

Freeman, S., & DiRamio, D. (2016). Elitism or pragmatism? Faculty hiring at top graduate programs in higher education administration. *The Journal of the Professoriate, 8*(2), 94–127. https://caarpweb.org/wp-content/uploads/2016/02/8-2_Freeman_p94.pdf

Harper, S. R., & Quaye, S. J. (Eds.). (2009). *Student engagement in higher education: Theoretical perspectives and practical approaches for diverse populations*. Routledge.

hooks, b. (2014). *Teaching to transgress*. Routledge.

Kniess, D. R. (2019). Moving into a faculty role from student affairs administration. In D. R. Kniess, K. Walker-Donnelly, & T. W. Cawthon (Eds.), *Managing career transitions across the lifespan for the student affairs* practitioner (New Directions for Student Services, No. 166, pp. 51–61). Wiley. https://doi.org/10.1002/ss.20307

Kniess, D. R., Benjamin, M., & Boettcher, M. (2017). Negotiating faculty identity in the transition from student affairs practitioner to tenure-track faculty. *College Student Affairs Journal, 35*(1), 13–24. https://doi.org/10.1353/csj.2017.0002

Kramer, G. L. (2003). Advising as teaching. In G. L. Kramer (Ed.), *Faculty advising examined: Enhancing the potential of college faculty as advisors* (pp. 1–22). Anker.

Love, B. (2020). *We want to do more than survive: Abolitionist teaching and the pursuit of educational freedom*. Beacon.

McCluskey-Titus, P., & Cawthon, T. W. (2004). The grass is always greener on the other side of the fence: Making a transition from student affairs administrator to full-time faculty. *NASPA Journal, 41*(2), 317–335. https://doi.org/10.2202/1949-6605.1336

Patton, L. D., & Catching, C. (2009). "Teaching while Black": Narratives of African American student affairs faculty. *International Journal of Qualitative Studies in Education, 22*(6), 713–728. https://doi.org/10.1080/09518390903333897

Patton, L. D., & Harper, S. R. (2003). Mentoring relationships among African American women in graduate and professional schools. In M. F. Howard-Hamilton (Ed.), *Meeting the needs of African American women* (New Directions for Student Services, No. 104, pp. 67–78). Wiley. https://doi.org/10.1002/ss.108

Smith, W. A., Allen, W. R., & Danley, L. L. (2007). "Assume the position…you fit the description": Psychosocial experiences and racial battle fatigue among African American male college students. *American Behavioral Scientist, 51*(4), 551–578. https://doi.org/10.1177/0002764207307742

Solórzano, D. G., Ceja, M., & Yosso, T. J. (2000). Critical race theory, racial microaggressions, and campus racial climate: The experiences of African American college students. *Journal of Negro Education, 69(1/2)*, 60–73.

Steele, C. M. (1997). A threat in the air: How stereotypes shape intellectual identity and performance. *American Psychologist, 52(6)*, 613–629. https://doi.org/10.1037/0003-066X.52.6.613

Strayhorn, T. L. (2019). *College students' sense of belonging: A key to educational success for all students*. Routledge.

A Return to the Administrative Side

David J. Nguyen

Careers are complex. Like many authors in this volume, I have taken many career paths. Never in my wildest dreams did I think I would work in higher education. Twenty years later, I now lead an academic college within a large public institution. This chapter describes my career path through a series of acts. I introduce some theoretical perspectives that help me understand my career development. I conclude with some lessons learned for professionals interested in pursuing academic administrative positions.

My Career Arc So Far

Lots of people: So...you were a financial consultant, and now you are an academic dean?

Dave: Don't forget that I also worked in student affairs and as a faculty member.

Lots of people: You've had a lot of very different jobs. What's your end game?

Dave: I like doing different things because my approach to work and careers is situated around how I can help improve things if I have only one chance in life.

This conversation represents many discussions about my career plans. I am currently an academic dean. The conversation also inevitably leads to the question of my long-term aspiration. I have never had a good answer to that question. I struggle to answer it because I want to do good, relevant, and interesting work. I want what I do to be meaningful and to help people along the way. Twenty years ago, I was introduced to an inspirational quote by Etienne de Grellet: "I shall pass this way but once; any good that I can do or any kindness I can show to any human being, let me do it now. Let me not defer nor neglect it, for I shall not pass this way again." Little did I know that my introduction to this quote during a service trip to the Boundary Waters would pay profound dividends in shaping how I think about my career.

To begin to unwind the relevance of this quote, it's important that I share a little about my background and college experiences. In thinking about my career planning, I liken it to theater, which may have one or multiple acts. In my case, the concept of acts comprises large chunks of time or scenes that I have dedicated to some form of career development. I also think about the way a protagonist navigates a story. Although my story has no specific antagonist, I think about situations where I have had to overcome a form of adversity or negative thinking to begin scripting the play in the way I would like to see it operate. Furthermore, as I share my story, I find great importance in offering an episodic approach for you.

College: The Prologue

Like so many first-generation college students from working-class backgrounds (see Ardoin, 2021; Bettencourt, 2021; Longwell-Grice & Longwell-Grice, 2021), my family valued education but did not know how we would pay for it or how to approach the process. I am the son of a car mechanic; many of my family conversations about college were to find a "practical career," like an engineer, and find "a good job" that paid more than my parents made. This seemed like solid, straightforward advice. I did not realize that I was not equipped with the discipline to be a good college student, let alone a student who needed to master certain mathematical and engineering concepts. I thought I was reasonably prepared for college, but I did not know how to prepare for class adequately and certainly did not use academic resources, like tutoring or supplemental instruction.

As I struggled in my courses, I had a fortuitous meeting with a career counselor who helped me better understand my skills and values. Through this interaction, I knew that leveraging analytical tools and program planning were things I enjoyed. However, I still had this gnawing feeling of not disappointing my parents, who had sacrificed so much for me to attend college in the first place. Consequently, I changed majors to marketing because I enjoyed the research aspect of the coursework. However, I added accounting to ensure I could meet my parental expectation of a "good job."

After College: Act I, the Non-Higher Ed Years

Eventually, I completed my undergraduate education (not in 4 years, by the way) and started working for a financial consulting organization. In this role, I learned how to apply tax regulations and create tax structures for large multinational organizations. The three areas I most enjoyed were helping people new to the organization learn about what it was like to work at the company through on-campus recruiting activities, helping people understand how to apply these complex rules and regulations to transactions, and helping people become part of the team. I had plenty of room for career advancement and worked well with clients; however, I needed to align better between what I enjoyed (hint: helping people) and the long hours working at client sites. So, I decided to leave on a whim and pursue work in higher education. Although I was relatively uninvolved as a college student, the collegiate environment allowed me to explore intellectual and personal ideas. I often thought about and described this time in my life as my altruistic moment where I was hoping to pay things forward for those who did not yet know they needed someone for guidance. These ideas prompted me to pursue a career in student affairs.

After College: Act II, Entering Student Affairs

I moved from one coast to another and found myriad jobs in campus life, orientation, and career services. To help support my career plans, I enrolled in a master's program to learn more about colleges' organizational behaviors and their students. Working with college students was so fascinating. For the first time in my career, I felt like I was actually *helping* people. Indeed, there were moments like supporting campus life events where students swam in a kiddie pool of cereal and milk. I supervised the student event staff but refused to clean up the mess made by their peers.

Furthermore, I worked with students in other situations to help them define how they would pitch themselves through their résumés and cover letters to prospective internship sites and employers. These developmental moments showed me that working in higher education had staying power for me; the work drew me in. I also noticed many people above me had terminal degrees. I would need an advanced degree to attain the roles I desired. I applied to and was accepted to a PhD program to meet this end.

When I entered my doctoral program as a full-time student, I did not know what career path I would take. Returning to administration was an option, becoming a policy analyst was another, and then there was this amorphous role known as a faculty member. A professor once asked our class if any of us wanted to pursue a faculty position, but I did not raise my hand because I did not envision myself in such a role. As with so many of my experiences, I had the fortuitous opportunity to join a research team—the National Study of LGBTQIA+ Student Success—where I entered as an affiliated researcher and eventually became the research project manager. At the time, I did not realize how essential research skills and a coherent agenda are to academic careers.

I received affirmation from several faculty members that I should consider a faculty career after completing my doctoral degree. Affirmation took many forms, including being invested in my skill development, having opportunities to coteach courses, and taking part in projects during the summer so I could pay my bills. The other form of affirmation came from the investment of time in reviewing drafts of papers, offering critique when necessary, and helping me in my job search. Unlike the hiring process for other entry-level positions, a faculty candidate may spend 1 to 3 days on campus delivering a teaching demonstration, giving a research talk, meeting with current students, connecting with other administrators, and answering questions from a search committee.

After College: Act III, Entering the Professoriate and Academic Administration

I am fortunate that I secured a higher education and student affairs faculty position upon completing my doctoral degree. In this role, I taught five courses each academic year, conducted research, and served the institution. The latter two responsibilities can be particularly challenging to quantify or qualify. For example, conducting research takes time to plan, execute, analyze, write, and publish. Service means serving on various department- and college-level committees with the option of volunteering for institutional ones. In my unit, the program coordinator role rotates among the program faculty every 2 years and goes according to who has been in the role and who still has not. Program coordinators are responsible for the day-to-day operations (e.g., course scheduling, organizing events, paperwork, recruitment) of a smaller academic unit inside a department. For example, the department I belong to is Counseling and Higher Education, and there are program coordinators for counselor education and higher education and student affairs.

As is often the case, the person who serves as program coordinator is only sometimes interested in these roles. Part of this reluctance comes from the time commitment and the lack of training for people in these roles. For example, in a doctoral program, little time is dedicated to how to run an academic unit or how to set up a schedule across seven faculty members with distinct desires for courses and teaching times. I stepped up and took on the role that the next in line did not want. I wanted to help recruit students to our program actively, whether through social media engagement or setting up a call with a prospective student. It was an opportunity to better connect the division of student affairs and the student affairs graduate program. Having a strengthened partnership would allow us to do more for the 20 to 25 students we onboarded each year. I also thought having a more tightly coupled relationship with the department would show students that the program was a theory-to-practice approach. I loved getting to know our graduate assistant partners and trying to help them find the best student for their available graduate assistantship. I had intended to keep doing this role until another opportunity presented itself.

(Enter interim associate dean role.)

Within the College of Education, the interim dean at the time put out a call for anyone who might be interested in serving as the interim associate dean for research and graduate studies. I applied because I had ideas about how the College of Education could improve its research engagement and processes around graduate education. I also applied because I needed a new career challenge but was still deciding whether to move into academic administration. I did not want to be another one of those people faculty had complained about as not listening to needs or having unrealistic expectations. Concerning the interim associate dean role, I was by far the most junior person in my college who could apply for the position. I was not even officially tenured when I applied for the position, but the interim dean believed in what I wanted to do with the role and offered me the position. This role challenged me professionally because I had to learn new jargon and negotiate meetings with faculty and academic leaders. I did not often work directly. This was challenging for a few reasons, including having a very youthful appearance and not knowing whether people would take me seriously. People often remark that I look like a student and may find it hard to relate. Nevertheless, I took on this challenge and changed some people's opinions about me and academic administrators.

I knew I might not be able to continue in this role after a permanent dean was named, but I enjoyed being able to do academic administrative work because I was tackling challenges that people so often complained about but never acted on. I sought out a role that had some level of permanence to it. Fortunately, a position I found ideal—the dean of University College—became available. At my institution, University College includes an academic department and nonacademic units (e.g., orientation, community engagement, major exploration). This kind of position appealed to me because it allowed me to leverage my previous experiences as a student affairs professional and faculty member in one position. I have been in this role for more than a year and have learned much (some insights are shared later in the chapter).

Analyzing My Experiences Through the Lens of Theory

Regarding my career planning, I think about the chaos theory of careers (CTOC) and self-authorship as valuable lenses for understanding how I went from a struggling college student to an academic dean.

Chaos Theory of Careers

Pryor and Bright (2011) developed the CTOC, which considers career development a lifelong process of complex influences, chance events, and change. *Complex influences* represent effects from a complicated interplay of individuals and environments (e.g., economy, sociocultural). People interpret these moments in various ways depending on the interplay; however, these influences can shift how people think about their lives and what they expect from life. Second, *chance events* refer to unintended happenstances that occur within the context of one's life. The individual does not anticipate these events but can guide career development. Finally, as a person experiences the world or experiences a particular set of events, the world they know evolves and can *change* what they expect from their careers.

Now I apply CTOC to some of my career development. Struggling academically as an undergraduate student was undoubtedly a complex influence on me. From the prologue as a first-generation student, I learned that the campus had resources to help people learn course content. Instead, I relied on the idea of group studying without knowing the fundamentals of the programs.

Furthermore, I thought group studying would mask my need for help and that perhaps I would learn the content through osmosis. I felt like I did not belong, but I did not want to communicate this concern to others for fear of being judged. Consequently, I struggled academically. This struggle culminated with a 29 on a Statics in Mechanical Engineering exam. After that, I had a chance encounter with a student affairs professional who let me know it was OK to struggle and that perhaps my major did not fit my strengths or personality. That person also introduced me to employment recruiters because they believed in my potential. Ultimately, I changed from engineering to a more applied field, business.

Self-Authorship

Baxter Magolda (2001) developed and applied self-authorship theory to college student populations. Baxter Magolda (2008) described self-authorship as a person's "internal capacity to define one's beliefs, identity, and social relations" (p. 269). The origins of Baxter Magolda's perspective emerged during a longitudinal study of 101 students, where she identified four key phases—following formulas, crossroads, author of one's life, and internal foundations—that students enter during their college and post-college transitions. Following formulas involves resisting listening to one's values and assuming the role others hold for them. In following formulas, the individual often looks to authority figures (e.g., parents) for guidance. Crossroads is a developmentally significant moment where a person struggles with balancing what other people expect (following formulas) and what the person expects for oneself (self-authorship). The incongruence of this experience can be jarring or call into question previously held beliefs. Self-authorship occurs when a person internalizes and operationalizes their belief systems in opposition to what others expect of them. During self-authorship, a person realizes they have control over how they respond to situations. Internal foundations refers to trusting the internal voice and forming a philosophy over one's belief systems.

Following Formulas

I grew up in Scranton, Pennsylvania, a working-class former coal-mining town. Scranton always seems to have a chip on its shoulder, and this permeated interactions I had in my youth. I was also involved with Boy Scouts of America. This program taught me much about leadership, helping everyone, and outdoor skills. I enjoyed the program so much that I worked at a local summer camp for six summers holding various positions. I enjoyed learning and sharing knowledge with people. Several hundred scouts would come to the camp each week, and I would teach them about camping, knot tying, orienteering, and many other outdoor skills. As I grew up, I decided to be involved in education. This way of thinking was incongruent with what my parents had hoped I would do with my life. One of my parents came to the United States as a refugee, so I felt indebted to both my parents for the sacrifices they made for me to pursue postsecondary education.

Crossroads

Although some might point to my poor academic performance during my undergraduate career as a crossroads-like moment, I had this experience only when I was trying to figure out what to do with my career. I was on the cusp of being promoted to a managerial role in the consulting firm, but if I had moved toward the promotion, I would find it easier to leave. So I started to think about what I might like to do and what I enjoy. Attending campus recruiting events provided me with the joy I had hoped for. I did not consider doing this on the employer side but wanted to be in the collegiate environment because I thought I would have more opportunities.

Authoring One's Life

I think I am beginning to self-author my career journey. As I progressed through my doctoral program and into my faculty career, I did what was expected of me to become tenured and promoted. I reviewed the guidelines and built a research agenda to meet the minimum scholarly productivity qualifications. I also tried to be innovative in teaching courses because I wanted students to engage with the material in new and exciting ways. Finally, I contributed to my program and department through collegiality and being a step-up colleague. I used these experiences as a jumping-off point for my academic administrative career. This situation taught me to trust my internal voice, which Baxter Magolda (2008) indicated is an essential element for self-authoring.

Lessons Learned in Returning to Administration

This chapter imparts a small amount of whiplash about the stream of positions I have held since graduating from college 2 decades ago. What has remained constant is the need to be able to *help*. This kind of need has led me in and out of careers and now from student affairs practice to academic administration. I have learned a few lessons about returning to administration.

The primary lesson is to apply principles of scholarly practice (Kupo, 2014; Nguyen et al., 2019; Sriram & Oster, 2012; Streitzel et al., 2020). When I worked in the corporate sector, we applied tax laws and regulations to transactions. When I worked in student affairs, I incorporated what I learned through my student affairs preparation program and applied it to the students with whom I worked. As a faculty member, I developed expertise in researching student success, including what helps students feel like they belong and can thrive in postsecondary environments. Now my team and I apply scholarship to help our students at University College succeed. Only some see themselves as scholars or feel like they have the time to be a scholar-practitioner, but everyone is capable. I draw on this during my conversations with my team to ensure the practices we use in our work move beyond anecdotes and draw from data to make certain our actions can be effective.

Connect with people internal to your institution. Having a strong network across your institution can help you be effective. My role as an academic dean comprises academic and nonacademic units, so I need a vast network across campus to understand how to accomplish a task or a job. I am guilty of not paying as much attention to the historical tensions or legacy of how a particular situation has emerged. For example, why might the institution do something a certain way? This intrainstitutional network can provide the foregrounding needed to avoid inadvertently creating a bigger problem for yourself. Sometimes people give too much credence to the past and continue to let things happen rather than actively seek to change something. The internal network can help you understand where flexibility exists.

Develop a network beyond your institution. Having noninstitutional peers can be helpful if you need to solve a problem or if you want to implement a particular program and need to learn about potential pitfalls. I strongly recommend attending conferences or convenings beyond your traditional sphere to develop connections outside your institution. For example, I frequently attend the NASPA–Student Affairs Administrators in Higher Education Annual Conference, but in my role, being an academic dean in a student affairs space might not allow me to maximize what I am looking to do in this kind of role. For this reason, I started to attend NASPA's Conferences on Student Success in Higher Education and one for university college deans to develop my network and to learn about initiatives that may make their way into the academic end of my portfolio.

Lessons Learned for Professionals Interested in Academic Administration

Although I can go in several directions regarding lessons learned for professionals interested in academic administration careers, I offer two low-risk suggestions: Take on the temporary role and seek out professional coaching to support you in this role. First, if you have an interest in academic administration but are not sure if it is something you want to do, then you should consider applying for a temporary commitment like an interim role (e.g., some program coordinator or department chair roles last for 1 to 3 years). Some studies and advice columns have explored interim roles, which often focus on the drawbacks or challenges of such positions (see Bain & Varela, 2020; Perlmutter, 2023; Vallancourt, 2018). However, I viewed my experience in a temporary role as an interim associate dean for research and graduate studies or the institution's student success fellow as an opportunity to challenge myself and activate change. Part of what led me to enjoy these roles was the amount of autonomy and flexibility. Much of this concerns the leadership of your supervisor, who may be the dean or the provost. However, taking on these kinds of roles can provide you with invaluable capital as well as give you a place and space to test your mettle.

Moving into an interim or temporary role can help you address the things that frustrate you or your colleagues. For example, there may be some process improvements or workflows that would make people much, much happier. One such example in my work was that many colleagues were often frustrated with how files were managed for doctoral students. I talked to some faculty members about what frustrated them and engaged them in ways they thought the process could be improved.

Using some of their suggestions, I met with the graduate records manager to discuss some of the frustrations and suggestions from the faculty while also listening to what might prevent them from making such a change. To help activate the change, my graduate research assistant and I scanned hundreds of files to create an online repository accessible to the faculty advisor so they could see the files' contents and would no longer need to ask what was in a folder. In doing so, the burden had shifted from an administrator to a faculty advisor while increasing accessibility to student folders for everyone.

Be open to professional coaching or mentoring in your academic administration role. You are talented, you are committed, and you are stretched personally and professionally in all things. However, you must invest in yourself (or you should at least ask your institution to invest in you). Academic administration is different from an administrative role in student affairs or the corporate sector. In these academic administrative roles where you work with faculty, the relationships can be different because of the way their contracts are structured, such as 9 months versus 12 months, or an "against the administration" attitude can permeate the interaction. Everyone can use a "guide on the side," whether it is through professional coaching or a mentoring arrangement. Having dedicated time to enhance your skill set and to learn more about yourself as a leader can be invaluable for understanding how you might work with people with different wants and needs than yours. Engaging with coaching is not to suggest that you have a shortcoming. It just might be that it can help you develop the repetition to learn how to actively harness and leverage these skills so that everyone can win. Seriously, no one will think less of you, and I can almost guarantee you will notice a difference in your confidence and leadership.

Conclusion

I have shared an unfolding story of how I have moved into student affairs, a faculty role, and administration. My story is still being written as I think about what will come next for me. One takeaway from this chapter should be that you can be the author of your story, journey, and career development. In some cases, you will play bit parts; in others, you can be the star. I wish someone would have told me that sooner. So go out there and make it your own and use some of my lessons learned so that you can be an influential member of your organization.

References

Ardoin, S. (2021). The nuances of first-generation college students' social class identity. In G. Longwell-Grice & H. Longwell-Grice (Eds.), *At the intersection: Understanding and supporting first-generation students* (pp. 89–99). Routledge.

Bain, S. F., & Varela, D. G. (2020). Navigating the interim role in higher education. *National Forum of Educational Administration and Supervision Journal, 38*(4), 1–8.

Baxter Magolda, M. B. (2001). *Making their own way: Narratives for transforming higher education to promote self-development.* Stylus.

Baxter Magolda, M. B. B. (2008). Three elements of self-authorship. *Journal of College Student Development, 49*(4), 269–284. https://doi.org/10.1353/csd.0.0016

Bettencourt, G. M. (2021). "I belong because it wasn't made for me": Understanding working-class students' sense of belonging on campus. *The Journal of Higher Education, 92*(5), 760–783. https://doi.org/10.1080/00221546.2021.1872288

Kupo, V. L. (2014). Becoming a scholar-practitioner in student affairs. In G. L. Martin & M. S. Hevel (Eds.), *Research-driven practice in student affairs: Implications from the Wabash National Study of Liberal Arts Education* (New Directions for Student Services, No. 147, pp. 89–98). https://doi.org/10.1002/ss.20103

Longwell-Grice, R., & Longwell-Grice, H. (Eds.). (2021). *At the intersection: Understanding and supporting first-generation students.* Routledge.

Nguyen, D. J., Mathuews, K., Herron, A., Troyer, R., Graman, Z., Goode, W. A., Shultz, A., Tackett, K., & Moss, M. (2019). Learning to become a scholar-practitioner through research experiences. *Journal of Student Affairs Research and Practice, 56*(4), 365–378. https://doi.org/10.1080/19496591.2019.1611591

Perlmutter, D. (2023, June 22). Admin 101: Your first day on the job as an interim leader. *The Chronicle of Higher Education.* https://www.chronicle.com/article/admin-101-your-first-day-on-the-job-as-an-interim-leader

Pryor, R., & Bright, J. (2011). *The chaos theory of careers: A new perspective on working in the twenty-first century.* Routledge.

Sriram, R., & Oster, M. (2012). Reclaiming the "scholar" in scholar-practitioner. *Journal of Student Affairs Research and Practice, 49*(4), 377–396. https://doi.org/10.1515/jsarp-2012-6432

Strietzel, J., Kaul, C. R., & Sriram, R. (2020). Overall effectiveness of a student affairs scholar practitioner workshop: A mixed methods study. *Journal of Student Affairs Research and Practice, 57*(4), 441–456. https://doi.org/10.1080/19496591.2019.1707091

Vallancourt, A. (2018, May 14). Are you sure you want that interim job? *The Chronicle of Higher Education.* https://www.chronicle.com/article/are-you-sure-you-want-that-interim-job

Going Global
Student Affairs Practitioners Abroad

Ainsley Carry, Baishakhi Taylor, and Raphael X. Moffett

Student affairs first emerged as a profession in the late 1800s (Deardorff et al., 2012). U.S. institutions adopted the positions of deans of women and deans of men to focus on student conduct and well-being. Initially, universities assumed *in loco parentis*—in place of parents—responsibilities. However, no formal preparation for deans of women and men was available until decades later. Professional networks and associations—such as the American Association of University Women, founded in 1880 (Levine, 1995); NASPA–Student Affairs Administrators in Higher Education, established in 1919 (NASPA, n.d.); and the National

Association of Appointment Secretaries transformed into the American College Personnel Association in 1931 (Cilente, 2011)—emerged to compensate for the informality of the work and to elevate the profession. The associations established roles and defined terms.

In 1913, Teachers College, Columbia University (n.d.) offered the first degree in student personnel administration. The program was a timely response to the growing need to professionalize student affairs work and integrate academic rigor. Graduate education for college and university administrators became increasingly crucial as veterans returned from World War I (1914–1918) and World War II (1939–1945), and the latter took advantage of the Servicemen's Readjustment Act (GI Bill) of 1944. Veterans needed more attention as they transitioned from battlefields to campus life. Student affairs degree programs and professional associations prepared practitioners for the work and legitimized the profession. Since the 1920s, hundreds of U.S. institutions have expanded graduate programs in higher education and student affairs administration and counseling.

By the late 1930s, universities began to define *student affairs* work in terms relevant to students' social, moral, and religious development (Deardorff et al., 2012). Deans of women and men focused on morals and prepared students for a life of high ethical standards. Outside the classroom, personal fitness and ethical behavior were prioritized. Weekly religious services and physical education requirements were a normal part of the curriculum. However, the deans' role shifted away from moral development as the research-intensive university model was adopted in the United States. The shift to the research university reduced attention on students' moral development. A new definition of *student affairs* was needed to explain the profession's relationship to research. In 1937, the American Council on Education hosted a 2-day meeting to develop professional standards. Scholars and practitioners created *The Student Personnel Point of View*. The document outlined how student affairs professionals should think about the work. Following is the central premise:

> The concept of education is broadened to include attention to the student's well-rounded development—physically, socially, emotionally, and spiritually—as well as intellectually. The student is thought of as a responsible participant in his development and not as a passive recipient of an imprinted economic, political, or religious doctrine, or vocational skill. As a responsible participant in the societal processes of our American democracy, his full and balanced maturity is viewed as a major end goal of education and, as well, a necessary means to the fullest development of his fellow citizens. From the personnel point of view any lesser goals fall short of the desired objective of democratic educational processes and is a real drain and strain upon the self-realization of other developing individuals in our society. (American Council on Education, 1949, p. 2)

The Student Personnel Point of View (American Council on Education, 1937, 1949) acknowledged the student as a holistic being with intellectual and social interests. Orienting toward research, universities devoted less time to students' social development and directed investments toward intellectual growth (e.g., teaching, research, academic advising, classroom facilities) and social needs (e.g., housing, dining, clubs, organizations, recreation, mental health). They reasoned that the student was not unidimensional but multidimensional—mind, body, and spirit—and thus neglecting one dimension could hinder the student's capacity to excel in others.

Further attempts to define the profession included the Council for the Advancement of Standards in Higher Education, established in 1979; *The Student Learning Imperative* (ACPA–College Student Educators International, 1996); the assessment and evaluation movement (early 2000s); and prioritizing student health and well-being. Each defining doctrine introduced new content and new professional requirements. As a result, an industry of conferences, workshops, seminars, institutes, and publications emerged to aid practitioners as they sharpen their skills. Professional development is a multibillion-dollar enterprise. Multiday professional conferences hosted in U.S. cities draw thousands of practitioners worldwide. Conferences are informative and help build professional networks, but content quality varies session by session.

Furthermore, dozens of universities and professional associations offer multiday institutes (e.g., Harvard Institutes for Higher Education, HERS Institute for Women in Higher Education, Aspen Institute College Excellence Program, AGB Institute for Leadership and Governance in Higher Education). Institutes, by design, are intensive, expensive, and rigorous; attendees delve deep into a complex theory or topic (e.g., enrollment management, leadership, fundraising, strategic planning). The institute model deepens professional competence of critical topics. Likewise, hundreds of for-profit companies also offer professional development products (e.g., consulting, coaching, data analysis, seminars) designed to address a specific personal or organizational competency. Depending on individual and institutional needs, all these products—conferences, institutes, and seminars—are meaningful options for professional development.

In this chapter, we build a case for global work assignments as an additional tool in professional development for seasoned student affairs professionals. Employment abroad is not a new idea. U.S.-trained student affairs professionals have worked outside the United States for decades. Here, we stress the strategic use of international assignments as professional development options. Few professional development experiences (e.g., conferences, seminars, workshops, institutes) match the transformational potential of total immersion in a foreign environment. Students learning a new language benefit most from immersion in the culture and being forced to communicate in the language, even if for a short time.

The same is true for student affairs professionals who practice in a foreign environment. Second, cross-pollination of experiences and ideas has benefits for all parties. Non-U.S. institutions are building more robust student services infrastructures, and U.S.-trained practitioners can offer new perspectives in international countries. Going global fosters conditions for deep learning and institutional change.

We acknowledge that working abroad may not be readily accessible for everyone. Every student affairs professional has a set of unique circumstances (e.g., income expectations, parental responsibilities, spousal support, marital status, social networks, health needs) that make working in a foreign country difficult, if not impossible. The privilege to accept an assignment abroad is not something to which everyone has equal access. In a sense, the same is true for all professional development opportunities (e.g., conferences, institutes, workshops). Still, the barriers to these are much lower than moving to a foreign country. Although going global is a life-changing professional development experience, it is *not required* to advance in the higher education profession. Generations of administrators successfully progressed in the academy without international employment. Universities advance and improve without the influence of foreign practitioners. But, for those who have the privilege to venture into unfamiliar territory, the reward is a mind-expanding and life-changing professional development experience.

Going Global as Professional Development

We, the authors of this chapter, had U.S.-based undergraduate and graduate educations. Like many professionals, we wandered into student affairs by accident. As college students, we were inspired by influential advisors, administrators, coaches, and mentors. While paying attention, solving problems, and helping others, we were introduced to the profession that would become a lifelong passion. Once we discovered student affairs as a profession, we delved into the literature and professional development experiences available through graduate programs and professional conferences. Like many others, we attended institutes, seminars, and professional conferences to sharpen our skills. Mentors and friends helped uncover blind spots and make essential connections. Our career experiences involve multiple institutions, including public, private, predominantly White, historically Black, small, and large universities. We all attest to valuable and sometimes painful learning experiences at nearly every stop along the journey. Building teams, managing budgets, solving complex problems, and negotiating conflicts are a small sample of important lessons learned from working at different institutions. Every stop was an educational experience. However, working in higher education outside the United States has been the most transformative and rewarding professional development experience we have ever encountered.

We provide first-person accounts of our student affairs experiences abroad in Abu Dhabi, United Arab Emirates (UAE), at New York University (NYU); in Vancouver, Canada, at the University of British Columbia; and in Kunshan, China, at Duke Kunshan University. Each of our experiences was unique, but similar learning outcomes emerged. You can use our insights to decide if going global is right for you.

■ ■ ■

A CANADIAN EXPERIENCE

Ainsley Carry

My parents immigrated to the United States from the West Indies, Trinidad, and Tobago. I was born in New York and grew up in Miami, Florida. As a teenager, I played sports in high school and wanted to continue playing in college. I attended the University of Florida to play football, but I soon discovered a passion for learning. I discovered this passion when I applied the same discipline from sports—exercise, practice, perform, and evaluate—to academics. I could learn anything. This discovery sparked my intellectual curiosity and led to a lifelong learning journey. My intellectual curiosity and career aspirations led to positions at Southern Methodist University, the University of Arkansas, Temple University, Auburn University, and the University of Southern California. My venture outside the United States to The University of British Columbia (UBC) in Vancouver, Canada, was initially driven by a desire to grow beyond my comfort zone. My career experiences in the United States included large and midsize universities, public and private institutions, and urban and suburban campuses. However, I sought an experience that was radically different. I wanted to practice in a different setting and to expand my knowledge by adopting new ideas and perspectives.

The vice president for students portfolio at UBC reports directly to the president. This reporting relationship is unique in Canada. In most cases, the vice president for students, or dean of students at most Canadian universities reports to the chief academic officer or provost. The portfolio includes more than 2,500 full-time employees, 1,500 student employees, and 70,000 students on two campuses. Departments within the portfolio include athletics and recreation, student housing, residence life, bookstore, parking services, conferences and accommodations, childcare, student health services, sexual violence prevention, career services, center for accessibility, international student development, center for community engaged learning, new student programs, and student leadership development. More than a dozen athletic and recreation facilities on two campuses are included in the portfolio. Student housing services supports more than 15,000 on-campus bed spaces. The portfolio is comprehensive and thus provides some significant advantages. Once students are admitted and enrolled, they are supported by a student-centered team through graduation. The capacity to offer a seamless cocurricular experience reduces friction common in institutions where revenue generation goals drive some student services.

U.S. and Canadian universities have many similarities and some significant differences. For example, academic rankings, degree programs, enrollment strategies, funding streams, and student services are relatively the same. Canadian universities, like U.S. institutions, rely on tuition, government funding, and fundraising to cover annual expenses such as salaries, infrastructure, and student services. Student concerns about mental health support, sexual violence prevention, racial and religious tensions, accessibility, and affordability are common on both sides of the border. Responding to these challenges from a different cultural perspective has been educational and has expanded my thinking on tackling these issues. My experience in Canada has been educationally transformational.

In terms of differences between the two nations' institutions, Canadian universities are less consumed by gun violence, overconsumption of alcohol, fraternity hazing, and intercollegiate athletics. Although Canadian students consume alcohol, binge drinking—excessive consumption of alcohol in a short period—is not a normal part of the drinking culture. The legal drinking age in Canada is 18 or 19, depending on the province. Therefore, when students arrive at college, they are usually casual rather than binge drinkers.

Similarly, incidents of violent fraternity hazing driven by excessive alcohol consumption are less common in Canadian higher education. The reduced emphasis on revenue-producing intercollegiate athletics, Greek life, and binge drinking creates a significantly different student experience.

Being cautious of overgeneralizations, I noticed the pace of work and forms of communication differed in Canada from my U.S. career experiences. Shared governance, financial management, decision-making, and direct versus indirect communication have different meanings in different educational environments. For example, in Canada, it is not uncommon to invest months or years discussing an important issue before making and implementing a decision. Advancing any important topic without adequate consultation is a recipe for disaster. Communication—direct versus indirect—is cultural and regional. Newcomers must notice communication cues and stifle urges to act before the agreement. Again, this is suggested cautiously as situations and environments may dictate otherwise.

Employed in Vancouver, I gained a new perspective and appreciation for Indigenous issues. Canada has a harsh history of residential schools. From the 17th century until the 1990s, the Canadian government and the Christian Church established residential schools to assimilate Indigenous youth into Canadian society. Ultimately, Indigenous children were sexually assaulted, stripped of their language and culture, and terrorized. In 2008, the Canadian government established the Truth and Reconciliation Commission of Canada to document the history and lasting impact of the residential school system on Indigenous students and their families. In 2015, the Commission issued an extensive report acknowledging the harms caused by residential schools and called for specific actions to reconcile those harms. The acknowledgment transformed conversations about equity, diversity, and inclusion. Land acknowledgments are one product of the Truth and Reconciliation movement. Nearly every meeting, big or small, begins with a land acknowledgment. As an African American man,

I learned to compartmentalize my internal struggle with American slavery and to appreciate the interconnectedness of the fight for human rights around the world.

I thought I was going global to share my education and experience. After graduate degrees and more than 25 years in college administration, I figured I had something to share with the world. However, my Canadian higher education experience has taught me far more than I imagined.

A UNITED ARAB EMIRATES EXPERIENCE

Baishakhi Taylor

My adolescent experiences and worldview shaped my career path. I grew up in Calcutta, India (now known as Kolkata). Calcutta was India's capital under the British Raj from 1772 to 1911 (Indian Statistical Institute, n.d.). The most formative years of my life were spent in the shadows of India's colonial past with the challenges of a newly formed nation-state. India, as a country, was barely 40 years old when I graduated from college. I grew up in a country with a palpable spirit of uncertainty, flexibility, and lingering burdens of colonialism and caste. Upon reflection, I inherited the traits of my home country, particularly flexibility and accepting uncertainty. Although my parents stirred my intellectual curiosity, they enforced gendered norms like not playing competitive sports or traveling alone. I grew up in pre-internet India, so my travels were limited to South Asian countries, particularly Nepal and Bhutan.

In 2000, I arrived in Waterloo, Iowa, as an international student. I had no family in the United States and did not know anyone when my flight landed near midnight in the small airport in the middle of nowhere. Arriving in the United States, I understood what it meant to feel marginalized. My first 6 months were filled with the excitement of being in a new place and profound homesickness. It was hard to explain or understand this contradiction of feelings. I enjoyed eating hot dogs and French fries and craved my grandmother's cooking. English was not my first language. Before coming to the United States, I wrote my college papers by hand or paid someone to type them. My learning curve was steep and long. I was ignorant of racial injustice and systemic oppression faced by Indigenous people and people of color in the United States. My experience as an international student, my cultural fluency, and my doctoral studies shaped my identity and career interests. I was attracted to uncertainty in foreign spaces. That said, I did not hesitate when offered a chance to advance my career in the Middle East.

My career spans more than 2 decades. In the first decade, I had roles in student and academic affairs. I served at state institutions, research universities, and small liberal arts colleges. My attention was focused on the intersection of curricular and cocurricular engagement. In the second decade, I transitioned to senior leadership roles, including vice presidencies at liberal arts colleges in New England. A turning point for my career came in 2020—the COVID-19 pandemic profoundly affected my psyche. I was the dean and vice president of campus life at a women's college. Reflecting on the human toll of the pandemic, racial unrest, and the war in Ukraine caused me to reexamine my contribution to the profession. I thought about my willingness to move beyond my comfort zone and knew I had blind spots and biases about non-U.S. universities.

The associate vice chancellor for student affairs position at NYU Abu Dhabi presented a professional challenge to push beyond my comfort zone. The role fit all the criteria for the professional challenge I needed. I was curious: What would it mean to build student life at a 10-year-old university in a country that is only 52 years old? How would I defend liberal arts education in the Middle East? I wondered what it meant to be a global university with no ethnic majority student group. How would we build a community where faculty, staff, and students hail from more than 100 countries? With more questions than answers, I pounced on the challenge to lead at NYU Abu Dhabi.

NYU Abu Dhabi is a degree-granting portal campus of NYU in the United Arab Emirates. Together with the main campus in New York City and NYU Shanghai, the portal campus is part of NYU's Global Network University. The academic program opened in September 2010 at the provisional site; in 2014, the campus was moved to its current location on Saadiyat Island, Abu Dhabi. NYU Abu Dhabi offers 25 degree programs in the arts and humanities, social sciences, science, and engineering. More than 2,000 undergraduates, 300 faculty, and 100 graduate students make up the community. Since its launch, the university has produced 17 Rhodes Scholars, more Rhodes Scholars per capita than any university worldwide. The 40-acre campus offers public spaces, a theater, performance halls, an art gallery, a conference center, and retail offerings. More than 60 student groups provide opportunities for student leadership and engagement. The associate vice chancellor reports to the vice chancellor and oversees residential life, athletics, career services, community outreach, orientation programs, student leadership and activities, class year experiences, student conduct, student success and well-being, health and counseling services, spiritual life, career services, and student accessibility.

The Middle East is not a single identity. A British colonial construct combined 13 countries and labeled them the Middle East. The construct blurs the region's history, culture, and uniqueness. More than 10 million people live in the United Arab Emirates, with about 1.2 million Emiratis—50% of the population hail from South Asia, with 30% from India. Hindi and Urdu are more frequently spoken than Arabic. In my role, I speak three languages every day (English, Hindi, and Bangla).

The United Arab Emirates faces higher education challenges similar to those in the United States, with a few nuances. For one, diversity and inclusion are more complicated at an institution of 2,000 students where more than 100 countries are represented. We have small numbers of students from many countries, and for most of them, coming to Abu Dhabi is their first time living away from home. Unlike in the United States, where most students are domestic, in Abu Dhabi, most come from other countries. These students require more time to connect with their roommates, with the institution, and with the greater UAE community. We also celebrate the abundant cultural traditions each group of students brings from their home countries.

Students who are Emirati nationals describe feeling like international students in their own country. Although located in Abu Dhabi, NYU still operates on a U.S. higher education model; this model is as foreign to Emiratis as it is to students from other parts of the world. A third challenge involves managing students' expectations. Many students come to NYU Abu Dhabi expecting a New York City experience, but that is not the case. The experience is more like that in a small college town. Helping students reconcile the difference between an urban campus mindset and a small college experience is a challenge. Finally, discussing diversity, equity, and inclusion in Abu Dhabi differs from U.S.-based versions of this discussion. Racial tension, systemic racism, and caste systems are not part of the NYU Abu Dhabi experience. Those topics are not the basis for inclusion and equity discussions. Instead, global events such as the floods in Pakistan, the earthquake in Turkey, or displacement in Yemen are foundations for diverse discussions.

My experience at NYU Abu Dhabi has forced me to reexamine the world through a non-U.S. lens. I am relearning the importance of traditions, celebrations, and culture. I also appreciate the differences among the Middle Eastern countries and rectifying my biases toward treating the Middle East as one entity. I am discovering commonalities I share with Emirati colleagues and students. For example, we collectively struggle with the lingering and harmful effects of colonial amnesia. India, my home country, and Abu Dhabi are still recovering from the lost cultural identity that is a byproduct of colonization. The national pride that upheld the country before colonization has been clouded.

A CHINA EXPERIENCE

Raphael X. Moffett

My parents were U.S. Armed Forces veterans and served 20 years in the U.S. Army. I was born in Stuttgart, Germany, while my parents were stationed in Europe. We moved to Lacey, Washington, when I was 7 years old; I spent my formative years there. My parents have always been advocates for higher education as a means to achieving upward mobility and giving back to my community. They were strict about academics and good grades. My grades were my passport to social activities and playing basketball. My kindergarten through twelfth grade educational experiences were influenced by classmates and teammates from various backgrounds, especially those from Asian cultures, because of the influx of military personnel worldwide. I attended school with Korean, Chinese, Filipino, Cambodian, Thai, Vietnamese, and Laotian classmates. As a result, I grew up with an appreciation and general understanding of the values and cultural norms my Asian friends held in high regard. Years later, these experiences were essential for my role as a chief student affairs officer in China. I enjoy working in higher education, but the most meaningful education for me has been the opportunity to travel and learn about people and cultures worldwide. The opportunity to serve Chinese and international students at joint venture institutions in China was an alluring new challenge that aligned with my higher education and personal experiences.

I took a nontraditional path into student affairs. Initially, I wanted to be a high school English teacher, but during my senior year of college, I decided to pursue graduate studies rather than teach full time. I attended Clark Atlanta University (CAU) to pursue a master's degree in educational leadership. The program focused primarily on students who wanted to become leaders in kindergarten through twelfth grade environments. While I was looking for housing at CAU, a staff member in residence life asked me to take on the resident director role. I did not choose student affairs; the profession chose me. I did not graduate from a traditional higher education program or work at an institution with a strong traditional student affairs ethos. Over time, I learned the nuances, culture, and skills of a practical student affairs professional. My residence life experience at CAU led me to serve at four historically Black colleges and universities (CAU, Morehouse College, Langston University, and Texas Southern University) and two predominantly White institutions (Georgia State University and Trinity University). All six of these institutions were different. Serving students from different cultural backgrounds has always been a guiding principle; it has drawn me to leadership roles in nontraditional and international environments. I believe an exceptional student affairs professional should meet the work that positively affects the student experience, no matter how complex or challenging the situation. This mindset made it possible to thrive in distinctly different institution types.

I worked at Duke Kunshan University (DKU) in Kunshan, China, from 2019 to 2022. DKU is a highly selective research-oriented liberal arts and sciences joint venture between Duke University and Wuhan University. The dean of students position reported directly to Duke University's executive vice chancellor. The portfolio included 30 full-time employees, 1,250 undergraduate students, and 200 graduate students. Departments within the portfolio included athletics, campus engagement, campus health services, case management office, Chinese student services, counseling and psychological services, international student services, residence life, and student conduct. The portfolio began when I arrived in 2019; DKU launched its undergraduate program in 2018. When I arrived, I expanded functional areas, implemented new policies and procedures, and created program initiatives. It was exciting to work with young professionals in a startup environment that was maturing into a sophisticated educational enterprise.

In 2022, I joined the Schwarzman Scholars program on the campus of Tsinghua University in Beijing, China. The Schwarzman Scholars program supports up to 150 scholars annually from the United States, China, and worldwide for a 1-year master's degree in global affairs. Scholars chosen for this highly selective global fellowship live in Beijing for a year of study and cultural immersion to develop a better understanding of leadership, global affairs, and China's impact on the world. The portfolio includes 18 full-time employees and 143 scholars. Departments within the portfolio include Chinese and English language programs, Chinese and international student services, counseling services (outsourced), deep dive experience (cultural and professional immersion), programs and events, residence life, student accessibility services, and student conduct. My portfolio is unique because the staff comprises traditional student affairs professionals and nonstudent affairs professionals in an academic college. It has been gratifying to work in a smaller environment because the work is high touch—it involves personal attention where trust between students and administrators is highly valued. I am also positioned at the intersection of philanthropy, international business, and higher education, which has been enlightening. Although I work at Tsinghua University, I am employed by the Stephen A. Schwarzman Education Foundation, a private nonprofit organization that funds the Schwarzman Scholars program.

The opportunity to serve at DKU and Schwarzman Scholars in China was a complete departure from U.S. higher education norms. Working in

Asia helped me leverage my career experiences in different institutions and prepared me to navigate the complex dynamics inherent in China. International and domestic students come to China with diverse geopolitical views, family dynamics, deep-seated cultural norms, personal priorities, and ambitious professional aspirations. My upbringing and professional experience in the United States complemented my work with Asian communities. The work has been rewarding because it deepens my personal and professional competencies. The cultural nuances and societal norms in China forced me to think creatively about how to serve students and the organization's mission. I learned how to work cohesively with colleagues and to support students with different lived experiences. I chose to work in China because I wanted to think outside familiar paradigms and to become adept at supporting the holistic development of students worldwide.

As an American working in China, I gained a deeper understanding of how student affairs professionals approach their work in traditional Chinese universities. For example, student affairs professionals at Chinese universities prioritize solving individual problems for students rather than facilitating broader student development programs. Younger Chinese faculty members work in student affairs as a collateral role in their professorship; full-time student affairs positions are uncommon. Conceptualizing Western and Eastern staffing models was initially a challenge, but it has been a great exercise to think beyond traditional workforce structures. At DKU, I implemented elements of Western staffing models while accommodating working styles and student support strategies from global perspectives, including the United States, China, Africa, South America, and Europe. At Schwarzman Scholars, I work within the structure of Tsinghua University. The Scholars program collaborates with senior administrators at Tsinghua University and is aligned with the student life team within the college that uses Western frameworks to support students.

In China, parent involvement has been an intriguing dynamic to navigate. Many Chinese parents expect frequent contact with high school instructors; this expectation continues into the university. Conversely, laws in the United States (e.g., Family Educational Rights and Privacy Act, Health Insurance Portability and Accountability Act) that limit universities' engagement with students' parents are less stringent in China. Therefore, administrators constantly balance parents' hands-on expectations with students' privacy.

■ ■ ■

Lessons Learned

Accepting a foreign work assignment is a transformative professional development experience. Each of us expanded our mind and leadership skills on assignments abroad. The nature of embedded learning forces learners to adapt and learn. For those who can consider going global as a next step, some advice is warranted:

1. **Ask yourself:** *What can I contribute to a foreign institution?* Inventory your skills and strengths. More importantly, what can you learn from the experience? Know your growth opportunities. Weigh the two—strengths and opportunities for growth—and consider whether the transition is worth it. Trust your intellectual curiosity to be a part of the decision.
2. **Gain financial literacy.** Research the currency exchange between the United States and the country you are considering. If you have expenses (e.g., student loans, car payments, mortgage) in U.S. dollars, the exchange rate will make a difference in your ability to pay those expenses. Some countries have stronger (worth more)

or weaker (worth less) currency compared to the U.S. dollar. For example, as of this publication, the Canadian dollar is $.77 to the U.S. dollar. At this exchange rate, a $100,000 salary in Canada equals $77,000 in the United States. Understand how the exchange rate affects your spending power.

3. **Understand the organizational structure.** Colleges and universities use unique terminology to describe components of their organization. Titles such as vice president, dean, director, provost, president, and chancellor mean different things in different places. Titles that seem low might be high-ranking in another system. Terminology differences are widespread and can create a steep learning curve initially. Do not get discouraged by a title that does not match your framework; focus on the scope of responsibilities.

4. **Use working abroad as a learning opportunity.** International assignments are risky and rewarding. Practitioners leave their comfort zones—extended family, friends, colleagues, and daily routines—to pursue a professional adventure marked by new challenges and opportunities. They enter situations where they might be misunderstood and unfamiliar with the terminology. They forgo rights and protections enjoyed in the United States that may be different in other countries. They enter countries where social customs and cultures may also be different. The confluence of comfort and discomfort offers a learning opportunity that will translate into a personal and professional asset.

5. **Put family first.** Foreign assignments take a toll on the family. It takes time to acclimate to a new environment. Homesickness, loneliness, weather patterns, and time zones affect the transition. When newcomers move to foreign countries with a family, the family experiences those same transitions. A trailing partner or

spouse might feel a more profound loss if they moved without employment or a social network. Children also need to adjust to a new school, new friends, and new academic standards. Partners must agree on the opportunities and challenges of a foreign assignment.

6. **Avoid preconceived notions.** Refrain from becoming narrow-minded in approaching student affairs work in non-Western environments because the challenges and opportunities will require unconventional strategies. Embrace cultural and geopolitical dynamics with the intent to understand without judgment.

7. **Seek first to understand.** Stephen Covey (1989), author of *The Seven Habits of Highly Effective People*, coined the phrase "seek first to understand, then to be understood" (p. 163). Listening is the most important asset a practitioner can bring to a foreign environment. Generally, people do not care what newcomers know until newcomers demonstrate that they care. Caring is listening to understand before trying to solve problems. Over listen in the first year. What appears as an obvious problem or solution is often not the answer.

8. **Know your trigger warnings.** Different customs and traditions populate the world. For example, race relations, gender norms, and religious freedoms vary worldwide. Newcomers might be offended by traditions and customs in other countries. Offenses might trigger deep emotions that are hard to ignore or overcome. Many customs will be beyond your scope of influence. Plan self-care ahead of time.

9. **Avoid copying and pasting.** "That is not how we handled that situation at my previous institution." Nobody wants to hear that. The statement elevates a prior institution and demotes a current employer. Avoid copying old solutions into new environments.

Take time to understand the unique nature of the current challenge and work collaboratively to discover a customized solution. Even if the idea is rooted in an experience, avoid the copy-and-paste approach. Try this instead: "I have an idea from experience." Sometimes, the journey is more valuable than the outcome.

10. **Embrace a different cultural struggle.** Every country has a unique cultural history. Slavery was a defining moment in U.S. history. Both Canada and the United States allowed religious organizations to remove and abuse Indigenous children in residential/mission school systems. Colonialism muddled many countries' histories and ruined cultural pride and identities. Respect the cultural struggle of the host country and observe their days of remembrance or significance. Realize the struggle may differ from the one you were acculturated to, which is no less critical. Also, be prepared for nonobservance of your cultural struggle. Your struggle may not be centered in the new environment.

Conclusion

Higher education administration is an evolving profession. Since its inception in the mid-1800s, every generation of student affairs administrators has faced new challenges from an evolving world and new definitions of student success and the academy. Deans of men and women focused on student conduct and moral development. Professional associations, degree programs, and institutes emerged to fill gaps in practitioners' knowledge. As colleges and universities became more research centered, character education was replaced by focusing on students' holistic development. Sluggish enrollment growth from domestic students, decreased state funding, and the rising costs of higher education have forced many institutions to rely on international student enrollment to generate revenue and meet enrollment expectations. International students now represent a significant portion of U.S. higher education. As a result, there is a growing need for practitioners to evolve again with the 21st-century demands of the academy.

The next generation of higher education practitioners and scholars must become fluent in international student engagement. The best way to build this competency may involve cultural immersion and embedded learning. The next step in professional development should involve expanding practitioners' global competence.

References

ACPA–College Student Educators International. (1996). *The student learning imperative: Implications for student affairs.* https://myacpa.org/wp-content/uploads/2022/09/ACPAs-Student-Learning-Imperative.pdf

American Council on Education. (1937). *The student personnel point of view.* https://www.naspa.org/files/dmfile/Student_Personnel_Point_of_View_1937.pdf

American Council on Education. (1949). *The student personnel point of view.* https://www.naspa.org/images/uploads/main/Student_Personnel_Point_of_View_1949.pdf

Cilente, K. (2011). *Fulfilling visions: Emerging leaders of ACPA* (2nd ed.). ACPA–College Student Educators International.

Covey, S. R. (1989). *The 7 habits of highly effective people: Powerful lessons in personal change.* Franklin Covey.

Deardorff, D. K., deWit, H., Heyl, J. D., & Adams, T. (2012). *The SAGE handbook of international higher education.* SAGE.

Indian Statistical Institute. (n.d.). *Calcutta: The city of palaces.* https://bit.ly/4efLdKX

Levine, S. (1995). *Degrees of equality: The American Association of University Women and the challenge of twentieth-century feminism.* Temple University Press.

NASPA–Student Affairs Administrators in Higher Education. (n.d.). *Our history leads to our future.* https://history.naspa.org

Teachers College, Columbia University. (n.d.). *About the higher and postsecondary education program.* https://www.tc.columbia.edu/organization-and-leadership/higher-and-postsecondary-education/about

Transitioning From Higher Education to PK-12 Education

Karen Warren Coleman

Considering a career transition from higher education to PK–12 education is exciting, and the sheer impact one can have from working with a younger population of students can be profound. At the same time, such a transition should prompt even the most experienced higher education practitioner to pause and reflect. Many similarities exist between the roles and environments—both involve educating students, after all—but the differences are also substantial. Although the skills and experience gained at a university or college are transferable and often highly desirable, this transition can be like learning another language or, at best, a different dialect. This chapter explores the motivations, rewards, and challenges of making such a change, as well as the skills and experiences that will help make the transition a successful one.

Day 1

I pulled into the school parking lot, cut the engine, and took a deep breath. After a quick mirror check, I gathered my belongings and stepped out of the car into the humid Texas air. I paused, taking in the campus's early-morning quiet, a stillness that soon would be buzzing with chatter, laughter, and activity as students in plaid skirts and forest green blazers arrived for the day.

I had experience teaching in a graduate school of education, but I had not set foot in a classroom with younger children since I was in high school, and the developmental distance between the two felt like a chasm. Yet here I was, after a career of 20-plus years in higher education, most recently as vice president of campus and student life at a top research university, taking the reins as head of an all-girls PK–12 independent school. It was a transition that surprised many of my colleagues—and, on some level, me.

I mustered my confidence, determined to let my first-day jitters dissipate in the Dallas sunshine. As I strode toward the school, the words of childcare expert Benjamin Spock (1946) came to mind: "Trust yourself. You know more than you think you do" (p. 1). Now, after 30 years in education and in my second headship, I can say with authority that he was right.

Why Make This Change?

My career trajectory in higher education was a deliberate, linear ascent. Armed with a bachelor's degree in psychology, I secured my first job out of college at Hobart and William Smith Colleges, where I was a live-in staff member responsible for six residence halls. Barely older than my students,

I relished my first opportunity to contribute to the field. It was a safe leap of faith. If the work was enjoyable and gave me meaning, I would stick with it. It was, and I did.

From there, I made the decision to pursue a master's degree in higher education and student affairs at the University of Vermont. My top-choice assistantship placed me in residence life, where I lived as an assistant hall director while completing my degree. While at the University of Vermont, I also was fortunate to intern in several areas, including admissions, development, and—my favorite—the office of the vice president for student affairs. The internship with the vice president exposed me to the day-to-day issues of a university and provided my first bird's-eye view of an institution—a perspective so valuable to senior leadership. It also delivered a mentor. I have carried this vice president's spirit of generosity and transparency forward as I, too, have mentored young professionals in the field.

After moving to The George Washington University, where I was director of student conduct, I joined the University of California, Berkeley, as student affairs director before becoming associate dean of students. I was technically at a higher level in the organization as student affairs director, reporting to the vice chancellor, but that position did not provide the direct supervisory and other professional experiences of the associate dean role, which reported to the dean of students. I knew that if I wanted to move up in the field, I needed to move down first.

After a decade at Berkeley, I joined the University of Chicago, where I was associate vice president for campus life and associate dean of students in the university for 3 years before applying as an internal candidate and being selected as vice president of campus and student life. During my 7 years there, I earned a doctorate in education from the University of Pennsylvania.

What drew me to higher education was the opportunity to work in the rich, stimulating space of a university environment. What kept me in higher education was the enormous satisfaction I felt from helping young people navigate often messy and confusing paths as they came into their own (McClellan et al., 2023). Yet I found that the higher I rose in the university, the further away I felt from that mission.

Assessing my skills as I considered the next step in my career, I realized I had a tremendous portfolio of experience that touched on most operations of a university: admissions, academic advising, diversity and inclusion, student engagement and development, health and wellness, housing, dining, facilities, security, finance, and curricular design. I wanted to figure out how to apply this experience in a way where I felt more at the center of lifting students up, in an environment that allowed me to focus on new approaches to teaching and learning, with intentional support for student well-being and more equitable and inclusive environments. It felt like the right time to explore how I might have a different kind of impact in the areas I care so deeply about.

When I met a colleague in my doctoral program who had recently made the transition from a career in higher education to independent school education, where it appeared that leadership could have a more immediate and lasting impact, I decided it was an avenue worth exploring. When the head of The Hockaday School in Dallas became available, I decided it was a position worth pursuing.

Still, I worried. If I was offered and accepted the position, how would this move be perceived? What if I did not find the sort of intellectual engagement I had come to expect and desire in my work? Would I be closing the door on a career in higher education? I agonized over the decision. I must have talked to 100 people about it. In the end, I decided that if I did not love the position, at least I would learn from it. And that would be OK.

When an opportunity presents itself, we get to choose whether we pursue it. Although we cannot control the outcomes, we have agency over the choices we make and the opportunities we pursue. Our decision-making wields enormous influence in our lives just the same. We give students this advice all the time. When this transition presented itself, the process worked for me because I was open to it and approached it with humility and vulnerability.

Questions to Consider

- What is your motivation for considering a career transition from higher education to PK–12?
- Assess your skills, experience, and exposure:
  - What skills directly translate?
  - What experience can you leverage?
  - What personal and/or professional experiences have given you a level of familiarity, if not specific skills?

Comparing the Environments

Transitioning from a career in higher education to a role in a PK–12 institution is not easy or even an apples-to-apples comparison. It is more like apples and oranges: they are both round fruit, but you would likely never bake an orange pie or eat apple sherbet. Yet, broadly speaking, the core mission of education is the same, and the skills and experience gained in the higher education environment are highly transferable.

And opportunity exists. Traditionally, the path to leadership in independent schools has begun with classroom teaching, but recent years have seen an increase in leaders coming from nontraditional backgrounds, including the nonprofit sector, higher education, and professions like business and law (Batiste & Riven, 2011). Couple this with the 2021 National Association of Independent Schools (NAIS, 2022) State of

Independent School Leadership Survey's findings that more than half of sitting heads intend to step down from their jobs by 2025–2026, and the potential opportunities widen.

Transitioning from a higher education environment comes with distinct advantages, most notably the experience of working within a complex organization. The structure of independent school governance has many parallels to colleges and universities, including admission and enrollment management, student health and well-being, residential life and boarding, academic departments and department chairs, student activities, athletics, student discipline, managing budgets, and making capital improvements like conceptualizing and building new facilities, which in turn often lead to engagement with the broader neighboring community. Careers in higher education—whether in student and campus life, admissions, communications, advancement, advising, or another area—typically provide exposure to a breadth of experience and a wealth of knowledge.

My first headship was at a day and boarding school, where I had the distinct advantage of working for many years in university housing, both as a live-in staff member and director. My higher education residential life experience translated directly to the independent school boarding program. This included roommate assignments, welcoming students and their families, supervision of hall proctors (resident assistants) and live-in hall directors, programming, supporting international students, dining, discipline, crisis management, student health and well-being (and a 24-hour health center), and hall government. Admittedly, the experience often felt markedly different because boarding students ranged in age from 13 to 18. For example, when we had a water main break in the courtyard adjacent to the residence halls, cutting off water to the halls, not only did we need to immediately relocate students to a nearby hotel, but we also needed to provide adult staffing and nurse coverage for the students while repairs were made.

In many ways, PK–12 independent schools can be like small colleges, particularly in terms of enrollment, size of the campus, number of staff, total endowment, and competitive marketplace (Baker, 2018). In fact, as I considered my next career move, I was advised that serving as head of a school would be a good way to test whether a college presidency might be a good fit in the future.

Both small colleges and independent schools tend to be close-knit, supportive communities in which the president or head of school is expected to be engaged across the community, highly visible, and accessible. They can be on par with their approach to academics and on the cutting edge of how they're thinking about education, albeit at different levels. Depending on the school, they may be deeply engaged with their neighboring community and city, which factored heavily for me in seeking the right fit.

Another similarity is that small colleges and independent schools typically share a deep sense of institutional history, culture, and tradition—strong values that can enrich the student experience but can also impede change, even if the change reflects positive progress. However, independent schools—should they choose—can be nimbler than colleges and universities and more adept at being able to change course. The PK–12 environment can operate on what I think of as a more human scale, with the administration able to use direct and timely access to student and teacher feedback to improve approaches that don't work. For example, independent schools, like universities, are filled with bright students whose schedules are often packed. When an upper school division director hears complaints from students that multiple assessments and papers across disciplines are scheduled within the span of a few days—making it impossible for them to adequately prepare given dawn-through-dusk schedules that may include competitive sports, fine arts rehearsals and performances, and community service—we can use that feedback to modify the schedule, if not in real time, at least for the next round of exams.

Likewise, heads get to witness the impact of their leadership, often in real time. For example, when deadly tornadoes tore through North Texas, destroying hundreds of homes and businesses and rendering several peer schools inoperable, my school was able to mobilize immediately. We were able to support affected families and neighboring schools in the hours, days, and weeks that followed. This included inviting the college counseling team from our brother school nearby to set up a satellite office on our campus to continue to provide timely guidance to their students when the tornadoes temporarily shuttered their school less than 10 days before the college application deadline. We can make decisions and act quickly to make a meaningful difference while also educating students about the power of community.

It's important to note that because independent schools often are steeped in tradition and culture, introducing and leading change must be handled with awareness and sensitivity. Although this can be true for any institution, and was certainly my experience in higher education, managing change can be particularly challenging for PK–12 independent schools. A school's multiple stakeholders include a board of trustees, to whom the head of school reports; parents, who are far more engaged in day-to-day operations and decisions than at the university level; and alumni, who are deeply vested in their school. Healthy relationships with each of these groups are vital to successful leadership in private PK–12 education (Batiste & Riven, 2011).

Questions to Consider

- How does your current environment compare to the PK–12 independent school environment?
- What specific professional experience would you bring to the table from your tenure in higher education?
- What will be your areas of growth?

Importance of Partnerships

Whereas a university's relationship and contract are primarily with the student, PK–12 schools, which support students ranging in age from 4 to 18, have a relationship and contract with the parents. (One exception is high school seniors who reach 18 before graduation; they generally receive a letter clarifying privacy laws and access to their records.) The age range that an individual school supports will vary depending on its composition. Some independent schools serve only grades PK–4, and others are freestanding middle schools that serve grades 4 or 5 through 8, stand-alone high schools, or comprehensive PK–12 campuses. Although university staff strive to keep parents at arm's length (because it is important for college students to learn to navigate the world as adults, and the legal relationship is with the student), at the PK–12 level, productive partnerships with parents and caregivers are essential.

As the PK–12 student grows and evolves through the grades, so must the relationship with parents and caregivers. The parents and caregivers are always engaged, but the level of engagement is deliberate at each stage of student development (Thompson & Evans, 2021).

For example, in the lower grades, conversations with parents and caregivers may often take place without the child present. Direct conversations with parents and caregivers continue in the middle grades but with the student engaged as appropriate. This ensures that students learn to self-advocate, for example, how to reach out to their teachers or advisors when they have an issue or need assistance. In the upper school years, schools typically communicate directly with the student, with parents informed on a need-to-know basis, thus paving the path to independent adulthood. As a leader committed to student development, I find it especially satisfying to help children develop resilience and self-advocacy as they prepare to graduate and move on.

In addition to parents, a strong partnership with the board of trustees is crucial for success in independent schools. Trustee relationships are among the most important for a head of school. Such relationships are not optional; trusted relationships with board members are essential to successful governance (Batiste & Riven, 2011). The board is responsible for hiring and evaluating the head of school, and the head is accountable to the board. The head works closely with the board to set strategic priorities, goals, and objectives for the school. It is worthwhile to note that PK–12 independent school boards often include significant parent and alumni representation, which means they may have greater knowledge of the school's operations and may bring those questions and ideas to the head more directly than a university board would typically do. Although board members are not involved with the day-to-day operational functions of the school, they are the long-term stewards of institutional and financial health, and they help identify and mitigate risk.

The board serves as the rudder to the head of school's sail. A board can be instrumental in advising whether the head of school is ambitious enough, moving too quickly, or not moving quickly enough. The board can provide guidance in responding to the most complex institutional decisions and can help set the school's strategic direction.

The relationship is not one way, by any stretch. Ideally, perspective and knowledge flow in both directions. For example, my experience and expertise in broadening diversity across the institutional spectrum have been valued in my headships. A strong relationship with the board has meant that I could make an impact by sharing best practices for increasing trustee diversity as they recruit new members.

The relationship with the board is of vital consideration for anyone thinking of moving into leadership at a PK–12 independent school. It is important for someone moving into this role to have worked with a board or to seek out the experience when planning a transition. Although you may not have had the opportunity to gain governing board experience in your career to date, NAIS has several publications focused on governance, including *The Trustee Handbook* (Orem & Wilson, 2022), *The Board Chair Handbook* (Creeden, 2019), and *Principles of Good Practice for Boards and Trustees* (NAIS, 2019). You may also benefit from research by leaders in the field of nonprofit governance, including Richard Chait et al. (1993). This kind of research can help you become familiar with board governance and understand what it takes to forge a strong and trusting relationship with your board.

In addition to the formal relationship between a board and head of school, board members can serve individually as resources and sounding boards. As head of a school, you will spend much time with your trustees. They will see you at your best and sometimes at your worst; if the relationship is a healthy one, they will be kind and clear in providing feedback and suggestions, and they will share responsibility for the extraordinary weight of the decisions you will inevitably be charged with making. The head of school can be a lonely role because essentially everyone at the school is subordinate to the head. Strong relationships with board members can be lifesavers (Batiste & Riven, 2011). I have found my relationships with individual trustees to be valuable in educating me about the culture, providing space to test ideas, and offering encouragement.

On the same note, relationships with other heads of schools serve an important role. Whether it is through associations like NAIS and its regional affiliates or by contacting the heads of peer schools, everyone in the role can benefit from relationships with leaders in similar circumstances. For example, during the early days of the COVID-19 pandemic, my peers and I had to make many urgent decisions in the face of uncertainty: whether to close or open, how to approach athletics and other cocurricular activities, how to support teachers through remote learning, and how to respond to shifting public directives. The ability to consult with one another and coordinate was a lifeline for us all.

Questions to Consider

- What is your relationship with parents in your current role?
- What experience, if any, do you have with boards?
- What is your experience with goal setting?
- How are you currently engaged with local, regional, and national higher education organizations? How might you see yourself forging similar relationships with PK–12 organizations?

Understanding PK–12 Education and Institutions

Of course, the primary focus of all educational institutions is students and learning. Although institutions of higher education are designed to have a broad impact on society through education, research, and intellectual inquiry, PK–12 schools have a much narrower focus: educating children.

What this looks like at each independent school is as different as it looks from college to college. Institutional mission and history (e.g., religiously affiliated, nondenominational, day or boarding school), educational approach (e.g., grades, no grades, Montessori, Reggio Emilia, Waldorf), when the school was founded and by whom (e.g., Ela Hockaday founded The Hockaday School in 1913; William Penn founded William Penn Charter School in 1689), campus culture, geographic region, and student composition (e.g., single sex or coed; elementary, middle, secondary, or comprehensive) are just a few of the factors that shape a school's unique educational identity.

A school's identity is also influenced by its role in the community and the broader region. Does it recruit primarily locally or from a broader geographic area? Is it financially accessible to students from an array of socioeconomic backgrounds, and do families from diverse communities see it as inviting and accessible or out of reach? Does it actively participate in local, regional, and national associations and coalitions of peer schools? Does the school see external partnerships as a central part of its teaching and student development model, or does it draw primarily from within its own school community for its core work of teaching and learning?

Caring for the Whole Child

At the PK–12 level, administrators and teachers must understand what a lower school student is experiencing, how a student moves through those early grades, and how to prepare students for the big transition that occurs during middle school: greater autonomy and the need to balance more academic work and student activities. Administrators and teachers then need to understand how students experience the final transition into upper school, which is a period where young people appropriately begin to separate from their families as they anticipate the transition to college.

Children experience massive developmental changes during the span of the PK–12 years. These changes often show up in the form of decision points (e.g., Who is in my friend group? Do I want to risk detention by going off campus with my friends without permission or let them go without me? My parents want to add schools to my college list; how do I tell them that I would prefer not to?). This period can be magical, heart wrenching, deeply satisfying, and agonizing all at the same time.

These developmental changes are all taking place in a world that continues to change exponentially. As students chart their path through this period of spectacular growth, their parents and caregivers painstakingly try to navigate their children's rapidly evolving needs, dispositions, and ever-diminishing willingness to share their private lives, all while questioning themselves and worrying about their children's futures.

The day-to-day lives and challenges children face today were unfathomable just a few decades ago. The stressors heaped on young people are keenly felt by parents and caregivers as well (Thompson & Evans, 2021). Higher academic pressure is just part of the equation. The proliferation of technology and social media has created new sources of stress, including cyberbullying (Twenge, 2017). Mental health issues such as depression, anxiety, and suicidal ideation have become significantly more prevalent (Damour, 2019), and these challenges were exacerbated by the social isolation of the COVID-19 pandemic. The seemingly unstoppable plague of gun violence and school shootings adds a layer of fear and anger. For students of every age, the importance of nurturing secure and supportive learning environments is amplified.

When researching independent schools, it is important to understand their student support structures as well as their safety and security resources. As discussed earlier in this chapter, each school is different—and these resources will differ from school to school. Many independent schools have learning support teams in each division (lower school, middle school, and upper school) that may include learning specialists, literacy coordinators, counselors, tutors, and on-site writing and math centers. Likewise, staff support students with academic accommodations, concussion protocols for return to school and play, and short- or long-term leaves of absence. Finally, this holistic approach to student support is buttressed with school counselors, who are typically trained mental health professionals.

Both independent schools I served have been fortunate to have a school counselor in each division; these individuals are an important part of a healthy and thriving school community. Traditionally, counseling support offered by the school is short term and not intended to function in place of professional, comprehensive counseling. Similar to higher education, but typically on a much smaller scale, each school has a safety and security director whose team is responsible for campus access control, visitor management, fire and lockdown drills, threat management, and overall community safety.

Today's best-in-class education is characterized by a commitment to the whole child—academically, socially, and emotionally. Although colleges and universities do much to address students' mental health and well-being, in PK–12 independent school education there is an opportunity to be deliberate in weaving wellness into the curriculum and cocurricular activities to help young people develop critical habits that will serve them well in college and beyond. Faculty in PK–12, including coaches, are often more closely connected to their students' sense of well-being and traditionally see it more squarely in their mission to support student wellness. Teachers and school administrators also have more direct connections with parents and caregivers, so they get a more active and nuanced view of what each student needs to thrive. One way this shows up in the curriculum is the integration of mindfulness education beginning in PK through to 12th grade. This holistic approach helps students gain important skills, including self-regulation, stress reduction, better attentiveness, and other long-term social and emotional benefits.

Shaping the Academic Environment

Transitioning from higher education to PK–12 independent school education presents an opportunity to shape children's education thoughtfully and comprehensively. A school can be a rigorous environment that engages students in the highest level of academic inquiry *and* can be a place that cares deeply about each child. The two are not mutually exclusive. Without question, independent schools are uniquely positioned to do this well, with a learning environment that optimizes best-in-class tools, including highly qualified teachers, smaller class sizes, diverse course offerings, a well-resourced instructional environment, and a commitment to teacher and staff professional development.

At the core of the academic experience is the classroom, where the tone and approach are shaped by teachers. Faculty members develop their individual course content, but the head is responsible for the entire school, including the curriculum. Whether your path to headship begins as a teacher or as a university administrator, the derivation of the title of head comes from the head teacher, or teacher of teachers, and who is responsible for setting the scholarly agenda (Batiste & Riven, 2011). This includes ensuring that the faculty (and administration) are aspirational, forward thinking, and strategic.

Having a doctorate in education was useful in preparing me for this academic role. Although I do not have classroom teaching experience at the PK–12 level, my advanced degree provided essential theoretical background and exposure to best practices in pedagogy. Equally important—perhaps even more so—was my breadth of exposure to diverse learning environments and being in roles that were always focused on supporting and the academic mission.

Being in immersive roles in support of educational values and priorities put me on solid footing as head to articulate a school's values and priorities and to set institutional expectations. These priorities and standards emerge from the school's long-standing initiatives, mission, strategic plan, and annual goals. As head, whether you join a school that is more than 300 years old or a school founded 25 years ago, you are part of a continuum (Batiste & Riven, 2011).

To this end, I created a mantra for my work: *To be a successful head, you must look back as you look ahead; it is important to honor the past, while being bold in your aspirations for the future.* This means spending plenty of time with alumni who will teach you about the past and what they hold dear. It also means asking what work (e.g., educational initiatives, academic decisions, special topic workgroups and task forces) preceded your arrival. You will want to ask about the scope of the work and who has been involved. This includes intentionally seeking out and learning from teachers who have been engaged in these efforts. Ask what accomplishments they are most proud of and what they believe to be the school's greatest untapped opportunities. Teachers and staff are an invaluable and rich resource of institutional knowledge, school history and culture, and general guidance.

The head of a school is also the leader of the administration, whose training, responsibilities, and expectations may be vastly different from those of the teachers. To add complexity, the lines among faculty, staff, and administration often blur in the PK–12 environment. Whereas the higher education environment tends to draw clear lines among those groups, in the PK–12 environment, staff and administration may also teach classes or coach teams. There is much more fluidity and a greater sense of *esprit de corps*. The university environment tends to be siloed, with individuals focused on a particular aspect of higher education, but the PK–12 environment tends to be united in a common goal, with the education and well-being of their young students at the core. As head of a school, it's essential to be flexible and inclusive while keeping in mind the many hats that faculty, staff, and administration wear.

Questions to Consider

- Are you interested in a comprehensive PK–12 or a subset? Single gender or coed? Religiously affiliated or nondenominational?
- What appeals to you about each school type?
- What other personal values are important for you to see reflected in your professional environment, and how are these reflected in the culture of a particular school?

Making the Change

Although many of the skills gained in a higher education career apply to the PK–12 independent school environment, success in this environment requires continual learning, beginning with research to decide whether it's the right move.

In the higher education field, I accrued knowledge and experience over 2 decades. I took for granted that I was intimately familiar with hundreds of colleges and universities and had colleagues across the country whom I could call on without pretense. I was deeply involved in ACPA–College Student Educators International and NASPA–Student Affairs Administrators in Higher Education, where I presented regularly and even chaired an ACPA Annual Convention. Suffice it to say, I understood the profession, and my peer network was vast and important to me as I navigated complicated situations and decisions. When considering the move to PK–12 education, I did not have that foundation or the luxury of time. I spent a fraction of the time—about 6 months—immersing myself in the independent school world.

I amassed a library of literature—books, magazines, and journals about independent schools. I did a deep dive into NAIS. I asked colleagues in the geographic regions I was considering about professional organizations and relationships with educators in the area and was deliberate in reaching out. I spoke to friends whose children attended independent schools. I connected with people who then opened the door to other connections. I contacted school leaders regardless of whether I knew them. For instance, when considering my current position at William Penn Charter School, I reached out to a half-dozen heads of school in the Philadelphia region in my quest to learn about the Philadelphia marketplace, Quaker education, and specifically Penn Charter.

In all these situations, people were generous, transparent, and helpful.

Their input helped me decide whether the community I was considering, academic and otherwise, was a place where I could thrive and do my best work. This outreach also helped me establish a set of education colleagues whom I now rely on as a sort of collegial think tank, helping me work through issues as they come up.

I also researched PK–12 education. I looked at master's programs and the materials and readings that were covered. I read the most current research on teacher preparation. Whereas I still maintain an impressive research library from my decades in higher education, I now have a growing library of resources focused on PK–12 independent school education, covering everything from early childhood development to artificial intelligence.

I stay aware of the conversations coming out of university schools of education around the country and keep abreast of emerging research and trends. I read all NAIS publications, subscribe to education periodicals that represent diverse perspectives, and deepen my perspective with sources like the *Harvard Business Review*, Pew Research Center publications, and *American Educational Research Journal*. I remain attuned to what is going on in higher education because it is not only the next step for PK–12 students, it is also a bellwether for emerging issues and shifting priorities in education generally.

Questions to Consider

- What local and national resources can you explore to help you learn more about the PK–12 environment?
- What further education or professional experience might you need?
- How else can you prepare?
- What connections and relationships do you have that can help you in your learning process and/or search?

Effective Leadership

Students at independent schools will earn a rigorous and comprehensive education and will be prepared for any academic environment. But how do we prepare them to engage in a world that is increasingly complex and polarized? How do we teach them not what to think but how to think? This is an area of particular interest that excites me about being in the PK–12 space, considering how I can contribute to advancing this complex and often fraught conversation.

Teaching students how to think is one component of effective leadership. To effectively lead a school, you must be committed to diversity and inclusion, know how to cultivate resilience, be a champion of critical thinking (among students, faculty, and staff), and be able to navigate a multitude of complexities daily. You have a responsibility to model these qualities in your own leadership practices.

Demonstrating Commitment to Diversity and Inclusion

Effective education begins with diversity, equity, and inclusion. Our responsibility as PK–12 educators is to prepare students for lives of purpose and impact. To do this, we must help everyone in our community feel respected and valued; sustain a culture of genuine inclusion and belonging; develop programs that support and enhance each student's physical, mental, social, and emotional well-being; and embrace and support a range of student learning profiles. These efforts are not just ethically sound; they are also fundamental to delivering an effective education. Children learn best when they truly feel part of a community. We know from a large body of research in education that learning in an environment with students from diverse experiences and perspectives strengthens the quality of the education (Hunt et al., 2020). As administrators, we need to cultivate environments where diverse perspectives are valued and understood as part of an exemplary educational environment.

In addition to a commitment to a diverse student body and workforce, students, teachers, and administrators must feel and believe their school demonstrates equality and fairness. An important aspect of diversity and inclusion in my work in higher education involved the recruitment and support of first-generation students, determining how to support the needs of these students and their families. How did these students use cultural capital, and how could the university ensure it was prepared to avail them of every opportunity? Were faculty and administrators adept at supporting these students? These were some of the questions I asked regularly while I was in higher education and continue to do so in the PK–12 setting.

The PK–12 environment is similar in ensuring the school is recruiting a diverse student body and reaching families who might not otherwise end up on its doorstep. Independent schools have a long history of generational attendance and families who have much pride in an institution that has so richly affected their lives and those of their parents and often their grandparents. It is always an affirmation of a school's mission and impact when a graduate chooses their alma mater for their own children. Likewise, families may not have any history with a particular school, and for some families, an independent school education might seem financially and socially out of reach. The mere perception that a school is too costly (often reflecting a lack of understanding about available financial aid) or is a place where you must already be an insider to be welcome may prevent families from considering a school that could be a great fit for their child. This can cheat the student of a fantastic education and the school community of a student and family who can add to the breadth of its learning community. Economic diversity is an important aspect of a diverse and inclusive school. Providing financial aid is one piece in helping make schools affordable and accessible, along with communicating effectively about how aid can put a school within reach of families, regardless of their means. Once a student matriculates, it is equally important for their experience to be equitable to their peers' and that they can avail themselves of all a school has to offer. Whether traveling for sports or purchasing a class ring, many components of the whole school experience have price tags associated with them. These costs should also be addressed.

Prioritizing diversity, equity, and inclusion for the student body, faculty, board, and curriculum is not about any one ethnic or socioeconomic group; it is about lifting up the entire community. Research shows that diverse environments yield much richer dialogue, more critical thinking, and more effective decision-making than homogenous environments (Wells et al., 2016). Conversations and work in this area have been going on in PK–12 for some time, and progress has been made. But children are growing up in a world that is evolving more rapidly than at any point in our lifetimes, and therefore we must sustain our commitment to this critical work.

Cultivating Resilience

When we educate children at the PK–12 level, we are not just preparing them for college; we are preparing them for life. The habits of mind they learn and the character traits they develop in their most formative years have the potential to shape the entire trajectory of their lives. Resilience is an essential life skill for thriving in this world, and it is a trait that seems to have been neglected in recent years (Lukianoff & Haidt, 2018).

Over the course of more than 2 decades in higher education, I witnessed a disturbing trend of college students turning to administrators to solve their dilemmas rather than trying to solve them on their own. Students increasingly seemed unwilling to or incapable of working out something as simple as a roommate dispute. This experience underscores that we can—and should—begin teaching and practicing resiliency and learning to navigate conflict in the PK–12 environment. The best way to teach this is through day-to-day work with students. These concepts can be integrated in ways that make sense. For example, what sort of decision-making authority do students have? How are they empowered to make developmentally appropriate decisions, whether they are a third-grader voting on a book for the class to read or a ninth-grader who is allowed to choose their own schedule for the next year? Students will not get everything they want, and they will inevitably be disappointed from time to time. And that's OK. It is important to create an environment and a decision-making infrastructure that teach students to be agents of their lives.

Championing Critical Thinking

Resilience is knowing how to navigate the world. It is also key to responding to opinions and actions that do not align with your own and to managing situations that are difficult or make you uncomfortable. It includes a skill set that is important to develop at a young age: how to hold a point of view while being open to another point of view and how to recognize that your truth probably is not the only truth.

Having resilience provides the foundation for learning to think for oneself. Teaching students how to think, not what to think, is perhaps the single most important skill we can cultivate in students. And a big part of learning how to think is learning how to listen and engage in respectful conversation, even when the subject matter is difficult.

These essential components of a student's education seem to be receding further out of reach. During my decades in higher education, I witnessed a disturbing trend: students demanding that a college or university uninvite a speaker with whom they disagree rather than finding a way to challenge that speaker, for example, by attending a speech and being prepared to ask hard questions. This should concern all education leaders regardless of personal political beliefs.

As Hanna Holborn Gray, president emerita of the University of Chicago, said, "Education should not be intended to make people comfortable, it is meant to make them think. Universities should be expected to provide the conditions within which hard thought, and therefore strong disagreement, independent judgment, and the questioning of stubborn assumptions, can flourish in an environment of the greatest freedom" (Committee on Freedom of Expression at the University of Chicago, 2014, p. 1). It is our responsibility as educators to teach students how to think critically, to prepare them to articulate what they believe and why, to provide them with tools for listening and hearing alternative points of view, to express their opinions and feelings with civility, and to question the various sides of a point of view or an argument.

This work is more complex in a PK–12 setting than in a university, given the range of student ages and development. However, we can and should begin this vital work early, even in the youngest grades. For a lower school student, it may begin with teaching a child the language to communicate their point of view. If a friend hurts their feelings, for example, we can teach the injured party how to express themselves in a way that gives their friend the opportunity to feel empathy, grow, and change. Middle school students can learn to identify the personal experiences, culture, and history that have helped shape their point of view and to develop skills in managing their emotions. High school students can develop more sophisticated skills in rhetoric—such as being able to identify the assumptions that underlie a particular argument or asking challenging but respectful questions—while also strengthening personal skills related to confidence and resilience, such as the ability to negotiate what they want in the face of opposition.

Critical thinking skills are essential for students and a key aspect of how faculty teach and administrators lead. It is human nature to be defensive in the face of challenging questions or critical feedback. Effective teachers and school leaders learn how to invite and respond to feedback as a welcome part of their toolkit. How do faculty respond when students challenge them in the classroom? How do administrators respond when parents, alumni, or colleagues ask questions or offer ideas for new approaches? The head of the school has a responsibility to model an open and encouraging response and to invite the school community to see self-reflection and growth as a core part of a healthy organizational culture.

On any given school day, myriad opportunities exist to live these skills and values. Several years ago, when a national discussion was underway about historical school yearbook photos depicting the use of blackface, I worked with my leadership team to review our school's archived yearbooks going back several decades. We discovered that they contained some photos with blackface and costumes that reinforce racist stereotypes. This was an extremely painful time for our community. Processing our institutional culpability and deciding what to do next were difficult. Ultimately, through dialogue, critical thinking, and self-reflection, it became clear that transparency and accountability were the only path forward.

Navigating Complexities

As you have likely discerned by now, the role of head of a school is among the most challenging in education. I have joked that the job is like running full speed on a treadmill while juggling balls, some of which are rubber and some of which are glass. And while you are running and juggling, you are giving a speech and your phone is ringing, and you need to know which balls you can drop, because guess what: You will drop some. You just try not to drop the glass ones.

Navigating complexities is part of the job, a presumed part of the day-to-day existence. As you consider whether a leadership role in PK–12 is for you, these are some of the questions you should ask yourself: *Do I enjoy navigating complexities, or is it anathema to me? Would I thrive in such an environment, or would I be miserable?* No matter what type of school you lead, you can be assured of one thing—no two days are the same. And the good days are truly great.

Questions for Consideration

- Are you prepared to create a diverse and inclusive environment? What additional skills or experience do you need?
- Do you consider yourself resilient? How can you build your resilience and that of others?
- Do you embrace an environment of open inquiry? Do you have the knowledge and skills to foster an environment of critical thinking?
- Are you prepared to navigate the complexities that come with a PK–12 leadership role?

Lessons Learned

Shifting from a career in higher education to the PK–12 educational environment is achievable and can be highly rewarding. The key to success can be found in a deliberate approach to the transition:

- Be clear about your motivations and desired outcomes.
- Be aware of the similarities and differences between the environments.
- Do a deep dive into the types of schools and positions available and PK–12 education in general.
- Leverage your relationships to learn all you can about an institution when considering a position.

- Be ready and willing to work in partnership with families and caregivers, board members, and other constituents.
- Embrace the expectations of leading and take the time to develop skills.
- Learn to juggle. While riding a unicycle. Backward. OK, that was a joke. Sort of. (A sense of humor is essential!)

Following are a few key lessons I learned during this process to keep in mind as well:

- **Plan ahead.** Making a successful change requires an honest assessment of your capabilities and a commitment to developing your knowledge, skills, and relationships. Although I spent an intensive 6 months absorbing the knowledge I needed, in many ways, I had been preparing for this move for years. Throughout my career, I made strategic decisions based on my likes as well as my "lacks"—where I perceived growth was needed to keep evolving and developing in my career. If you, too, are a person who is continually assessing your skills and looking for growth opportunities, you will be well suited to making such a change.
- **Respect what you do not know.** Once I made the transition, I had a tremendous sense of deference to the fact that although I brought extraordinary experience to the table, and the faculty and staff would benefit from that, I had, and still have, much to learn. No matter how intensively I threw myself into learning about PK–12 education and institutions before leading one, it could never be a substitute for years in the classroom and is not meant to be. The good news is that as head of a school, you are surrounded by teachers. New administrators should take advantage of that.

- **Value the work and learning.** To best understand your teachers and to value the work that they do every day, you need to be in their spaces and see how they engage with their students and ask informed questions. I spend a lot of time in the classroom. I schedule regular classroom visits on my calendar. If you do not schedule these vital activities as an administrator, your time is consumed by other things.
- **Treasure the schoolhouse.** Electing to work with children is an enormous privilege and responsibility. Treat it as one of the most important jobs in the world because it is. As a leader in PK–12 education, you have an opportunity to have an indelible impact on many lives. You also have a reason to play hopscotch again. How great is that?

Resources

National Association of Independent Schools. (n.d.). *NAIS jobs-to-be-done research: What are boards searching for when they hire an independent school leader?* https://www.nais.org/articles/pages/research/nais-jobs-to-be-done-research-what-are-boards-searching-for-when-hiring-a-head-of-school

National Association of Independent Schools. (n.d.). *NAIS research: Jobs-to-be-done study on independent school parents.* https://www.nais.org/articles/pages/research/nais-research-jobs-to-be-done-study-on-independent-school-parents

National Association of Independent Schools. (n.d.). *Trustees' guide. Section 7: Partner with the head of school.* https://www.nais.org/trustees-guide/partner-with-the-head-of-school

National Association of Independent Schools. (2021, August 1). *2021 NAIS state of independent school leadership survey.* https://www.nais.org/articles/pages/research/nais-research-2021-state-of-independent-school-leadership-survey

Rowe, M. A. (2021). *NAIS research: State of independent school leadership survey.* National Association of Independent Schools. https://www.nais.org/articles/pages/research/nais-research-2021-state-of-independent-school-leadership-survey

Watchorn, V. (Ed.). (2018). *The NAIS head search handbook* (2nd ed.). National Association of Independent Schools.

References

Baker, C. (Ed.). (2018). *The NAIS enrollment management handbook: A comprehensive guide for independent schools.* National Association of Independent Schools.

Batiste, G., & Riven, J. (Eds.). (2011). *The head's handbook: A guide for aspiring, new, and experienced heads of school.* National Association of Independent Schools.

Chait, R. P., Chait, R., Holland, T. P., & Taylor, B. E. (1993). *The effective board of trustees.* R&L Education.

Committee on Freedom of Expression at the University of Chicago. (2014). *Report of the Committee on Freedom of Expression.* University of Chicago. https://provost.uchicago.edu/sites/default/files/documents/reports/FOECommitteeReport.pdf

Creeden, J. (2019). *The board chair handbook: An essential guide for board leaders at independent schools.* National Association of Independent Schools.

Damour, L. (2019). *Under pressure: Confronting the epidemic of stress and anxiety in girls.* Ballantine Books.

Hunt, V., Prince, S., Dixon-Fyle, S., & Dolan, K. (2020, May 19). *Diversity wins: How inclusion matters.* McKinsey & Company. https://bit.ly/47FN8Vy

Lukianoff, G., & Haidt, J. (2018). *The coddling of the American mind: How good intentions and bad ideas are setting up a generation for failure.* Penguin.

McClellan, G. S., Kiyama, J. M., & Stringer, J. (2023). *The handbook of student affairs administration* (5th ed.). Jossey-Bass.

National Association of Independent Schools. (2019). *Principles of good practice for boards and trustees.*

National Association of Independent Schools. (2022). *How to prepare for headship: Key takeaways for aspiring heads from the 2021 NAIS state of independent school leadership survey.* https://www.nais.org/articles/pages/research/nais-research-2021-state-of-independent-school-leadership-survey

Orem, D., & Wilson, D. (2022). *The trustee handbook* (11th ed.). National Association of Independent Schools.

Spock, B. (1946). *The common sense book of baby and child care.* Duell, Sloan and Pearce.

Thompson, M., & Evans, R. (2021). *Hopes and fears: Working with today's independent school parents.* National Association of Independent Schools.

Twenge, J. M. (2017). *iGen: Why today's super-connected kids are growing up less rebellious, more tolerant, less happy—and completely unprepared for adulthood—and what that means for the rest of us.* Simon & Schuster.

Wells, A. S., Fox, L., & Cordova-Cobo, D. (2016, February 9). *How racially diverse schools and classrooms can benefit all students.* https://tcf.org/content/report/how-racially-diverse-schools-and-classrooms-can-benefit-all-students

Boundaries, Balance, and Moving Forward

Darryl Lovett and Marcella Runell

Although most of this book discusses transitioning to a new job or assuming different responsibilities, this chapter explores methods for enhancing job satisfaction without having to make a change. Reinvigorating your career path doesn't always require a drastic leap; it can often be achieved through intentional efforts within your current role. In certain situations, taking a big leap may be necessary, but this chapter offers some direction before reaching that point. Student affairs professionals have the ability to mold their workplace, encourage teamwork, and inspire positive relationships. Such efforts require organizations to recognize the importance of cultivating a supportive culture that enables employees to thrive and grow.

Reinvigorating Your Career

Reinvigorating career paths in student affairs is a pressing need in today's rapidly evolving higher education landscape. Traditional career paths in student affairs were often linear and hierarchical, offering limited prospects for growth and advancement (Biddix, 2013). However, the field has undergone significant changes, particularly because of the COVID-19 pandemic (Chessman, 2021), and now faces new challenges and expectations. When reflecting on the history of student affairs career paths and considering the current challenges in the field, a compelling need for change and innovation in the approach to career development becomes clear.

Professionals in student affairs encounter a range of challenges that require adaptive skill sets, including addressing mounting mental health concerns within the campus climate, fostering inclusivity and diversity in the face of divisive politics, adapting to technological advancements, and navigating the evolving needs of students. To meet these challenges, the field of student affairs must adopt a more flexible approach to career development. Such an approach requires the creation of opportunities for multidimensional growth, the promotion of cross-functional collaboration, and an emphasis on continual learning and skill development; it also includes a commitment to policy, programs, and people who actively support a sustainable model for work–life integration. Stephen Kohler, CEO and founder of Audira Labs, said that "work–life integration is centered on the belief that there is no distinction between the two and that both must coexist in harmony" (Fallon-O'Leary, 2021, para. 2). What does this approach mean for student affairs professionals who often work and live on campus or who have on-call responsibilities?

Reimagining Career Paths

By embracing innovation, cultivating growth and adaptability, and directly addressing the unique challenges of the field, we as a profession can establish a vibrant and fulfilling career environment that supports the holistic development and success of students in higher education. Institutions can no longer can create unrealistic expectations for student affairs professionals. In *Creating Sustainable Careers in Student Affairs: What Ideal Worker Norms Get Wrong and How to Make It Right,* Kristen A. Renn (2020) related, "Before I started my master's program, I was primed as an 'ideal worker' for student affairs. I knew how to prioritize multiple and competing demands, how to run a meeting, and how to work 14 hours a day" (p. ix). Unfortunately, this is the culture many professionals have been mentored into, and it does not reflect the need to establish boundaries to focus on both work and life.

To redefine success and foster professional growth in student affairs, it is crucial for institutions to adopt a holistic approach that recognizes the diverse talents and aspirations of individuals in the field. Ardoin et al. (2019) emphasized the significance of redefining success and professional growth in student affairs to overcome the limitations of the traditional model. It is important to acknowledge and appreciate the different career pathways in student affairs, including specialized roles across various departments and units. By expanding the range of career options, professionals can explore and pursue paths that align with their unique skills and interests. This approach enables individuals to find fulfillment in their work and to make an impact on their campus communities.

By embracing a multidimensional perspective, student affairs educators can prioritize personal and professional growth beyond the conventional success metrics. This effort may involve seeking opportunities for skill development, engaging in continual learning, and fostering collaborations across disciplines; additionally, it requires that both student affairs leadership and team members recognize the importance of personal well-being, work–life integration, and consistent self-care in achieving sustainable professional growth. Redefining success and professional growth in student affairs requires a shift toward a more thoughtful approach that values diverse talents and career pathways. By broadening the scope of career options and encouraging multidimensional progress, professionals can find fulfillment and make a meaningful impact in their field. The following are some examples of work–life integration strategies.

The Right Institutional Fit

A new vice president for student affairs has young children and chooses to accept a role at an institution that provides opportunities for on-campus housing to reduce commute time. There is also on-campus childcare, which allows for building stronger community ties. This work–life integration enables flexibility in terms of attending evening events and building relationships with students.

168 hours

Laura Vanderkam (2011) wrote a book called *168 Hours*, which is all about how to maximize time each week. Her recommendations include adjusting daily schedules in order, for example, to attend an early-morning parent and child dance class as a standing commitment to time with a young child before they reach school age—or splitting work time to create windows of opportunity after school to do pick-up, homework, and dinner, and then resume email later. With her supervisor's support, a dean of students with a school-age child at a small liberal arts college made that split schedule a reality during her child's elementary school years as a way to maximize her time. These choices about time reflect seasons and chapters that will change. They are meant to be creative solutions for what will work best at any given time in our lives.

Creative Side Hustles

Sometimes the best way to stay invigorated is to serve on a board or start a new project that brings joy and uses a skill set different from that of your primary work. An assistant dean made a choice to start a consulting group that focused on managing life transitions after the death of a parent. This was a way to find meaning in a tragedy, incorporate work she loves, and find integration in her life.

Creative side hustles have become a growing trend in the realm of student affairs and higher education. Professionals are increasingly leveraging their expertise to develop side hustles that resonate with their passions and skills. These individuals, who have dedicated years to building and supporting campuses and empowering students, are branching out to offer personalized services. These side hustles provide the opportunity for elevated professional standing within the student affairs community as well as supplement income, which can be used for more leisure at a later date, also increasing work–life satisfaction.

Creating Sustainable Workplaces

The goal of sustainability in student affairs is to establish and maintain a campus environment that is not only healthy and inclusive for all members of the community but also considers the needs of current students while ensuring the ability of future generations to meet their own needs (Michel et al., 2023). This commitment requires the integration of various aspects of student affairs, including policies, programs, and operations.

Creating sustainable workplaces is no longer a choice but a necessity for organizations seeking long-term success, and the field of student affairs is no exception. To fully comprehend the concept of sustainability, leaders must acknowledge the intricate relationship the field has with the environmental, social, and cultural facets it encompasses. Senior-level student affairs officers play a pivotal role in shaping both a sustainable workplace and its impact on staff.

Creating a sustainable workplace requires that leadership implement various strategies and practices. One involves promoting work–life integration by encouraging flexible work arrangements, such as remote work options or flexible hours, which allow employees to better manage their personal and professional responsibilities. Additionally, investing in professional development programs and resources that foster continual learning and growth for staff members empowers them to enhance their skills and make more meaningful contributions to the organization.

Senior-level student affairs officers can also prioritize employee engagement and job satisfaction by fostering a work culture that values diversity, equity, and inclusion. They can, for example, offer opportunities for open communication, feedback, and recognition; these moments foster a positive work environment—one that prioritizes collaboration, innovation, and overall well-being. By adopting these sustainable workplace practices, senior-level leaders contribute to the long-term success and flourishing of both the organization and the individuals within it (Allworth et al., 2021).

Creating sustainable workplaces goes beyond environmental considerations to encompass social ones. By promoting inclusivity, diversity, and equity, institutions can cultivate a sense of belonging and ensure equal opportunities for all campus community members, establishing a work culture that supports personal growth—which ultimately contributes to an institution's sustainability.

Furthermore, incorporating ethical practices into the economic aspects of student affairs, such as responsible financial management and innovative processes, can further aid the overall sustainability of the student affairs unit and institution. By adopting a holistic approach to sustainability that incorporates environmental, social, and economic concerns, student affairs professionals can create workplaces that thrive in the long run.

Strategies for Employee Retention and Satisfaction

Implementing strategies for employee retention and satisfaction is vital. Extensive research has consistently highlighted the costly and disruptive nature of employee turnover (McNaughtan et al., 2023; Rattrie et al., 2020). To enhance retention rates, institutions should prioritize several factors:

1. Leaders must institute competitive compensation to attract and retain top talent. Employees who feel properly compensated are more likely to remain committed to their organization and have higher job satisfaction (Rattrie et al., 2020).
2. Employees are more likely to stay with an organization that provides clear career paths, training programs, and chances to develop their skills (Rattrie et al., 2020). By investing in their employees' professional growth, organizations demonstrate a commitment to staff development and increase the likelihood of retaining valuable talent.
3. Organizations that prioritize a healthy balance between work and personal life create a positive and supportive environment. Flexible working arrangements, family-friendly policies, and supportive management all contribute to employee well-being and job satisfaction (McNaughtan et al., 2023).
4. Building a positive workplace culture, fostering effective communication, and recognizing employee achievements are all crucial to enhancing job satisfaction and retention rates (McNaughtan et al., 2023).

By considering these strategies, organizations can create sustainable workplaces that attract and retain skillful individuals while minimizing the costs and disruptions associated with high employee turnover and poor staff morale (McNaughtan et al., 2023; Rattrie et al., 2020). Taking proactive measures to address employee retention and satisfaction not only benefits the organization but also contributes to a positive and productive work environment.

Recent media attention has been paid to the concept of "quiet quitting." At its core, it is about employees deciding to create boundaries. This is a complicated idea when it is applied to student-facing roles; the notion that quiet quitting is subversive or even insubordinate is equally complex. If systems and structures were fully staffed for their stated priorities, if policies allowed for appropriate use of paid leave time, and if organizations supported growth and development, then would quiet quitting be such a phenomenon? Or is it a natural outcome of better boundaries? In *Set Boundaries, Find Peace: A Guide to Reclaiming Yourself*, author Nedra Glover Tawwab (2021) reminded readers that not everything can be resolved or fixed. She identified six types of boundaries: physical, sexual, intellectual, emotional, material, and time. Student affairs preparation programs and professional development spaces should address these boundaries; they are what allow the completion of this complex work in ways that do not lead to chronic and habitual burnout. Tawwab put forth these questions to consider:

- Whose standard am I trying to meet?
- Do I have time to commit to this?
- What is the worst thing that could happen if I do not do this?
- How can I honor my boundaries in this situation?

Organizational Culture Must Improve

To understand and effectively navigate the intricacies of student affairs work, practitioners must explore the complexities of the institution's multifaceted culture. Organizational culture encompasses the shared values, beliefs, norms, and practices that actively shape the behavior and interactions within an institution. It plays a significant role in determining the experiences and outcomes of students, staff, and faculty members. According to Schein and Schein (2017), organizational culture affects an institution's decision-making processes, communication patterns, and overall functioning. Furthermore, it influences how student affairs professionals engage with students, design programs, and create inclusive environments.

Analyzing the various layers and dimensions of institutional culture is essential for professionals seeking to understand its impact on student affairs work. Schein and Schein's (2017) model of organizational culture outlines three levels: artifacts and behaviors, espoused values, and underlying assumptions. Artifacts and behaviors are the visible aspects of culture, such as physical spaces, rituals, and ceremonies. Espoused values represent the stated beliefs and goals of the institution. Underlying assumptions are the deeply ingrained and often unconscious beliefs and attitudes that guide behavior. By examining these layers, student affairs professionals can identify patterns, norms, and potential areas for improvement in their institution's culture.

Cultural Transformation

To promote cultural transformation and navigate change in institutions, student affairs professionals must implement specific strategies tailored to their unique roles and responsibilities. These strategies should engage all stakeholders, including students, staff, and external partners, while emphasizing institutional leadership's commitment to drive cultural change. By actively involving individuals at all levels and seeking their input on decisions, student affairs professionals can foster a sense of belonging and collective responsibility (Allworth et al., 2021). This participatory approach empowers students and staff to contribute their perspectives and ensures their buy-in to the efforts.

Leadership commitment is crucial for achieving cultural change. Student affairs professionals play a vital role in championing and embodying the desired cultural values and behaviors. They must communicate the vision for change, serve as role models for the expected cultural norms, and align institutional processes and policies accordingly. Consistent and visible commitment from student affairs leaders sends a powerful message to students and staff, establishing trust and cultivating a shared commitment to the transformative journey (Allworth et al., 2021).

In *Work Won't Love You Back: How Devotion to Our Jobs Keeps Us Exploited, Exhausted, and Alone,* Sarah Jaffe (2021) made the case that helping professions, such as student affairs, have been undervalued in a capitalist framework, and much of the above-and-beyond work is perceived as appealing, with employees performing these duties for the greater good. This perception can create a systemic cycle that may abuse the time and talents of people in helping professions. Often they are also primary caregivers for others in their families or communities. In *Pay Up: The Future of Women and Work (and Why It's Different Than You Think)*, Reshma Saujani (2022) put forward an innovative plan related to paid leave, affordable childcare, parenting and caregiving, and more government support for the unpaid labor it takes to run homes and families. For the student affairs profession to survive, the field needs to be more vocal and strategic about workforce conditions and the future of work.

The profession will not continue to thrive if it does not radically commit to questioning the idea of the "ideal worker" in student affairs—today and in the future. This is a unique moment to shift the view to what is possible for future student affairs professionals. A nonexistent professional pipeline will persist if cultures and systems are not created to address burnout, compassion fatigue, and inadequate compensation, all of which erode optimal work–life integration. Effectively leading student affairs divisions during crisis moments, finding the time to build joyful and essential relationships, and participating in the intellectual and community life of an institution are achievable goals, but they must be taken seriously.

Leaders must develop a culture of openness and accountability for managing change effectively and driving cultural transformation in student affairs departments. This approach encourages students and staff to take responsibility for their actions, embrace new ideas, and adapt to evolving circumstances; it fosters an environment where innovation is valued, allowing professionals to seize opportunities for growth and remain competitive in the ever-changing landscape of higher education (Allworth et al., 2021).

More Effective Leadership in Student Affairs

Progressive leadership in student affairs plays a crucial role in shaping the profession and influencing employee experiences, team dynamics, and professional development. Open-minded leaders favor management styles that emphasize transformational leadership, open communication, and mentorship. They inspire their teams, stimulate intellectual growth, and consider each individual, which is both useful and impactful.

Research consistently shows that transformational leadership has a positive impact on employee job satisfaction, commitment, and performance (Bass & Riggio, 2006; Schaufeli et al., 2009). Transformational leaders set a compelling vision, encourage creativity and innovation, and promote critical thinking and learning opportunities, inspiring and motivating their teams. These leaders also recognize the unique strengths and needs of each team member and foster a sense of belonging and commitment.

In line with progressive leadership, open and transparent communication is essential. Leaders who prioritize clear and frequent communication create a culture of trust and inclusivity, enhancing teamwork and organizational effectiveness (Dirks & Ferrin, 2002). Transparent communication values employees and facilitates collaboration and the exchange of ideas, leading to more effective decision-making and problem-solving.

Mentorship and ongoing support are crucial aspects of progressive leadership in student affairs. Such leaders invest in mentoring relationships and offer continual support, contributing to their employees' growth and success (Ivey & Dupré, 2022). Through mentorship, leaders offer guidance, feedback, and professional development opportunities, enabling employees to enhance their skills and advance in their careers. By fostering a supportive environment, supervisors create a sense of loyalty and commitment among employees, resulting in higher job satisfaction and retention rates.

Student affairs professionals should create a culture that truly encourages and expects everyone to take all their vacation days without guilt about leaving colleagues to bear the burden. The cultural norm should be that everyone at the institution uses paid time off regularly—without guilt or repercussion. Senior leaders should explore the opportunity for sabbaticals. These leaders may have a substantial amount of accrued paid leave or may have the ability to live on a reduced salary for a short time. It would be an innovation in higher education leadership to socialize a culture of sabbaticals for student affairs professionals.

By incorporating these progressive leadership practices and changes to institutional culture, leaders and supervisors shape the student affairs profession and foster their employees' growth and development (Bass & Riggio, 2006; Dirks & Ferrin, 2002; Ivey & Dupré, 2022; Schaufeli et al., 2009).

At its core, work–life integration is about flexibility. It means bringing family members to community events, leaving work in the middle of the day to volunteer on a school field trip, or signing off to attend a doctor's appointment with a loved one. Work–life integration is often the default for student affairs staff because the nature of the work—especially the community-building opportunities—seeps into nights and weekends. Living on campus, eating in the dining hall, and walking on campus for exercise are visible ways that these professionals demonstrate a version of work–life integration. Work–life *balance*, however, calls for clearer boundaries between roles and is often harder to achieve in student affairs work, especially among employees who live on campus. The balance necessitates a commitment to firm boundaries at the individual level and a good-faith effort to honor them. Boundaries are important. Work–life integration may blur responsibilities, but it still requires boundaries.

Conclusion

The evolving nature of student affairs work, amplified by the challenges brought about by the pandemic, necessitates a reimagining of career paths, the creation of sustainable workplaces, the implementation of strategies for employee retention and satisfaction, the analysis of organizational culture, and the adoption of effective leadership practices. This chapter sheds light on these critical aspects, offering insights and guidance for professionals in the field.

Employees must embrace alternatives to traditional success metrics and adopt new ways of thinking about work and purpose. The field of student affairs demands a more flexible approach to career development—one that promotes multidimensional growth, cross-functional collaboration, and continual learning. By recognizing the diverse talents and aspirations of professionals in the field, redefining success, and expanding the range of career options, individuals can discover fulfillment and make an impact on campus communities.

Creating sustainable workplaces is no longer a choice but a necessity. Organizations must prioritize work–life balance, invest in professional development programs, foster inclusive cultures, and incorporate ethical practices to promote the long-term success of both the institution and its employees. Competitive compensation, opportunities for growth and advancement, and a supportive work environment are vital for attracting and retaining top talent and cultivating a positive and productive workforce.

By embracing these insights and implementing the recommended practices, professionals can navigate its evolving landscape, find contentment in their work, and create a positive impact on the lives of students and the higher education community as a whole. It is through collective efforts and a commitment to innovation, inclusivity, and personal well-being that the field will continue to thrive and evolve, shaping the future of student affairs for the better.

References

Allworth, J., D'Souza, L., & Henning, G. (2021). *Design thinking in student affairs: A primer*. Stylus.

Ardoin, S., Crandall, R. E., & Shinn, J. (2019). Senior student affairs officers' perspectives on professional preparation in student affairs programs. *Journal of Student Affairs Research and Practice, 56*(4), 379–393. https://doi.org/10.1080/19496591.2019.1614938

Bass, B. M., & Riggio, R. E. (2006). *Transformational leadership*. Psychology Press.

Biddix, J. P. (2013). Directors, deans, doctors, divergers: The four career paths of SSAOs. *Journal of College Student Development, 54*(3), 315–321. https://doi.org/10.1353/csd.2013.0056

Dirks, K. T., & Ferrin, D. L. (2002). Trust in leadership: Meta-analytic findings and implications for research and practice. *Journal of Applied Psychology, 87*(4), 611–628. https://doi.org/10.1037/0021-9010.87.4.611

Chessman, H. M. (2021). Student affairs professionals, well-being, and work quality. *Journal of Student Affairs Research and Practice, 58*(2), 148–162. https://doi.org/10.1080/19496591.2020.1853556

Fallon-O'Leary, D. (2021). Work-life integration is the new work-life balance: Is your team ready? *CO*. https://www.uschamber.com/co/grow/thrive/work-life-integration-vs-work-life-balance

Ivey, G. W., & Dupré, K. E. (2022). Workplace mentorship: A critical review. *Journal of Career Development, 49*(3), 714–729. https://doi.org/10.1177/0894845320957737

Jaffe, S. (2021). *Work won't love you back: How devotion to our jobs keeps us exploited, exhausted, and alone*. Bold Type Books.

McNaughtan, J., Garza, T., Eicke, D., Garcia, H. A., & Bodine-Al-Sharif, M. A. (2023). Being our best: Understanding the relationship between empowerment and employee engagement among midlevel student affairs professionals. *Higher Education Quarterly, 77*(4), 774–791. https://doi.org/10.1111/hequ.12432

Michel, J. O., Buckley, J., Friedensen, R., Anderson-Long, M., & Garibay, J. (2023). Infusing sustainability into graduate level higher education and student affairs coursework. *About Campus, 27*(6), 4–11. https://doi.org/10.1177/10864822231151878

Rattrie, L. T. B., Kittler, M. G., & Paul, K. I. (2020). Culture, burnout, and engagement: A meta-analysis on national cultural values as moderators in JD-R theory. *Applied Psychology, 69*(1), 176–220. https://doi.org/10.1111/apps.12209

Renn, K. A. (2020). Foreword. In M. W. Sallee (Ed.), *Creating sustainable careers in student affairs: What ideal worker norms get wrong and how to make it right* (pp. ix–xi). Stylus.

Saujani, R. (2022). *Pay up: The future of women and work (and why it's different than you think)*. Atria/One Signal.

Schaufeli, W. B., Bakker, A. B., & van Rhenen, W. (2009). How changes in job demands and resources predict burnout, work engagement, and sickness absenteeism. *Journal of Organizational Behavior, 30*(7), 893–917. https://doi.org/10.1002/job.595

Schein, E. H., & Schein, P. (2017). *Organizational culture and leadership* (5th ed.). Wiley.

Tawwab, N. G. (2021). *Set boundaries, find peace: A guide to reclaiming yourself* (N. G. Tawwab, Narr.) [Audiobook]. Penguin.

Vanderkam, L. (2011). *168 hours: You have more time than you think*. Portfolio.

Presidential Perspectives on Student Affairs Careers and Preparation to Move On

Kenneth Elmore, Thomas Gibson, Ajay Nair, Ellen J. Neufeldt, and Lori S. White

This book is chiefly a set of narratives of exceptional professionals who have served higher education for all or part of their careers. These trajectories boast successes and challenges. This chapter is a microcosm of those perspectives within a unique community: university presidents and chancellors.

First and foremost, we seek to inspire readers by offering reasons to pursue a presidency. Second, each of us has had a long and successful career in student affairs. We share examples of how our career paths prepared us for our presidencies. Third, and most important, this chapter includes personal reflections of self-doubt and unique histories intended to address stereotypes of who gets to be "in the seat."

■ ■ ■

DREAM!

Kenneth Elmore
14th President of Dean College

"Dream!" is what I have often told people—especially young folks and students—to do when I am asked for advice to carry them through their careers and life's work. I counted, and I was startled: I had 10, maybe 15, years of work life left. (I also recognized that 10 to 15 years would pass swiftly.) A few short years and I had not taken my advice. I never dreamed.

Like everyone, I was surrounded by racial violence, political chaos, and global pandemics that kept me in my head and forced me to finally ask myself the big questions: *Who am I? What is my work?* I was calling out my struggles with anger, sadness, and lots of joy to find meaning and life in my work in law and student affairs. I had to permit myself to grapple with my healing and the care of others. I came away from my personal retreats even more human and with an appreciation that my soul was asking me to continue my work in a more mission-driven space—one that contributes to more people finding meaningful participation in society.

Discovering Meaning in Career Ramblings

My work has been in breaking barriers of divisiveness—via programs, reflection with others, and meaningful connections and conversations.

For decades, I have been engaged in building inclusive communities. I have been about belonging and inclusion before those were buzzwords. My work has entailed making creative spaces that catalyze the sharing of our humanity—discourse centered on listening, conversations, and action. I believe in places where folks can be folks and disagree and face one another. People can enter spaces to claim and reclaim themselves without denigrating one another. My work involves challenging perceptions and questioning easy, comfortable answers.

I did not think I could get the sense of fulfillment I knew I needed from higher education. Although I was still curious, optimistic, and enthusiastic about the field, I also felt battered at the time. Moreover, I was not confident that I would find fulfillment anywhere else because I was sure that my work seemed heady, ill-defined, and strange to people, institutions, and businesses outside of higher education. I explored other jobs for 18 months and realized I was already in my next vocation: higher education. Years ago, I briefly left higher education to be a lawyer. I returned to higher education (that is another story that I will share when we meet). I recognized that I was wired and built for education and needed to shift how I did my work to have the greatest impact. I decided to seek a presidency at a college, leadership at a nonprofit, or a head-of-school position in a secondary school.

I Found My People

Colleges run and succeed on business models, culture, and mission. I sought a presidency where I could fight for a mission—a living and breathing mission that operates as a college. I was in a place that allows multiple stories to live and thrive. The community at Dean College is full of different thinkers: artists, the neurodiverse, people whose perspectives are rarely highlighted in popular media, people with disabilities, poor folks, the working class, people who are the first in their families to experience education beyond high school, and high achievers. Dean College excels at placing people in the world who beat the odds or challenge the status quo. All of us at the institution believed that people, our students, deserve the opportunity to discover and exceed their greatest aspirations. Ultimately, my colleagues and I shepherded philanthropic dollars, partnerships, and resources in service to society. We were and still are proud of our excellence at transforming students and providing social mobility and exposure to the world.

Recruiting on Mission

I believe—perhaps as an act of hubris—that I am part of a long human-rights struggle. This struggle needs us to come to know ourselves and each other. The way to those interactions is to make spaces for all of us to be engaged in business, science, medicine, technology, entertainment, sports, our communities, society, and life. I work with others to provide launches and leadership pipelines to this life and society, especially for people who have been pushed away from the launchpads or told that they are underserving. I am proud to be a contributor to this fight.

I also believe that Dean College's mission is valuable to everyone; a democratic society needs all the multiracial-ness, multiethnic-ness, and any other "ness" it can get. I recruited people to be on my team who had thought about doing the work of this mission and saw it as a personal fulfillment. Furthermore, I remain impressed by the people who were there before I arrived, and who had been deeply engaged in the mission. I am humbled that they let me join them and saw me for what I could contribute. I am still thrilled that we came together and proud that we fought together. I hope to recruit you to join me on my journey and am open to joining you on yours.

Presidential Perspectives

FROM CAMPUS ENGAGEMENT TO STRATEGIC VISION

Ellen J. Neufeldt
President, California State University, San Marcos

Commencement weekend is my favorite time of year. Over my career in higher education, I have participated in dozens of these ceremonies. A joy permeates the air, and the atmosphere is electric with a profound sense of accomplishment—not only among the graduates but also among their families and loved ones who gather to celebrate. Witnessing and being a part of this outpouring of pride and love are an incredible experience that never gets old—nor does it fail to remind me of the transformative power of education and why it is such a privilege to play a part in supporting students' upward trajectory and social mobility.

My first commencement as a university president at California State University, San Marcos (CSUSM), in spring 2020, came with the unexpected plot twist of a once-in-a-lifetime pandemic. Instead of walking across the traditional commencement stage, our graduates decorated their vehicles and drove through campus in a car parade. At the same time, staff and faculty volunteers lined the sidewalks—6 feet apart—with signs, pom-poms, and banners to cheer them on. We handed diploma covers through car windows, and I briefly congratulated every graduate. The silver lining of this unusual celebration was seeing vehicles packed with proud parents, grandparents, spouses, children, and siblings—even dogs and cats—all thrilled to experience commencement with their graduates. It was an unusual way to mark the conclusion of my first academic year as president, but it is a day filled with memories I will always cherish.

My first year as president brought a global pandemic and many other challenges and opportunities. Now, in my fifth year, I am grateful for the unusual yet incredibly fulfilling presidential pathway I took via student affairs. Although all career pathways—whether via academic affairs, finance, or advancement—bring with them essential perspectives, I often encourage student affairs leaders to consider the exciting possibilities of university leadership because of the broad spectrum of student-centered experiences these individuals bring to the table. Their backgrounds benefit not only the institution but also the student experience on campus.

Making Meaningful Impact From the Start

When I entered student affairs nearly 30 years ago, I did not know that university president would one day be my job title; at the time, it was rare to see vice presidents of student affairs transition into the executive office. Although I could not imagine where my career would eventually take me, from the beginning, I always sought to make a meaningful impact—both on the institution and students' lives.

When I accepted my first job as an assistant dean of students, I changed my career from the private sector to higher education. This was a return to my roots. I had the enormous privilege of growing up on the campus of Tennessee Tech University, and I witnessed firsthand the dedication my father, a history professor, and my mother, an administrative assistant in the college of engineering, had toward their students. They exemplified the idea of "leading from where you are" and taught me that authentic leadership is not confined to titles or positions but emanates from a deep sense of caring and commitment.

At the time, the concept of student success had yet to gain prominence. Still, my parents embodied its core principles in the compassionate way they supported their students, often inviting them to join us for meals at our dining room table or showing concern for their academic achievements and personal growth.

As the newly hired assistant dean of students at the University of Tennessee at Chattanooga, I immediately began drawing upon the lessons I learned from watching and listening to my parents as well as from the many mentors I was fortunate to have. As assistant dean, I quickly found myself navigating the complexities and nuances of Title IX investigations, training resident assistants, handling issues in housing, investigating and resolving conduct cases, and organizing student activities and events, including wellness educational programming.

Extraordinary Skill Development Inherent in a Student Affairs Career

In student affairs, you quickly realize that student issues transcend the confines of university business hours; at any given moment, an email or call can arrive, signaling a student in need. I will forever remember the first time I rushed to a hospital to sit with dazed parents after a fatal accident and the weight of responsibility I felt in providing comfort and support during immense grief. Nor will I forget when I was on call to support incidents that occurred in housing or related to Greek life. I was challenged to think on my feet, find creative solutions, and collaborate with colleagues from various divisions to ensure students felt supported.

The point of view I gained in these often-unpredictable situations became an important asset that I continue to lean on as a university president. Navigating complex issues of access, academic support, personal health and safety, wellness, campus climate, diversity, equity, and inclusion requires a deep understanding of the student experience and a profound commitment to student success.

Bringing a student affairs lens to these matters allows me to approach them with the sensitivity and understanding that come from firsthand experiences in the field. It reminds me of the urgency and personal impact behind our policies and decisions. It prompts me to work with my leadership team as well as others across all levels and divisions of our university to seek out innovative solutions, prioritize student well-being, and champion inclusivity and equity in all aspects of the university.

As my career progressed to the role of vice president of student affairs, first at Salisbury University and then at Old Dominion University, I witnessed the increasing complexity of contemporary issues and challenges in the field. My teams and I grappled daily with campus safety issues, crisis response, emergency preparedness, campus climate, inclusion and equity, student activism, and mental health. And they were on top of other priorities: I oversaw matters related to budget, enrollment, facilities, construction projects, program assessment, community engagement, and even fundraising. As I balanced these responsibilities, I recognized the comprehensive skill set and knowledge base required of a university president.

With this understanding, I encourage those student affairs leaders contemplating a future presidency to seek opportunities to broaden their portfolio beyond their division. Embracing projects and initiatives that transcend student affairs and rise to the institutional level allows aspiring leaders to gain invaluable insights and experiences. For example, I supported the university's strategic planning and budget committee at Salisbury University, work that gave me a broader perspective on institutional priorities and financial decision-making. Additionally, I immersed myself in major construction projects related to student housing, developing expertise in facilities management and contributing to enhancing the campus environment. These experiences served me well when I was charged with a universitywide strategic planning process shortly after arriving at CSUSM and oversaw the opening of new student housing and the successful proposal for a new affordable housing complex that was awarded $91 million in support from the California legislature.

Similarly, I engaged in strategic partnerships with the university advancement team at Old Dominion University to fundraise for student scholarships. I will never forget closing a $5 million scholarship gift to support low-income students. Furthermore, I delved into governmental affairs to support initiatives such as the Online Virginia Network, advocating for changes in campus conduct practices, Title IX legislation, and financial aid disbursement. These experiences not only deepened my understanding of philanthropy and resource development but also allowed me to cultivate relationships with donors and alumni as CSUSM's chief "storyteller" and "cheerleader"—essential skills for a university president. As my team and I now prepare to launch an effective philanthropic campaign to support CSUSM capital projects as well as student success initiatives, I am grateful to have had these experiences.

I encourage student affairs leaders to garner experience in the classroom. My time teaching counselor education and a higher education program gave me a perspective of the academic environment. It allowed me to observe and experience the faculty–student dynamic while gaining an understanding of the teaching and learning process, curriculum development, and educational policies. This insight has helped me be a stronger partner in shared governance and a more effective collaborator.

Future-Proofing Student Affairs Skills and Experiences

Moreover, I have not even touched yet on the much-needed trend—accelerated in the face of the COVID-19 pandemic as well as changing student demographics—of colleges and universities becoming "student ready." Student affairs leaders are vital to aiding the institution's vision and creating a strategic direction to support student success and enhance the student experience. At my former institutions, I had the challenge and the opportunity to support many student populations and learning modalities, including traditional destination students, commuters and distance learners, international students, military-affiliated students, and adults. My experiences in enrollment planning and with practices that help students persist and graduate—partnering with academic affairs colleagues every step of the way—have all come deeply into play in my presidential role as my team and I have partnered across campus to launch new CSUSM initiatives such as a student success coaching program; a new strategic enrollment plan; a master campus facilities plan; a long-range academic plan; and new policies that support retention and graduation success within a framework of diversity, equity, and inclusion.

Many years ago, I committed to a career in student affairs because of my passion for student success and for supporting student social mobility. This passion is now only elevated in my role as president, where one of my proudest recent accomplishments was CSUSM being named the top university in the country for social mobility on the Social Mobility Index. My student affairs career and perspective have made me a better president, and the experiences, competencies, and values I learned in the profession continue to be my compass. I sincerely hope that more student affairs leaders ascend to the presidency, supporting our collective institutions as they evolve and become even more student-centered and supportive of academic communities that prepare leaders to be tomorrow's change-makers.

Presidential Perspectives

KEEPING STUDENTS AT THE CENTER

Ajay Nair
President, Arcadia University

With a professional background in student affairs and academics, I often find it bemusing when academics view me more as a student affairs expert and when student affairs professionals see me more as an academic—sometimes simultaneously. My experiences in both areas have given me a well-rounded background in two crucial areas that are equally important in understanding the student experience and in working on ways to enhance that experience. I have sought to leverage this background in my current position as president of Arcadia University, especially in my vision to keep students at the center of everything we do.

The students led a protest in the center of campus on my first day as president of Arcadia University. The protest was not about me. Rather, students and others in the university community had gathered in response to personnel decisions that had been planned before my arrival. Some colleagues attempted to steer me away from the scene, but I wanted to be there. Not only did I want to know more about the gathering itself, but, even more important, I wanted to learn what was *behind* the chants and the signs.

That day, April 2, 2018, took me back a few years to my previous position as senior vice president and dean of campus life at Emory University. In 2016, students protested with demands to improve the racial climate on campus amid racial tension at the University of Missouri and Yale University. While leaders at Emory worked to address the students' demands point by point, I felt that if we looked at the demands just at face value, then we'd miss something—in particular, an opportunity to directly engage with students on issues that were vital to their sense of well-being and their sense of an authentic university experience. We also were missing out on the chance to educate and be educated.

At Emory, the student protests were an opportunity for us to embark on a weeks-long engagement process where we developed working groups for each demand. Then they worked together as a community to resolve the core issues and create action steps, timelines, and accountability measures. That collaboration, and the willingness of the university to dedicate the appropriate amount of time and resources to address systemic issues rather than merely respond to demands, helped me realize—and this was after 20 years serving as an administrator—that we in leadership roles can truly change how a university operates. And it does not have to take 5 or 20 years—a time nearly no student has to wait.

Three weeks after the protest at Arcadia in April 2018, we convened the first of several campuswide working sessions. These led to establishing committees to address issues such as budget, communications, transparency, shared governance, and the campus's aspirational vision, because, as I had suspected, there were issues beyond those that were being chanted on the green that first day. We needed to work toward systemic change.

Change Is Possible

In summer 2020, I was in the middle of a protest—this time, alongside marchers after the murders of George Floyd, Breonna Taylor, and Ahmaud Arbery. I was joined by hundreds in our university community who agreed that change was needed and that it would start at Arcadia. We gathered Arcadia's Commission on Justice, Equity, Diversity, and Inclusion, which had been created the year prior. We shared a desire to improve the experience of students of color at Arcadia and to address anti-Black racism.

Once again, out of protest came progress.

Before the fall 2020 semester started, we had approved and implemented dozens of initiatives to combat anti-Black racism and oppression.

These initiatives stretched across the entire university—academics, athletics, campus climate, alumni engagement, finances, and faculty and staff recruitment and retention processes. However, the most heartening aspect was that students were at the center of these efforts and ideas; their vision, passion, and energy helped enact the change that Arcadia needed.

Change at the university level is possible, mainly when it follows a sustained engagement with students and university community members. All and any change my team and I have exacted at Arcadia has been done by keeping students at the center, which has become our unofficial mantra.

A Consistent Feedback Loop

My student affairs leadership positions also revealed that university administrators must be listeners—not just listen but be listeners—and facilitate a university practice that appreciates the lived experiences of all students. We also must engage in difficult conversations, if necessary.

I encourage and seek constant interaction with students—a consistent feedback loop to help us address who we as an institution are and want to be. Students contact me directly—via email, on social media, stopping me on campus—to express their thoughts, concerns, or questions. Some of these conversations are innocuous, and nearly all are amicable. Others, though, are more difficult, and these are the discussions that I want to explore. These are the conversations that we as leaders often need to have with larger groups, such as students, administrators, faculty, staff, and others in the university community. No matter the subject, these interactions are opportunities to evaluate campus practices in real time. What is working? What is not? Where are the gaps? How can we fill them?

Since becoming president, I have remained focused on building a university for the future. How can we maintain a university that meets students at the heart of their lived experiences while preparing them for fulfillment and success after graduation? How can we adapt and remain flexible to the changing landscape of a global society that becomes more interconnected daily? How can our colleges and universities reflect the world in which we want to live, while working to address injustice within our local, national, and global communities? The answers to these questions may vary from institution to institution, but I hope all colleges and universities remain committed to keeping students at the center of all they do.

Keeping students at the center seems so simple that it will always be at the forefront of the minds of college and university administrators. This strategy should always be prioritized regardless of the institution—and even more so at colleges and universities that focus on personal attention. My bedrock conviction of keeping students at the center has been nurtured and strengthened through my years of directly engaging with students, learning about their concerns and vision, hearing where they saw or felt injustice, and approaching issues with cultural humility. These moments have made an indelible impact on my current role and focus; they have helped me want to reimagine how a university operates and question how it should be.

I SAID YES TO THE DRESS

Lori S. White
President, DePauw University

I said yes to the dress—that is, the academic gown with the four stripes worn only by the president or chancellor of a college or university. How is it that I ended up being whisked from St. Louis, where I was serving as the vice chancellor of student affairs at Washington University in St. Louis (WashU), to Greencastle, Indiana, where I would formally be presented as DePauw University's 21st president? I would be the first woman and the first person of color to hold that position at DePauw—and one of the relatively few female and African American presidents in the country and the only African American female president at a 4-year college in the entire state of Indiana. (But the good news is that there are increasingly more presidents of color [Melidona et al., 2023].) As the car sped east on Interstate 70 (a 3-hour direct route from St. Louis to Greencastle), I was overwhelmed. Who am I to have the audacity to think I can do this big ol' job?

Breaking the Glass

When I started my first position in higher education almost 40 years before—my first job in higher education was at the University of California, Irvine, staffing their information booth—I never imagined a college presidency was in my future. I loved my work in student affairs and as a vice president for student affairs; I'd held the role for 8 years at two universities. Also, while in that role, I had seen very few people who looked like me ascend to the position of president. The messages I received were that presidential jobs are for *other people*, not someone with my demographic and student affairs profile.

Sadly, often women and people of color tend to minimize what they think they are capable of achieving, for a whole host of reasons: We think we need more experience before we are ready for the next opportunity; we receive feedback from supervisors and hiring committees that we are not a *fit* for certain kinds of jobs; we have a hard time shutting off the self-doubt; we are not mentored, sponsored, or encouraged; we do not have the right networks; we are not in the proverbial "room where it happens."

I am a college president for various reasons: I was fortunate to have mentors along the way who told me I should aspire to do more; one of those mentors nominated me for the DePauw position. The chair of the DePauw presidential search, herself an African American and a chair of the board of trustees, encouraged the search committee to look beyond the stereotypes for outstanding candidates. And an institution needed what I could bring to the table in terms of my experiences and talent. Now, 3 years into the role, I can attest that all of my student affairs and collective higher education experiences were a perfect fit for the job. I serve as president of a small, residential liberal arts college, where the student experience is central.

Preparation for the Presidency

Vice presidents for student affairs (VPSAs) make good college presidents because we typically manage a multifaceted division—one that requires us to work across the university in support of the student experience, thus giving us a perspective on the university broader than that afforded to most other vice presidents or academic deans. VPSAs oversee programs, facilities, people, resources, and critical institutional decisions. We are often responsible for managing large budgets and those composed of varied fund sources (e.g., tuition revenue, fees, auxiliary income, grant funding, endowment funds). VPSAs regularly respond to any number of campus crises; most of us played a lead role in helping to lead our institution's pandemic response. We frequently interact with a variety of stakeholders—students, parents, alumni, boards of trustees, and community members—and some of them, at one point or another, are upset with us because of a decision we have or the university has made. We have reputations as collaborative problem-solvers and great communicators. We raise money. Many of us hold faculty positions. But, most important, we care about and understand the student experience.

I call upon those skills and experiences daily as president of DePauw. And, for any readers considering the presidency, I share this piece of advice: The more proficiency you develop regarding budget oversight, strategic planning, fundraising, academic affairs (e.g., shared governance, the tenure process curriculum), enrollment management, athletics, and board of trustee relationships, the more competitive you will be in a presidential search process and the better prepared you will be for the actual job. It is also important to note that the first presidential appointments for those who serve as VPSAs before becoming presidents (and there seem to be more of us every year) are more likely to be at liberal arts colleges, regional universities, and religious schools; major research universities still tend to hire presidents who come from the tenured faculty ranks.

Experience as a President

DePauw formally announced me as their 21st president on March 10, 2020, and a week later, the COVID-19 pandemic turned the world upside down. I had to quickly reorient how I would spend my first year on the job. There would be no grand tour of the country introducing myself to and meeting with our alumni, no opportunity for me to attend in person the Harvard New Presidents Institute (a rite of passage and cohort bonding opportunity for new presidents in a given year), no slow onboarding for me as a rookie president. Immediately, I had to work with my cabinet leadership team (only one of whom I had hired) to make tough decisions about whether we would open the campus in the fall to in-person teaching, require the COVID vaccine, allow employees to work remotely, and for how long we would continue remote options.

Furthermore, as all of us who worked in any area of higher education at that time know, those COVID-related decisions were constant, ever-changing, and endless. Also, in that first year as president, the board asked me to deliver a new strategic plan. I had to think about creating a collaborative strategic planning process virtually with a community to whom I was unknown and then deliver the bold, inspiring strategic plan to the board that hired me to lead. I also had to build and sustain a leadership team with my cabinet—a mix of folks who had already been at DePauw serving as vice presidents and new vice presidents I was in the process of hiring.

Further, the board expected me to increase enrollment and deliver a new class of students after 2 years of much lower-than-expected first-year student enrollment. And, most important, I had to reassure and uplift my new community during the most challenging times for higher education generally and for liberal arts colleges in particular. I honestly wondered whether there was still time for me to rescind my offer letter, to take back the dress I was not sure I wanted to wear in the first place. I took a deep breath (well, several each morning when I rose), said my daily affirmations ("And still I rise," said the great Maya Angelou), and gave myself the advice I regularly give to my mentees: "Don't worry about what you don't know. Focus on what you do know, and you will figure out the rest as you go along."

In all my previous higher education leadership roles, I'd never had to make a decision as consequential as whether the university would reopen in the fall for in-person instruction. However, in those previous roles, I certainly had decision-making experience and knew the importance of seeking counsel from my team; reviewing the consequences of opening or not opening; and, with a decision of this magnitude, making sure the higher-ups (in this case, the board of trustees) fully supported our decision. Like many colleges, we ultimately chose a hybrid model. I leaned on my experience leading divisional strategic-planning processes at three institutions to develop a strategic planning model for DePauw. That model incorporated the idea that people across the university, including coordinators, administrative assistants, and new faculty (not just senior members of the university or the usual players), should have the opportunity to serve on strategic planning committees. I also knew the importance of demonstrating presidential vision and carefully balancing my ideas while encouraging ideas to be generated communitywide.

In moments when I feel the need to call upon the spirit and wisdom of my African American ancestors to guide me forth or to convey an important message, I often turn to one of my favorite old Negro spirituals. "My Soul Looks Back in Wonder, How I Got Over" is one that captures my first 3 years as a college president. Somehow, given the circumstances, we accomplished more over the first 3 years of my presidency than I or anyone else thought possible. As a virtual community, DePauw faculty and staff worked hard through cross-functional teams to identify and recommend incredibly bold ideas that are now the centerpiece of DePauw's (2022) new strategic plan: DePauw Bold & Gold 2027. To date, each year I have been president has seen the largest class of first-year students in DePauw's history, and this past year, we had the highest number of applications to DePauw—ever! I hired five new powerhouse vice presidents (including four women, at least two of whom have indicated their interest in becoming college presidents), and my new team has great synergy. We also moved up a notch on the *US News* rankings and were named one of the country's most innovative colleges.

Even with the pandemic now mainly in the rearview mirror and the considerable good news to celebrate at DePauw, higher education still faces many, many challenges. All of us are familiar with the evolving demographics in higher education: fewer traditional college-aged students (Grawe, 2018); the belief held by many families that college is too expensive and perhaps not worth the investment; the notion that college is fundamentally about preparing for employment and not also about intellectual enlightenment; and the complaints voiced by some who see colleges as inhibiting freedom of expression, particularly expressions of more conservative viewpoints (Blake, 2024). Compounding these challenges for small liberal arts colleges like mine is that students are flocking to enroll in only the most highly ranked or well-endowed institutions. Some predict that, as a result, many small colleges will be forced to close their doors or merge with other colleges (Moody, 2023).

All of this means that college presidents, particularly at institutions like mine, must reimagine the education model (Marcy, 2020), including adding new academic programs and perhaps sunsetting others; considering new methods of education delivery (e.g., traditional residential liberal arts colleges having fully online degrees); recruiting different students (and providing the level of support necessary for those students); linking the curriculum more directly to workforce needs; making the tough decisions about directing limited resources to the highest institutional priorities; and deferring others until additional resources are garnered through fundraising, increased student revenue, and reduced spending.

Furthermore, college presidents are regularly asked by legislators (at public universities), boards of trustees, parents, alumni, and the public to defend their commitment to educational experiences that are more accessible, equitable, and inclusive for the diversity (race, ethnicity, culture, income, identity) of individuals, all of whom should be provided an opportunity to study at one of the more than 4,000 institutions of higher education in the United States. The 2023 Supreme Court ruling restricting the use of race as an admission criterion and legislation in many states outlawing diversity, equity, and inclusion offices will further complicate any focus on diversity-related initiatives on college campuses.

It's a Calling

Each week, I receive a call or email from someone who indicates an interest in becoming a college president and seeks my perspective and advice. The college presidency is not an easy job, and it is lonely, as no one, other than other college presidents, truly understands this all-consuming experience (presidents are *always* on). For those readers who decide to go for it, the most important factor is to discern whether you are genuinely interested in the *work* of being a college president, not just the fancy title. Presidential leadership as a woman and/or a person of color comes with another set of layers. The decisions we make are often viewed through a gendered or racial lens. Moreover, for some of our constituents, our advocacy in support of what are perceived as women's or diversity issues is either too much or too little (with both perspectives often being true simultaneously).

Given what I have shared about the role, why have I chosen to be a college president? I have a good friend who left his dream job as dean of admissions at one the best universities in the country to become a priest. When I asked him why, he said he felt called to serve the church. His calling was to make an impact on the world by ministering to those who needed spiritual guidance. I think I have been called to serve higher education as a college president—but not for me. I have been called to serve because representation matters, particularly as the demographics of our country change. Future generations need to believe that someone who looks like me can become a college president, and I look forward to the day when we have moved well beyond "the first." I have been called to serve because, according to the executive summary of the 2023 ACE American College

President report, "The complex issues facing colleges and universities today need diverse, informed and well-supported leaders to address the changes and developments of tomorrow" (Melidona et al., 2023, p. 7).

And that is why I said yes to the dress.

A NONTRADITIONAL PATH

Thomas Gibson
Chancellor, University of Wisconsin, Stevens Point

I earned a bachelor's degree in communication and aspired to a career in broadcast television. Most of my time was spent either in the campus's television studio or chatting up student affairs professionals in their offices. This time led to working in several positions as a student employee—first as a peer advisor and then as a resident assistant during the summers, a peer student orientation counselor, and eventually a student patrol officer for the university's police department. My intrigue with the student affairs profession was born. I believed that I had discovered my purpose.

However, I could not deny my fascination with media and entertainment. So, I continued my pursuit of a communications degree. After graduation, I was fortunate to secure a position as a technical director and video editor for a small television station in Connecticut. I was proud of my accomplishment. I enjoyed this role for approximately 3 years before the novelty of working in broadcast television began to wane. I began to think about when I felt most fulfilled and of service to others. It was when I was an undergraduate student serving in student employment and volunteer roles.

At that moment, I realized a career change and graduate study were necessary. After earning my master's degree, I secured my first professional position in higher education as a residence hall director at a private college in Connecticut. The experience of supervising student staff, managing a budget, mentoring students, creating inclusive programming, and teaching affirmed that I had made the right decision to leave broadcast television for a career in higher education. Additionally, working as a resident hall director helped to shape my professional interests and competencies.

I was energized by the prospect of helping more students succeed during my next role as an academic coordinator for an opportunity program at Connecticut's flagship public university. However, I was unprepared for the seemingly unintentional institutional roadblocks that first-generation, underrepresented, and lower-income students would encounter. The attitudes of some colleagues suggested that providing too much support was unhelpful to students and would foster overdependent behaviors. According to Hecht et al. (2021), 4-year university administrators tended to value student independence more than interdependence, as the latter created a barrier that affected first-generation students' college experiences and educational outcomes. I understood this dynamic early on in my career, so I was committed to pursuing growth opportunities that would allow me to create and influence policy. A college presidency or chancellorship was not yet a professional goal.

Contextual Aspects

My higher education journey would provide opportunities to serve as an associate dean of students, associate vice president for student affairs, and vice president for student affairs and vice provost. Each role afforded professional experiences that prepared me for the college presidency or chancellorship. As an associate dean of students, I gained key competencies in managing crisis response, interpreting institutional policies and procedures, and supporting faculty and staff about issues affecting students. Mitroff et al. (2006) suggested that effective crisis management is an operational imperative for university leaders. According to Treadwell (2017), student affairs leaders are more likely than not to lead crisis response efforts and serve as the primary advisor to the university president/chancellor.

As an associate vice president for student affairs, I taught in a graduate student affairs preparation program. This position brought more significant insights and responsibilities for leading institutional student success priorities, including student retention, persistence, and completion goals. Student affairs professionals are the most knowledgeable about student needs, and thus their teaching and scholarship have implications for student success (Gilbert & Burden, 2022). Indeed, there is student learning and institutional value for the student affairs practitioner–scholar. As vice president for student affairs, I had responsibility for the student experience. This leadership role included fostering student engagement, beginning with new student orientation, student involvement, residential education, and preparation for life after graduation. Specifically, I led resident life, student conduct, recreation and wellness, counseling, the health care center, Title IX, leadership programs, Greek life, Trio programs, and equity and inclusion programs.

As vice provost, I led undergraduate student success priorities, including student retention, persistence, and completion outcomes. Being intellectually curious and having academic leadership characteristics help demonstrate an understanding of the academic enterprise. This dual operational linkage of student affairs and academic affairs role is still somewhat unique; however, higher education thought leaders have been increasingly interested in better academic and student affairs collaborations to improve student success (Commodore et al., 2018). Moreover, as vice president for student affairs and vice provost, I was an ex officio senator of the faculty senate with rights for debate and voting. Serving the institution in this role provided a window into faculty issues and decision-making procedures. Furthermore, it allowed for the development of the following competencies that have served me well: shared governance, strategic planning, assessment and accountability, fundraising, risk management, budget and resource management, community and business engagement, and teaching.

As a vice president and officer of the university, I finally thought I could do more "good" on behalf of students. I was now in the room where decisions were made as a senior university leader. But that is not always the case for many vice presidents for student affairs. I have heard many colleagues relate their feelings about their work not being as valued by their institution and cabinet colleagues. I was fortunate to have student-centered leadership and support across my institution and opportunities to contribute to many institutional success efforts. "At strong performing institutions, student affairs professionals recognize their primary obligation is to support the institution's academic mission and view themselves as full partners in the enterprise" (Kezar 2005, p. 3). In the most unprecedented moments, colleagues begin to recognize the importance of student affairs professionals.

In late March 2020, our world and the higher education sector were forever changed. COVID-19 was declared a global pandemic by the World Health Organization. Many colleges and universities ceased in-person classes and moved to online instruction, on-campus housing and dining were closed, intercollegiate athletics and campus events were canceled, and many faculty and staff were asked to work remotely. Institutions became worried about the implications for student enrollment and the future of higher education. Proactively, the institution where I worked at the time began modeling budget implications for likely enrollment decline and the number of positions that would need to be eliminated to address a financial shortfall. Subsequently, approximately 120 faculty and staff were nonrenewed or laid off a few months later. I had already begun thinking of presidential and chancellorship opportunities and decided to pursue a few select opportunities. Feeling optimistic about possible outcomes and given the uncertainty of additional faculty and staff reductions, including my position, I resigned, thinking that might help the institution. However, I continued my teaching assignment in the higher education administration PhD program. I also accepted an invitation to serve as a presidential leadership fellow at Robert Morris University in Pennsylvania. There, I gave guest lectures to faculty, staff, and student groups about leadership challenges and opportunities in the higher education sector. I also shared my experiences fostering a culture and community of belonging and provided advice on supporting underrepresented student retention, persistence, and degree completion.

Then, in what seemed like a perfect storm, a wave of presidents and chancellors announced their retirements. Many presidents and chancellors suggested that the pandemic was not a direct cause of their retirement (Whitford, 2020). Many delayed their retirement plans because of the pandemic. Regardless of their reasons, executive leadership vacancies during the crisis presented a compelling opportunity for me to raise my hand to serve and further influence the policies that affect students' academic outcomes. This leadership pursuit was timely and reaffirmed my personal and professional purpose.

Nontraditional Landscape

As the complexity and demands of leading a higher education institution continue to grow, some governing boards are seeking more diverse skill sets and competencies in their institutional leaders. Beyond being the face and voice of the institution to students and families, college and university presidents and chancellors are expected to be mission-driven leaders for faculty and staff; maintain positive relationships with local and state legislative delegations, donors, business, and industry; steward budgets and resources; and manage reputational risks. Student affairs professionals, often the most experienced campus leaders in many areas, are well prepared to assume the college or university president or chancellor role.

Recommendations for Ascending to the Presidency or Chancellorship

In no ranked order, I offer the following recommendations for professional experiences you should seek to aspire to college presidency or chancellorship.

Enjoy the work you do. You will spend significantly more time with students, faculty, staff, and other constituency groups than your family. Work–life balance is indeed essential, but it must be prioritized.

The ability to attract institutional resources through philanthropic efforts is necessary for sustaining and developing the institution. This work often requires travel and attendance at evening and weekend events. Plan accordingly. Exercise is essential for building endurance for these roles.

Institutional leaders must understand strategic planning and assessment and have a good facility with data. I earned a certificate in strategic planning from the Society of University Planners. The training has been helpful.

Demonstrated intentional commitment to informed decision-making and advancing university goals are critical to delivering on your institution's mission. Institution leaders must be thoughtful and decisive. However, do not be pressured to decide before you are ready. Instead, think about the type of institution you would want to lead. Be able to articulate your vision for that institution. Where would you like to take your respective institution? What would be your institutional priorities? Answering these questions often involves input from a board, campus governance groups, and campus community stakeholders.

Nonetheless, the vision begins with the institution's leader. Institution leaders must be good storytellers. Therefore, it is imperative to know as much as possible about the success and impact of your institution.

A solid communication strategy can create a shared purpose, articulate values and priorities, and introduce stability during crises. Developing cultural intelligence is becoming increasingly more critical for presidents and chancellors desiring to lead equitably as students and other constituency groups, rightfully so, demand a more inclusive campus learning environment. Being adaptable and relatable and engaging with high emotional intelligence are no longer considered soft skills; more commonly, they are considered hard skills. Nevertheless, they remain important for aspiring college presidents and chancellors.

Embrace and practice a commitment to shared governance. Fostering mutually beneficial relationships takes time, but my investment in such relationships has served me well—particularly when confronted with making complex and unpopular decisions or in a crisis. Sharing your leadership with your campus community invites accountability for resolution among campus community members. Although this notion of collaboration may not be easy or always practical, it is essential for institutional democracy.

Continue to do good work in your current role. Let your president or chancellor know of your ambition. Seek their mentorship or let them recommend others to you.

Seek professional development opportunities. I have participated in the Association of Governing Boards Institute for Leadership and Governance in Higher Education. This experience has brought invaluable preparation and encouraged self-reflection and assessment in leading an institution of higher education.

My 26-year ascension to the university chancellorship certainly contradicts my youthful appearance. My student affairs background and academic leadership experiences laid a solid foundation for pursuing the college presidency. There is no specific pathway to the presidency or chancellorship. Instead, nontraditional leadership roles and experience are perhaps what an institution needs to advance its mission at a particular moment. Make no mistake that the college presidency or chancellorship is among the most challenging and complex jobs in higher education, and this sector is in a watershed moment. Many colleges will need to address institutional pressures such as declining student enrollments, which have resource and budget implications; persisting COVID-19 disruptions; the declining perceived value of a college degree; and growing legislative interest in eliminating diversity, equity, and inclusion programs and related curricula. I encourage you to raise your hand to do the work of a president. The profession needs you.

■ ■ ■

Conclusion

These five narratives are unique for their diversity but also for their commonalities. Each of us has had successful careers by any measure, but our journeys were not always smooth. You may have begun reading this chapter for advice on ascending to the presidency. You should dream about a position or a job not yet earned. A broad student affairs background prepares leaders for the presidency. Regardless of the institutional context, your success is predicated on keeping students at the center. Even with a dream and proper preparation that centers students, you will face doubts and need a calling to say yes to the dress. Know that each institutional leader has their own nontraditional, purpose-driven pathway that serves as the foundation of their career.

References

Blake, J. (2024, February 28). Workforce development, state funding among higher ed leaders' policy priorities. *Inside Higher Ed.* https://www.insidehighered.com/news/government/state-policy/2024/01/09/survey-state-higher-ed-officials-outlines-policy-priorities

Commodore, F., Gasman, M., Conrad, C., & Nguyen, T. (2018). Coming together: A case study of collaboration between student affairs and faculty at Norfolk State University. *Frontiers in Education, 3,* Article 39, 1–10. https://doi.org/10.3389/feduc.2018.00039

DePauw University. (2022). *DePauw bold & gold 2027.* https://www.depauw.edu/about/president/strategicplan

Gilbert, C., & Burden, S. (2022). Student affairs practitioner scholarship: Structural barriers and opportunities for institutional leadership. *College Student Affairs Journal, 40*(2), 129–142. https://doi.org/10.1353/csj.2022.0020

Grawe, N. D. (2018). *Demographics and the demand for higher education.* Johns Hopkins University Press.

Hecht, C. A., Priniski, S. J., Tibbetts, Y., & Harackiewicz, J. M. (2021). Affirming both independent and interdependent values improves achievement for all students and mitigates cultural mismatch for first-generation college students. *Journal of Social Issues, 77*(3), 851–887. https://doi.org/10.1111/josi.12416

Kezar, A. (2005). *Promoting student success: The importance of shared leadership and collaboration.* Indiana University Center for Postsecondary Research. https://hdl.handle.net/2022/23532

Marcy, M. B. (2020). *The small college imperative: Models for sustainable futures.* Stylus.

Melidona, D., Cecil, B. G., Cassell, A., & Chessman, H. M. (2023). *The American college president: 2023 edition; executive summary.* American Council on Education.

Mitroff, I. I., Diamond, M. A., & Alpaslan, M. C. (2006). How prepared are America's colleges and universities for major crises? *Change: The Magazine of Higher Learning, 38*(1), 61–67. https://doi.org/10.3200/CHNG.38.1.61-67

Moody, J. (2023, January 18). A harbinger for 2023? Presentation College to close. *Inside Higher Ed.* https://www.insidehighered.com/news/2023/01/19/more-colleges-will-likely-face-closure-2023-experts-say

Treadwell, K. L. (2017). Learning from tragedy: Student affairs leadership following college campus disasters. *Journal of Student Affairs Research and Practice, 54*(1), 42–54. https://doi.org/10.1080/19496591.2016.1206019

Whitford, E. (2020, September 30). Retirement wave hits presidents amid pandemic. *Inside Higher Ed.* https://www.insidehighered.com/news/2020/10/01/many-college-presidents-are-leaving-say-pandemic-isnt-driving-them-out

Values as a Framework for Career Realignment

Amie K. Hammond

"We're here for the students" is a common refrain among professionals working in student affairs. Unfortunately, this other-focused mindset, coupled with demanding workloads in environments often plagued by insufficient resources, makes it easy for busy student affairs professionals to lose sight of what brings them career fulfillment and satisfaction. However, it is not too late to engage in career realignment. Ensuring the sustainability of the student affairs profession and its people is more crucial than ever.

Realigning an individual's career is worthwhile, considering how much time is spent at work throughout a lifetime. However, career realignment is an iterative and ongoing process that requires time and mental energy. It involves examining the individual's existing or desired work environment. To be effective, it also requires self-reflection to achieve deeper understanding of one's values.

For many professionals, the COVID-19 pandemic created conditions that were ripe for self-reflection and assessment of workplaces. The pandemic spawned what is now called the Great Resignation, where the highest rate of resignations occurred in the United States since the U.S. Bureau of Labor Statistics began tracking such data (Gittleman, 2022). The student affairs profession is not immune. A social media group dedicated to supporting student affairs professionals who are considering leaving the field (or have left already) boasts more than 24,000 members (Expatriates of Student Affairs, n.d.).

Rather than focus on those who lament what could be or who make rash career decisions out of desperation, this chapter promotes intentional reflection and decision-making to achieve greater career fulfillment. It offers strategies and considerations for any student affairs professionals interested in promoting their or others' job satisfaction. It provides a framework and tools for employees ranging from job seekers to seasoned professionals to reflect on their values and to assess fit within their workplace. Student affairs leaders will find this chapter helpful in supporting their current employees' job satisfaction and attracting new employees.

Understanding Values Congruence

Values congruence refers to the degree to which an individual's values match the values found in their work environment. For more than a century, the person–environment fit theory has been noted in organizational and vocational psychology (Dawis, 2000). Dawis and Lofquist (1984) introduced values into the person–environment fit theory when they developed the theory of work adjustment, which is indicated by the satisfaction of the individual with the work environment and by the satisfaction of the work environment with the individual. Values are a key factor in the theory of work adjustment, which can be used to understand career decision-making and satisfaction. The relationship between an individual and their work environment is a system that must maintain equilibrium to be effective. When the system is balanced, both the employee and employer are satisfied. When the system is out of balance, possible consequences involve the employee quitting or the employer reassigning or terminating the employee.

Dawis and Lofquist (1984) posited that the employee and their environment have needs that must be met. The employer requires that specific tasks be fulfilled through the employee's skills. The employee's needs include compensation and fulfillment of their values. When their needs are met, the outcome is job satisfaction and commitment to the work. To maintain balance, employees can make adjustments to their work environment.

A Case Study of Student Affairs Professionals

Hammond (2022) used Dawis and Lofquist's (1984) theory as the framework for a study that examined how student affairs professionals in a large public university system in the United States experienced values congruence and its influence on job satisfaction and work commitment. The study included an analysis of student affairs position descriptions to identify the prevalence of stated values. The conceptual framework used for this research situated the theory of work adjustment within the context of neoliberalism.

Neoliberalism is an economic–political agenda that began in the 1980s, when government support of programs serving the public good was decreased in favor of a more capitalistic, market-driven approach (Harvey, 2007). This trend of decreased government-sponsored funding for social programs, including education, has persisted to the present day. Within higher education, it has manifested as so-called academic capitalism, where colleges and universities are forced to operate like businesses, with students viewed as customers (Saunders, 2010; Slaughter & Rhoades, 2000).

As a result of neoliberalism, institutions have been forced to generate revenue through increased tuition and student fees, the commercialization of research, athletics advertising agreements, outsourcing, and public–private enterprises (Kezar, 2004; Uslu et al., 2019). Within student affairs, evidence of academic capitalism can be seen in self-supporting financial models for programs, fundraising initiatives, and auxiliary-run departments, to name a few (Hamrick & Klein, 2015; June, 2017; Slaughter & Rhoades, 2000).

Hammond's research highlights how neoliberalism influences student affairs professionals' values congruence. This concept is explored more in depth throughout this chapter. Additionally, other findings from the study illustrate ways that student affairs professionals can leverage their understanding of values and values congruence to enhance job satisfaction. Finally, this chapter presents ways in which student affairs leaders can promote values congruence with their employees.

Enhancing Job Satisfaction Through Values Congruence

Student affairs professionals at all career stages can strive to enhance their job satisfaction by strengthening their values congruence at work. Those in the job-seeking stage can optimize their values congruence by taking proactive steps. Established employees can use values congruence strategies to enhance their satisfaction and commitment to their current work environment or apply the strategies to determine whether they would be best served by seeking a new opportunity. Finally, student affairs managers and leaders can use their position and influence to support others' values congruence.

The following sections present strategies established professionals, managers, and job seekers can use to improve their own and others' values congruence. Although there is a dearth of research on values congruence in student affairs relative to other industries (Hammond, 2022), studies indicate that values congruence affects one's sense of fit within an organization (Perez, 2017) and work commitment (Wilson et al., 2016). Therefore, the first step is to reflect on and clarify values. This step is beneficial for professionals at any stage of a career or job search.

Clarifying Values

Values are connected to career selection and job satisfaction (Dawis & Lofquist, 1984; Rounds & Jin, 2013). Renowned social psychologist Milton Rokeach (1968) defined *values* as "a type of belief, centrally located within one's total belief system, about how one ought to or ought not to behave, or about some end-state of existence worth or not worth attaining" (p. 124). Countless other definitions of values, types of values, and instruments measure values. More than 9,000 values measurement instruments are listed in the American Psychological Association PsycTests database.

Values assessments and activities can clarify an individual's core values. Two widely used tools include the Knowdell Career Values Card Sort (Careerplanner.com, 2023) and the O*Net Work Importance Locator (https://www.onetcenter.org/WIL.html). Many others are online or can be administered by a career coach or counselor.

A less structured approach begins by reflecting on the prompt "What is important to me?" through writing, visual journaling, dialogue with a close friend or family member, or whatever form of reflection is preferred. Then, the reflections can be translated into words that convey the expressed values. Many comprehensive lists of values are available online, which can be helpful resources in this process.

Another approach involves considering what drew a person to the student affairs profession. Reflecting on past experiences and prior employment can also be helpful. In doing so, one should identify the values they felt were fulfilled or not fulfilled in past roles.

For example, consider Mary, who was previously a resident director. Although she enjoyed her most recent position, she felt frustrated by her highly structured work environment and the many approval processes and check-ins with her supervisor. In contrast, Mary recalls a different position where she enjoyed the independent decision-making she was afforded. Reflecting on these two experiences, she recognizes that autonomy is a value she holds.

Regardless of the process used to clarify values, once identified, the objective is to pare them down to a set of core values. The number of core values for a person can vary. However, a good recommendation is to narrow the identified values down to five core values. Pinpointing the values most important to an individual will enhance clarity when undertaking values-based decision-making. Some people also opt to prioritize or rank their core values to provide greater focus and intentionality when making decisions.

Coexisting With Neoliberalism

Research conducted by Hammond (2022) identified that some of the tension student affairs professionals experienced between their values and work environments stemmed from the effects of neoliberalism. Most notably, participants widely reported having unrealistic expectations of efficiency and productivity in the workplace. These expectations were generally the result of insufficient resources within the organization. In addition, more than half of those interviewed were aware of or directly supported revenue-generating activities within their departments, such as grant writing and fundraising. However, despite the participants' experiencing such aspects of neoliberalism, a review of position descriptions across the case revealed that these types of duties and expectations were frequently underrepresented in position descriptions or were absent altogether.

The prevalence of neoliberalism in higher education has consistently risen since its inception in the 1980s (Saunders, 2010). By the late 2010s, it was considered pervasive (Kezar et al., 2019). Neoliberalism is now so deeply rooted in higher education that it will likely persist unless significant government reform or structural changes in higher education occur. The reality is that student affairs professionals will be forced to coexist with neoliberalism. With such a significant force affecting their prospective work environments, job seekers should take a proactive approach. They can minimize potential values incongruence by understanding what neoliberalism is, what causes it, and how it might manifest itself in their work. This understanding will help them evaluate the fit of a prospective environment.

Career Realignment Through Values Congruence

The following sections offer practical career realignment strategies and considerations for professionals at all stages of their careers. The strategies and examples presented center values congruence in the career assessment and decision-making processes. To begin, strategies for established employees are presented. This group is the broadest category of student affairs professionals, and many of the strategies presented for them are helpful for professionals at all stages of their careers. Next, recommendations for student affairs leaders are offered. The final section addresses the needs of job seekers, which include both emerging professionals in the student affairs field and established employees who seek new opportunities.

Most student affairs professionals experience a sense of fulfillment in their work. Some feel fulfilled after finishing a significant project or successfully executing an event. For many, this fulfillment is achieved by helping students. This feeling is part of why they were drawn to the profession, and it reinforces a feeling of fitting into their work environment.

In contrast, most student affairs professionals also experience times when the work is not fulfilling or they have negative feelings about their workplace. Applying the theory of work adjustment (Dawis & Lofquist, 1984) as a framework, an employee's satisfaction—or lack of it—can be traced to two causes. Either the employee's skills do not align with the work environment's needs, or their values are not fulfilled.

Identifying discrepancies between an employee's skills and the job requirements is typically easier than recognizing values incongruence. Unlike skills, values incongruence is more challenging to diagnose. Values cannot be measured. Moreover, unfortunately, some employees may not have a strong awareness of their values.

Established student affairs professionals should intentionally reflect on their values in their work environment. Using strategies mentioned in the previous section, they should first clarify the core values they expect to be fulfilled in their workplace. Then, they can assess how these values are fulfilled. Finally, if incongruence exists between the professional's values and their work environment, they should consider whether they or their workplace can adjust to address the incongruence.

For example, Maria is an admissions counselor who holds innovation as a core value. However, she feels dissatisfied at work; after considering her values, she realizes that the absence of innovation in her job is a contributing factor to her dissatisfaction. Empowered with this new insight,

Maria jumps at the opportunity to join a newly formed committee that is updating the department's outreach strategy. She can help the committee develop new ideas to support the department's mission.

Maria also notices that after being in her role for several years, she has fallen into a rut of doing things the same way. With a new, heightened awareness of her values, she sees an opportunity to make a change. Maria decides to prioritize dedicated time in her schedule during the off-peak admissions cycle to refresh her presentation to prospective students that she has been delivering for the past 3 years. She becomes excited about the possibility of adding audience participation activities, creating an updated slide deck, and integrating new technology into the presentation.

These are examples of employee-initiated changes that can promote values congruence. However, because values congruence is about the relationship between the employee and the work environment (Dawis & Lofquist, 1984), the workplace also has a role in influencing values congruence. To be optimally effective, the process relies on the workplace receiving input. Student affairs professionals are encouraged to communicate their values to their supervisor and to regularly engage in active dialogue about how their values are or are not fulfilled at work.

Student affairs professionals who want more values congruence should work with their supervisors to explore potential adjustments to improve alignment between themselves and their work environment. Employees should come prepared to offer solutions rather than just point out where more alignment is needed. A manager or supervisor will be more receptive to adjusting how the employee approaches their job or what responsibilities they prioritize if the changes benefit the organization, not just the employee.

Hammond's (2022) study on the values congruence of student affairs professionals indicated that some employees found ways to reinforce their values by taking on pet projects to promote their values congruence.

Similarly, others self-advocated to hold on to job responsibilities that reinforced their values even as their roles changed. One study participant initiated a collaborative program with a campus cultural center to fulfill her value of equity. Another insisted on retaining oversight of her department's peer mentor program because she found it rewarding.

The theory of work adjustment (Dawis & Lofquist, 1984) asserts that within the system of the employee and work environment is a threshold of how much tension can be tolerated. If this threshold is surpassed, the resulting outcome is the employee leaving the work environment. In some cases, the workplace initiates this transition (e.g., terminating, transferring, promoting the employee). In others, the employee initiates it, resulting in resignation or retirement.

Ideally, the tension threshold will be achievable if the employee makes proactive adjustments with their supervisor's support. However, sometimes a shift is not possible because of the employee's lack of agency, an unsupportive supervisor or workplace, rigid job requirements, or other confounding factors. Under circumstances when the values incongruence cannot be resolved, the employee will need to consider their options.

The least desirable option is to persist in the work environment despite the high level of tension. Excessive tension perpetuates job dissatisfaction.

Supporting Employees' Values Congruence

Student affairs leaders, including supervisors and managers, have a unique opportunity to realign their careers through the lens of values congruence and to use their position to support others in doing so. Hammond's (2022) research found that student affairs professionals believed leaders could influence employees' values congruence positively. Leaders can bolster their employees' values congruence by honoring and supporting individuals' values and by promoting shared values within their organizations.

This finding aligned with Seggewiss et al.'s (2019) research, which showed that employee work commitment could be affected by perceptions about their supervisor's values.

Even before an employee is hired, leaders can communicate the organization's values through the position description. Beyond simply stating the organization's values, the position description should include specific job duties or requirements that demonstrate how values will be applied in the position. Here are a few examples:

- Value of supporting students: "Guide students through the career decision-making process, with consideration for their backgrounds and identities."
- Value of ethics: "Maintain confidentiality of sensitive and protected information."
- Value of lifelong learning: "Regularly participate in professional development activities such as faculty and staff book circles, online training, and professional conferences."

Leaders should develop position descriptions that provide transparency for prospective employees. Through document analysis of 46 position descriptions and interviews with 12 student affairs professionals, Hammond (2022) found that the espoused values of the student affairs profession needed to be more present in position descriptions. Additionally, Hammond's research revealed that job duties related to neoliberalism (e.g., revenue generation, competition) were frequently absent from or veiled within position descriptions. As a result, some study participants felt they spent an unexpected proportion of their time supporting tasks that detracted from their values congruence. These findings illuminate a need to closely review and update position descriptions to provide employees with more explicit expectations and to amplify the position's values-driven aspects.

The organization's values can be highlighted in other ways during the employee recruitment process. Intentionally crafted interview questions can communicate the organization's values to candidates. Likewise, hiring committee members' responses to candidate questions can demonstrate the organization's values. Of equal importance, the recruitment process itself can demonstrate the organization's values. For example, if diversity, equity, and inclusion are espoused values of the organization, the hiring manager should consider whether these values are reflected in the composition of the hiring committee, accessibility accommodations offered to the candidate, and fairness and equity demonstrated to all candidates in every recruitment stage.

Throughout the hiring process, it is critical that hiring managers and student affairs leaders ensure that any espoused values of the organization can be substantiated with evidence of the values enacted. Research by Garcia et al. (2021) supports this recommendation. The study revealed how student affairs professionals experienced a contradiction between their institutions' stated values of diversity, equity, and inclusion and the institutions' demonstrated commitment to upholding these values. For example, some institutions stated that they prioritized this value but did not allocate sufficient resources to support it. Furthermore, institutional policies impeded the ability to advance equity-based initiatives. Mission statements about the stated values of diversity, equity, and inclusion were commonly performative.

Regularly articulating their values to employees reinforces that the leader centers values in their work. However, this behavior is effective only if the leader consistently demonstrates their commitment to upholding these values. Discrepancies between statements and actions will weaken trust and morale among employees.

Leaders committed to centering values within their organization should engage their team in developing a set of shared values. A strong sense of shared values within employee teams supports individual values congruence and work commitment (Hammond, 2022). Also, as colleagues engage in dialogue and reflection, the process can illuminate examples of values-driven work and can draw attention to gaps and opportunities.

Once a shared set of values is identified, the team should revisit it regularly. These values can be used to determine priorities, infuse new and existing initiatives with meaning and impact, and help employees achieve enhanced satisfaction in their work. Creative leaders can find endless opportunities to infuse a values-centered mindset into the workplace. Examples include using values as a framework for collaborative decision-making, connecting values to symbolism within the organization (e.g., traditions, staff recognition), and aligning values with the organization's brand and communication points for external stakeholders.

On an individual level, student affairs leaders can promote their employees' values congruence by fostering open dialogue. If a manager learns of employees who are experiencing tension between their values and the work environment the manager should actively listen and be open to making adjustments that will enhance values congruence while still fulfilling the organization's needs. An example is a mid-level manager named Elena, who was recently promoted from a role as a program coordinator. Elena spent most of her time directly supporting students in her prior position. However, since being promoted, she feels disconnected from students. Elena shares her frustration during a weekly check-in with her supervisor, Nan.

Elena and Nan explore opportunities for Elena to reconnect with her value of supporting students. One idea they have is for Elena to invite students to join a committee she leads. This solution will allow Elena to spend more time directly connecting with students and will enhance the committee by bringing in the student perspective.

Nan also points out that since receiving her promotion, Elena has effectively supported the program coordinators she supervises, yet she rarely makes time to attend their programs. Elena tells Nan she feels too busy with the new administrative duties she has assumed as a manager. Together, they identify some ways that Elena can manage her time differently so she can attend her staff members' student programs. Elena realizes her presence shows her employees that she supports them and allows her to experience the fulfillment of her values. At the events, she observes how students are affected by her work because her leadership and support of the program coordinators contributed to the program's success.

In the example of Nan and Elena, the supervisor and employee collaboratively identified solutions that improved Elena's values congruence and were appropriate for her position and the organization's needs. There may be circumstances, however, where it is not within the scope of reason or possibility for the work environment to make adjustments that will adequately address an employee's lack of values congruence. In those cases, the outcome is that the employee leaves the work environment.

Termination of the employee is the most unfavorable course of action. Alternatively, leaders can support employees in securing a job in a different work environment. One option is to identify a different position within the organization that better aligns with the employee's values. Both a transfer and a promotion fall into this category. Another option is to help the employee find employment outside of the organization. Supervisors can support an employee in this circumstance, including normalizing the transition, serving as a job reference, or acting as a career sponsor who actively advocates for the employee and facilitates networking connections.

Supervisors also must advocate for extrinsic motivators that contribute to employees' feeling valued. According to Hammond (2022), student affairs educators reported that factors such as compensation, training, and advancement pathways—or the lack of these factors—significantly affected how they experienced values congruence. As such, student affairs leaders should use their position and influence to support and advocate for competitive salaries, professional development for staff, and advancement opportunities. Increased job satisfaction and commitment benefit the workplace by reducing turnover and cultivating employee engagement.

Values Congruence as a Tool for Job Seekers

Whether a student affairs professional is thinking about searching for a new job or is actively doing so, values play a central role in securing a position that is a good match. Assessing the fit of a prospective work environment through the lens of values congruence can be an empowering process.

Once individuals have clarified their values, they can evaluate their job options. The process begins with closely reviewing the position description of any job they are considering. Has the employer explicitly stated the organization's values in the job announcement or position description? What about the job duties? Do these connect to the job seeker's values (e.g., diversity, equity, and inclusion; helping others)? Through additional research, the job seeker can also discover evidence of aligned values in the employer's mission statement, strategic plan, annual report, and other information on their website.

Beyond reviewing the information found online and in the position description, asking targeted questions of the employer during the hiring process can help job seekers gain additional insight into how the workplace will fulfill their values. Findings from a study by Garcia et al. (2021) exposed instances of new student affairs professionals discovering, upon being hired, that their institution's diversity statements were merely performative. Therefore, when inquiring about values, job seekers need to ask questions that provide evidence of the values enacted. For example, rather than ask whether the institution (or department, manager, or team) holds equity as a value, the job seeker should inquire about specific actions the institution has taken to promote equity.

In addition to the values typically associated with student affairs, such as ethical behavior; diversity, equity, and inclusion; and helping others (Bureau, 2018; NASPA–Student Affairs Administrators in Higher Education, 1997; Young, 1993), Hammond's (2022) study revealed that participants valued approaching work using their strengths and preferred work style. Regarding the latter finding, job seekers can use strategies similar to the ones shared here. In particular, the supervisor of the prospective position and the department or unit's top manager are ideal sources of information. The job seeker should ask how their preferred work style and individual strengths align with the job expectations and the organization's team dynamics, structure, and needs.

To illustrate the role of preferred work style, consider a job seeker, Kai, who is applying for positions as an academic advisor. Kai wants to work in an environment where he can be creative and frequently collaborate with others. He is deliberate in his search to maximize the potential for values congruence in his future workplace. First, he closely reviews job descriptions he is interested in to identify evidence of how the position will allow him to approach work in his preferred work style. More specifically, he looks for statements in the position description that convey that collaboration and creativity are desired traits in the role. Kai also tries to identify stated job duties and responsibilities that use collaboration and creativity, such as committee work and developing new programs for students.

In the interview process, Kai asks academic advisors in the workplace to describe how they collaborate with others and how much time they spend collaborating in an average week. When he meets with the position's supervisor, Kai mentions how he likes to be creative and asks about opportunities for creativity in the role. In addition, throughout all interview stages, he looks for examples of collaboration and creativity within the department (e.g., services, programs, initiatives). As a result, Kai can better ascertain whether the position will meet his needs by actively gathering information and seeking clarification about how collaboration and creativity are or can be incorporated into the job.

Hammond's (2002) study also indicated that student affairs professionals valued opportunities for professional development, advancement pathways, and compensation increases. Therefore, job seekers should consider asking about these topics during the hiring process (see Table 14.1). However, remember that some hiring managers may find it off-putting for a candidate to ask questions of this nature too early in the hiring process. Therefore, when there is doubt about the timing of bringing up these topics, the most prudent approach is to raise these questions after a job offer is made.

Table 14.1

Sample Questions Job Seekers Should Ask During an Interview

Topic	Questions to ask
Professional development	• What types of professional development are supported for this position? • How much release time is provided to participate in professional development? • How are funding allocations for individual staff members determined?
Advancement opportunities	• What advancement opportunities are possible in this department? In the institution? • Does this position have a predetermined advancement pathway? • What support is provided to employees who aspire to advance in the organization? • What positions have former employees in this position moved on to secure?
Compensation	• Is this position eligible for merit-based increases or bonuses? If so, how are they determined? • Does this position receive an annual step increase and/or cost-of-living adjustment? If so, how much? • Are increases or bonuses awarded for additional degrees or certifications earned?

The institution's human resources department is a potential source of information and clarification. At institutions where a union represents student affairs professionals, the collective bargaining agreement (usually found online) or a union representative may have information about policies or practices related to compensation, salary increases, and career advancement. The structured nature of unionized work environments can mean limited flexibility in terms of compensation and advancement pathways. However, collective bargaining agreements offer employees clarity and predictability about the pathways. Furthermore, unions use membership strength to negotiate with employers for improved working conditions, including pay and benefits.

Additionally, asking clarifying questions about job duties potentially connected to neoliberalism will help the job seeker better understand the position. The Values Alignment Worksheet for Job Seekers (see Appendix) can be a useful resource in this process. Understanding neoliberalism, its causes, and how it might manifest in one's work can empower a job seeker. This knowledge allows them to clarify expectations and evaluate whether specific neoliberalism-influenced job duties will contradict their values. Case study research by Carducci (2010) explored how student affairs administrators at three higher education institutions understood neoliberal behaviors occurring within their functional areas. Participant interviews indicated that administrators expressed commitment to the espoused values of the student affairs profession, yet many accepted marketlike behaviors as a necessary means to support student programs and services.

Once a job seeker has secured employment, they will likely be consumed with learning the job and acclimating to their new work environment. They are encouraged to regularly reflect on their values and evaluate how they are (or are not) being fulfilled. As described earlier, the relationship between an employee and their work environment is a dynamic system in which adjustments are made to maintain equilibrium. Minor, proactive adjustments can help prevent tension within the system from increasing beyond the threshold for tolerance.

Conclusion

Student affairs professionals can use values as a powerful framework for realignment at any point in their careers. This chapter underscores the importance of proactively enhancing job satisfaction by developing greater awareness of values and understanding of how values congruence affects job fit. This process is now more critical than ever given the rapidly changing landscapes of higher education and work.

Job seekers and current student affairs professionals should be empowered to engage in activities and reflection, leading them to clarify their core values. Then, through research about a position and work environment, inquiry, and open communication with others, including hiring managers and supervisors, they can become well equipped to determine the fit potential between their values and their workplace. When applied regularly and intentionally, the strategies offered in this chapter can help readers enjoy a more satisfying career.

Student affairs leaders are encouraged to integrate values into their management approach to support their employees' job satisfaction. Articulating their values and promoting the development of shared values among their team members will demonstrate their commitment to centering values within the workplace. Furthermore, they can support individual employees by regularly discussing values and crafting positions to promote values fulfillment. When an employee experiences conflict between their values and the workplace that adjustments on either party's side cannot resolve, supervisors can support their employees in seeking a position that is a better fit.

The importance of values congruence for student affairs professionals cannot be overstated. By taking the time to reflect and understand their values and to assess how they align with their workplace, professionals can work toward achieving greater satisfaction in their careers. Although the profession exists to serve students, it can be sustained only if the needs of the people it employs are also met.

References

Bureau, D. A. (2018). Grounded in their work: Interpreting perceptions of professional values by participants in student affairs preparation programs. *Journal of College and Character*, *19*(3), 215–228. https://doi.org/10.1080/2194587X.2018.1481098

Carducci, R. (2010). *Academic capitalism in student affairs organizations: Examining the business of student development* (Publication No. 3450988) [Doctoral dissertation, University of California, Los Angeles]. ProQuest Dissertations and Theses Global.

Careerplanner.com. (2023). *Knowdell career values card sort*. https://www.knowdellcardsorts.com/Career-Values.cfm

Dawis, R. V. (2000). The person-environment tradition in counseling psychology. In W. E. Martin Jr., J. L. Swartz-Kulstad, & W. E. Martin (Eds.), *Person-environment psychology and mental health: Assessment and intervention*. Routledge. https://doi.org/10.4324/9781410605580

Dawis, R. V., & Lofquist, L. H. (1984). *A psychological theory of work adjustment: An individual-differences model and its applications*. University of Minnesota.

Expatriates of Student Affairs. (n.d.). *Members* [Facebook page]. Facebook. Retrieved April 16, 2022, from https://www.facebook.com/groups/749836875175930/members

Garcia, C. E., Walker, W., Morgan, D., & Shi, Y. (2021). Aligning student affairs practice with espoused commitments to equity, diversity, and inclusion. *Journal of College Student Development*, *62*(2), 137–153. https://doi.org/10.1353/csd.2021.0013

Gittleman, M. (2022, July). The "great resignation" in perspective. *Monthly Labor Review*. U.S. Bureau of Labor Statistics. https://doi.org/10.21916/mlr.2022.20

Hammond, A. K. (2022). *Understanding values congruence between student affairs educators and their work environments in a neoliberal context* (Publication No. 29168612) [Doctoral dissertation, California State University, Fresno]. ProQuest Dissertations and Theses Global.

Hamrick, F. A., & Klein, K. (2015). Trends and milestones affecting student affairs practice. In E. J. Whitt & J. H. Schuh (Eds.), *New directions for student services, 1997–2014: Glancing back, looking forward* (New Directions for Student Services, No. 151, pp. 15–25). Jossey-Bass. https://doi.org/10.1002/ss.20134

Harvey, D. (2007). *A brief history of neoliberalism*. Oxford University Press.

June, A. W. (2017, May 25). 5 forces that drive administrative "bloat." *The Chronicle of Higher Education*. https://www.chronicle.com/article/5-forces-that-drive-administrative-bloat

Kezar, A. J. (2004). Obtaining integrity? Reviewing and examining the charter between higher education and society. *The Review of Higher Education*, *27*(4), 429–459. https://doi.org/10.1353/rhe.2004.0013

Kezar, A. J., DePaola, T., & Scott, D. T. (2019). *The gig academy: Mapping labor in the neoliberal university*. Johns Hopkins University Press.

NASPA–Student Affairs Administrators in Higher Education. (1997). *Principles of good practice for student affairs*. https://www.naspa.org/images/uploads/main/Principles_of_Good_Practice_in_Student_Affairs.pdf

Perez, R. J. (2017). Enhancing, inhibiting, and maintaining voice: An examination of student affairs graduate students' self-authorship journeys. *Journal of College Student Development*, *58*(6), 833–852. https://doi.org/10.1353/csd.2017.0067

Rokeach, M. (1968). *Beliefs, attitudes and values: A theory of organization and change*. Jossey-Bass.

Rounds, J., & Jin, J. (2013). Nature, importance, and assessment of needs and values. In S. D. Brown & R. W. Lent (Eds.), *Career development and counseling: Putting theory and research to work* (pp. 417–447). Wiley.

Saunders, D. (2010). Neoliberal ideology and public higher education in the United States. *Journal for Critical Education Policy Studies*, *8*(1), 41–77.

Seggewiss, B. J., Boeggemann, L. M., Straatmann, T., Mueller, K., & Hattrup, K. (2019). Do values and value congruence both predict commitment? A refined multi-target, multi-value investigation into a challenged belief. *Journal of Business and Psychology*, *34*(2), 169–187. https://doi.org/10.1007/s10869-018-9534-0

Slaughter, S., & Rhoades, G. (2000). The neo-liberal university. *New Labor Forum*, *6*, 73–79.

Uslu, B., Calikoglu, A., Seggie, F. N., & Seggie, S. H. (2019). The entrepreneurial university and academic discourses: The meta-synthesis of higher education articles. *Higher Education Quarterly*, *73*(3), 285–311. https://doi.org/10.1111/hequ.12198

Wilson, M. E., Liddell, D. L., Hirschy, A. S., & Pasquesi, K. (2016). Professional identity, career commitment, and career entrenchment of midlevel student affairs professionals. *Journal of College Student Development*, *57*(5), 557–572. https://doi.org/10.1353/csd.2016.0059

Young, R. B. (1993). The essential values of the profession. In R. B. Young (Ed.), *Identifying and implementing the essential values of the profession* (New Directions for Student Services, No. 61, pp. 5–13). Jossey-Bass. https://doi.org/10.1002/ss.37119936103

Appendix

Values Alignment Worksheet for Job Seekers

This worksheet will help individuals seeking jobs in student affairs to align their values with a prospective work environment, considering neoliberal influences.

Step 1

List three to five core values that you want to fulfill within your work environment. (Tip: Use activities and tools introduced in the Clarifying Values section of Chapter 14 of this book to determine your core values.)

My Core Values

-
-
-
-
-

Step 2

Assess how neoliberalism might manifest itself in your prospective work environment. For each neoliberal characteristic listed, seek out information[1] that will help you clarify the following questions.

Neoliberal characteristic	Questions	Notes
Accountability	• Are there specific performance targets for this position? Are salaries or salary increases tied to these targets? • To which agencies or entities is this department accountable? What does accountability look like? • What role do data play in decision-making and resource allocation in this department? • Does the department or division produce data and reports? What do these materials tell you about the organization's priorities? • If the person in this role supports students via individual appointments, how many students are they expected to meet with? How much time is allotted for each visit, and is there a limit on this expectation?	
Competition	• Is the person in this role expected to showcase the department's services or resources to attract students as "customers"? • Does this department engage in activities that increase the institution's reputation or rankings? • Does this position support student enrollment activities?	

---

[1] Examples of information sources include position description; observations made during the hiring process; conversations with current or former employees; information found on the organization's website, strategic plan, or reports; and the organization's mission, vision, and values.

Revenue generation[2]	- How is this department funded? Are the funding sources consistent and stable? - Is the department's funding allocated based on performance targets and/or output? (Note: This question relates to accountability, too.) - Is the department's funding affected by how it performs compared with other departments? (Note: This question refers to competition, too.) - Is this position responsible for performing revenue-generating activities such as grant writing or fundraising? If so, what training and resources are provided to support an employee's success? - Are goals or target outcomes associated with revenue-generating activities? What happens if they are not met?	
Productivity and efficiency	- Are all positions in this area currently staffed? When a vacancy occurs, what happens to that individual's job duties? If the duties are distributed to others, do staff who assume them receive additional compensation? - How do employees experience work–life balance? What does the organization do to help employees maintain work–life balance? What aspects are the responsibility of the employee? - Is productivity or efficiency measured in this job? Are output expectations adjusted when resources are lacking? - Does this position involve evening, weekend, or on-call duties? Are these hours compensated? Can employees adjust their schedules to regain these hours in their personal lives? - When there are competing priorities, how is the importance or urgency of each determined, and by whom?	

---

[2] Revenue generation also relates to accountability and competition, respectively.

Step 3

Respond to the following reflection questions:

- Considering what I know about the position and the work environment[3], I foresee that my values will be fulfilled in the following ways: *(Example: "My value of work–life balance will be fulfilled because this department does not require weekend responsibilities.")*

- Where do I notice potential tension or misalignment between my values and the work environment? Is this a nonstarter for me, or are my expectations flexible?

- How will I navigate and keep my values central in this role, particularly if I foresee potential misalignment (even if it's slight)?

- How will the organization support me in keeping my values central?

---

[3] Examples of information sources include position description; observations made during the hiring process; conversations with current or former employees; information found on the organization's website, strategic plan, or reports; and the organization's mission, vision, and values.

Step 4

Review and reflect on your responses in Steps 1 and 3 and the information gathered in Step 2. Consider the degree to which you feel your values will be congruent with the work environment. Use this insight to help you determine if the new work environment is a good fit based on how you want your core values to integrate with your work.

Editors and Contributors

Editors

Amy Hecht is the vice president of student affairs at Florida State University. Before that, she was the vice president of student affairs at the College of New Jersey and has held positions at Auburn University, Temple University, Cabrini College, and the University of Pennsylvania.

A professional in the field of student affairs since 2001, Hecht has served on executive leadership teams in student affairs organizations and has extensive experience leading and managing in higher education. She is a colead facilitator with LeaderShape, a national nonprofit organization, and has held volunteer leadership positions with NASPA–Student Affairs Administrators in Higher Education. Hecht launched her career with Alpha Chi Omega national sorority, serving as a traveling consultant, and was awarded Alpha Chi Omega's Woman of Distinction honor in 2018. Hecht serves as the Florida Region Director for the Children's Heart Foundation and is a member of Leadership Florida's 40th Cornerstone Class. She has published book chapters and articles focused on organizational learning, change, executive transitions, and the role of assistant and associate vice presidents in student affairs organizations. Hecht earned a bachelor's degree from Florida State University in mass communications and a master's degree and doctorate in higher education administration from the University of Pennsylvania.

Jason B. Pina is senior vice president for university life at New York University. He has served higher education for over 30 years, most recently in senior student affairs, enrollment, and diversity roles at Ohio University, Bridgewater State University, the University of Rhode Island, and

Roger Williams University. As a former NASPA Board of Directors member, he was the 2019 and 2020 NASPA Annual Conference Chair. He has been recognized with several awards, including the NASPA Foundation's 2022 Pillar of the Profession Award, and the Ohio College Personnel Association's Phillip A. Tripp Award for Distinguished Service in 2020 and the Gerald L. Saddlemire Mentor Award in 2019. In addition to serving on national higher education boards and various institute faculty, Pina has authored numerous articles and book chapters and coedited *AVP: Leading from the Unique Role of Associate/Assistant Vice President for Student Affairs* (NASPA, 2016). He holds an EdD in educational leadership from Johnson & Wales University, master's and specialist's degrees in educational leadership from the University of Northern Colorado, and a bachelor's degree in economics from Occidental College.

Contributors

Pauline Burke is the vice president of student affairs at Stonehill College. She has served in higher education since 1994 at both Stonehill College and Wentworth Institute of Technology. She has also been an engaged leader with NASPA in numerous capacities, including Region I Massachusetts state director, Region I conference committee chair, Region I director, National Knowledge Communities director, and faculty member for the Aspiring VPSA Institute. Dobrowski's research centers on organizational leadership, and she contributed to *AVP: Leading from the Unique Role of Associate/Assistant Vice President for Student Affairs* (NASPA, 2016). Dobrowski earned a bachelor's degree in psychology from Boston College, a master's degree in social work from Simmons University, and a doctoral degree from Northeastern University.

Constanza Cabello is an equity-minded leader committed to strategically positioning organizations to advance justice in their organizations and with their constituents. With foundations in leadership, facilitation, and counseling, she has spent her career working with organizations on their goals to advance diversity, equity, and inclusion. She is the vice president of equity programs at an asset management and financial services company. Cabello applies an equity lens to initiatives and leads the development and implementation of strategies to build more significant equity related to human capital and business practices, services, and products. Before moving into the corporate space, she spent 13 years in higher education (student affairs, institutional diversity, and community affairs). She has a Doctor of Education in organizational leadership from Northeastern University, a Master of Science in counseling from Central Connecticut State University, and a Bachelor of Science in social policy and planning from the University of Connecticut.

Ainsley Carry has served in administrative and teaching roles at Southern Methodist University, the University of Arkansas, and Temple University. He accepted his first vice presidency at Auburn University in 2009 and has held similar positions at the University of Southern California (2013–2019) and the University of British Columbia in Vancouver, Canada (2019–present). Carry has authored several articles and two books: *Executive Transitions in Student Affairs: A Guide to Getting Started as the Vice President* (NASPA, 2014) and *Washington Next? Disputed Monuments, Honorees, and Symbols on Campus* (Kindle Direct Publishing, 2021). His areas of research include the intersection of history, law, and race in American higher education. Carry earned bachelor's, master's, and doctoral degrees from the University of Florida. He also earned master's degrees in business administration and law from Auburn University and the University of Southern California, respectively.

Michael N. Christakis is vice president of student affairs at the University at Albany (UAlbany). Since his arrival at the university in 1999, Christakis has held numerous positions in student affairs, having served as associate vice president before his appointment as vice president of student affairs in 2015. Christakis currently serves as chair-elect of the NASPA Board of Directors and chair of the Association of Public and Land-grant Universities' Council on Student Affairs. He previously served as director for NASPA Region II, national president of Omicron Delta Kappa, and cochair of NASPA's Assessment, Evaluation, and Research Knowledge Community. A fellow of the State Academy for Public Administration, he was appointed public service professor in 2013 and teaches undergraduate courses in public policy, public administration, and political science, for which he was honored with Rockefeller College's Outstanding Teaching Award in 2010 and the UAlbany Student Association's Outstanding Teaching Award in 2014. Christakis holds a BA in political science and history from Alfred University and an MPP and PhD from the University at Albany Rockefeller College of Public Affairs and Policy.

Karen Warren Coleman is the first female head of William Penn Charter School in its 334-year history. Before transitioning to PK–12 education, she served in higher education for 24 years, including at the University of Chicago; the University of California, Berkeley; The George Washington University; and Hobart and William Smith Colleges. Her first headship was at the Hockaday School. Coleman has been an adjunct faculty member for Loyola University and has been an active member of ACPA and NASPA, including as Annual Conference chair. Her research interests include diversity and inclusion, student activism, leadership, and governance. Coleman earned a bachelor's degree from the University of Massachusetts–Amherst, a master's degree from the University of Vermont, and a doctorate from the University of Pennsylvania.

Natasha N. Croom is associate dean for academic and student affairs in the Graduate School and associate professor of higher education and student affairs in the College of Education at Clemson University. She has worked in higher education for more than 18 years as staff, a faculty member, and an administrator at Texas A&M University, the University of Maryland, and Iowa State University. Croom's work has been shared in *The Review of Higher Education, Negro Educational Review, Equity & Excellence in Education, About Campus,* and the *Journal of Student Affairs Research and Practice.* She has coedited several books and is also coeditor-in-chief of NASPA's *Journal of Women and Gender in Higher Education.* Croom earned her PhD from Iowa State University, her master's degree from Texas A&M University–College Station, and her bachelor's degree from Texas A&M University–Kingsville.

Shannon Ellis has been the vice president of student services at the University of Nevada, Reno, since 1998. She has worked in the field of higher education for more than 40 years as a faculty member and administrator at the University of Massachusetts–Amherst, the University of Southern California, Seattle University, and Evergreen State College. Ellis has served as president of NASPA and has been active on several NASPA boards, institutes, and advisory committees. She has published numerous articles and chapters in several professional journals and books, and has authored and edited several books on student affairs and student affairs administrative leadership. Her ongoing research focuses on organizational transformation and the role of student services in tomorrow's colleges and universities. Ellis received her PhD from the University of Southern California, her master's degree at the University of Massachusetts–Amherst, and her bachelor's degree from the University of Illinois Urbana-Champaign.

Kenneth Elmore served as the 14th president of Dean College from 2022 to 2024. With nearly four decades of higher education experience as an accomplished leader, connector, and community builder, Elmore has throughout his career been an institutional catalyst dedicated to making and keeping the common ground compelling. He has received several honors and professional distinctions, including being named a Pillar of the Profession by the NASPA Foundation and a Diamond Honoree by ACPA–College Student Educators International for outstanding work in higher education and student affairs. In 2019, Elmore was selected by the Boston mayor to deliver the annual, historic Fourth of July Oration at Faneuil Hall. Recently, he was inducted into the Martin Luther King, Jr. Collegium of Scholars at Morehouse College. Elmore holds a bachelor's degree in physiological psychology from Brown University, a master's degree from Boston University, and a Juris Doctor from New England Law.

Michael S. Funk is a clinical associate professor and director of the Steinhardt School of Culture, Education, and Human Development, Higher Education and Student Affairs program at New York University (NYU). Funk's scholarship focuses on social justice. He coauthored a chapter on racism and White supremacy in the fourth edition of *Teaching for Diversity and Social Justice* (Routledge, 2023) and is coeditor of the upcoming fifth edition of *Readings for Diversity and Social Justice* (Routledge, in press). Funk has received the 2023 NYU Martin Luther King Jr. Faculty Award, the 2022 New York University Center for Multicultural Education and Programs Nia Award for Faculty Excellence, the 2018 Steinhardt Teaching Excellence Award, and a Lifetime Achievement Award from the NYU College of Arts and Science's Academic Achievement Program in 2017. He earned a bachelor's degree from Edinboro University, a master's degree from New York University, and a doctorate from the University of Massachusetts Amherst.

Thomas Gibson serves as chancellor of the University of Wisconsin–Stevens Point (UWSP) and is a tenured professor. Prior to joining UWSP, he served as vice president for student affairs and vice provost at Bowling Green State University and as associate vice president of student affairs at Ball State University. He held several roles at York College/CUNY, including associate dean for student development. He also led academic support services at Queens College/CUNY and the University of Connecticut at Stamford. He currently serves as faculty for the Association of Governing Boards' Institute for Leadership and Governance in Higher Education. His research interests include student achievement, higher education governance and organization, presidential leadership, and leadership development. He earned a bachelor's degree in communication from Eastern Connecticut State University, a master's degree in education from the University of New Haven, and a doctorate in educational leadership in higher education at Johnson & Wales University.

Stephanie A. Gordon is the vice president for professional development at NASPA–Student Affairs Administrators in Higher Education. She joined the association in 2003 as the director of educational programs. She supervises the professional development team and serves as the NASPA Board of Directors liaison at the largest, most comprehensive student affairs association in the United States. Prior to NASPA, Gordon served as director of residence life and coordinator of first-year programs at Chatham University; assistant director of residence life, staff development, and training at Colgate University; and assistant director of undergraduate admissions at Simmons College. Her scholarly research includes the professional competencies of chief student affairs officers and persistence of first-generation and historically excluded student populations. Gordon holds an EdD in higher education management from the University of Pennsylvania Graduate School of Education, an EdM in higher education administration from Harvard University Graduate School of Education, and a BA in English literature and political science from Simmons College.

Amie K. Hammond is the executive director of career services at California Polytechnic State University. During her career in student affairs, Hammond has worked in a variety of functional areas: residential life, fraternity and sorority life, student activities, advising, and career development. She is an active member of the Mountain Pacific Association of Colleges and Employers, where she has been on several standing committees and served on the board of directors. Her research interests include neoliberalism in higher education, individual and organizational values, and career development. Hammond earned a bachelor's degree in kinesiology from Occidental College, a master's degree in student personnel administration from NYU, and a doctorate in educational leadership from Fresno State University.

Erin Hoffmann Harding is a management consultant specializing in strategy, transformation, and executive counseling for higher education and public sector clients. She served as vice president for student affairs at the University of Notre Dame for 9 years, and she was also the founder and inaugural leader of the university's Office of Strategic Planning and Institutional Research. Hoffmann Harding has extensive experience at McKinsey & Company, where she advanced to associate partner, served as the core expert on student success for McKinsey's global education practice, and continues to serve clients as an independent consultant. Hoffmann Harding has also held long-term board leadership roles at the Stanley Clark School, a premier regional independent day school. She received her Juris Doctor from Harvard Law School and her bachelor's degree from the University of Notre Dame.

Martino Harmon is the vice president of student life at the University of Michigan. For over two decades, he has served in a variety of public higher education settings ranging from small 2-year institutions to large 4-year universities. His leadership experience includes enrollment management, student success, and student affairs. In addition, he has held numerous leadership roles in professional associations, including ACT, the Association of American Universities, the Association of Public and Land-Grant Universities, the College Board, the Melvin C. Terrell Educational Foundation, NASPA, and the Ohio Association for College Admission Counseling. He earned a doctorate in higher education and administration, a master's degree in education, and a bachelor's degree in business administration from the University of Toledo.

Tamara Bertrand Jones is professor of education policy, organization, governance, and leadership and associate dean for faculty affairs in the College of Education at the University of Illinois Urbana–Champaign. She uses qualitative methods and critical and Black feminist theories to examine how culturally responsive environments and structures of support in education influence the intersectional experiences of historically underrepresented populations, particularly Black women, in academia. Her work as a higher education administrator and program evaluator for more than 25 years has also shaped her research on culturally responsive evaluation, higher education leadership, and faculty development. Bertrand Jones' scholarship and praxis has broad implications for recruitment, retention, advancement, and professional development of emerging scholars in higher education.

Darryl Lovett is the director of people and culture for student affairs at Florida State University. With over a decade of experience in higher education, he brings extensive knowledge and a deep commitment to fostering an inclusive campus environment. Before his current role, he gained valuable experience in facility operations, programming, employee and student well-being, and the municipality and private sector. Additionally, Lovett served as an adjunct faculty member, teaching a leadership and well-being course while fulfilling his administrative responsibilities.

His research interests include sense of belonging, mentorship, emotional intelligence, leadership development, and organizational culture. Lovett is currently pursuing a doctorate at Florida State University, where he earned both a bachelor's and a master's degree.

Jeanna Mastrodicasa is the senior associate vice president for agriculture and natural resources at the University of Florida, where she is the chief operating officer for the statewide Institute of Food and Agricultural Sciences. She has worked at the University of Florida for more than 26 years in five positions, including academic advising, new student orientation, honors program, and student affairs. Mastrodicasa has held leadership roles in NASPA, including national chair of the Public Policy Division; the AVP Steering Committee; and cochair of the Assessment, Evaluation, and Research Knowledge Community. She serves on several nonprofit and advisory boards and was previously a two-term city commissioner in Gainesville. Mastrodicasa earned bachelor's and law degrees from the University of Georgia, a master's degree from the University of Tennessee, and a PhD from the University of Florida.

Raphael X. Moffett is the chief student affairs officer at the Schwarzman Scholars Program at Tsinghua University in Beijing, China. In this role, he is responsible for the holistic development of scholars while creating a sense of belonging in the college. A native of Washington State, Moffett began his career in student affairs at Clark Atlanta University in 2002. Before joining Schwarzman Scholars, Moffett served in executive leadership roles as the dean of students at Duke Kunshan University in Kunshan, China, vice president of student services at Texas Southern University, and vice president of student affairs at Langston University. He has more than two decades of higher education experience serving in progressive leadership roles at Trinity University, Morehouse College, Georgia State University, and Clark Atlanta University. Moffett also is the president and founder of Inspire YOUniversity, LLC, a consultancy supporting universities, sport teams, corporations, faith-based groups, and nonprofit organizations to become the best versions of themselves. He holds a bachelor's degree in English from Washington State University, and a master's degree and doctorate in educational leadership from Clark Atlanta University.

Ajay Nair has been president of Arcadia University since 2018. He has served in higher education since 1999 at Pennsylvania State University, the University of Virginia, Columbia University, the University of Pennsylvania, and Emory University. His research interests include quality assurance in educational systems, service-learning and civic engagement, second-generation Asian American identity, and the state of multiculturalism in university communities. Nair has served on a range of university and civic boards and organizations, including as director of NASPA's Justice, Equity, Diversity, and Inclusion Division. He earned a Bachelor of Science in human development and family studies and a doctorate in workforce education and development from The Pennsylvania State University.

Ellen J. Neufeldt is the fourth president of California State University, San Marcos (CSUSM). Before joining CSUSM, she was vice president of student engagement and enrollment services and vice president of student affairs at Salisbury University. Neufeldt has received numerous awards in the field of student affairs, including the 2016 Howard Davis Senior Award by the Southern Association for College Student Affairs, as well as several awards from NASPA, including the 2020 Outstanding Enrollment Management Professional Award, the 2018 Melvene D. Hardee Dissertation of the Year Award, the 2017 Pillar of the Profession Award, and the 2014 Scott Goodnight Award for Outstanding Performance as a Dean. A champion of student success and student social mobility, she founded the national Social Mobility Symposium (now hosted annually at CSUSM) as well as a center dedicated to social mobility at Old Dominion University. Under Neufeldt's leadership, CSUSM was recognized as the top university in the nation on CollegeNet's Social Mobility Index. Neufeldt received a Doctor of Education degree from the University of Tennessee at Knoxville, a Master of Arts degree in educational psychology and counselor education from Tennessee Technological University, and a Bachelor of Science degree in business administration from Tennessee Technological University.

David J. Nguyen is the dean of University College at Ohio University. In addition to this academic administrative role, he holds a tenured faculty appointment in the Higher Education and Student Affairs program. He has worked in different academic and student affairs units at institutions including Tufts University and the Massachusetts Institute of Technology. As an academic, he has published more than 40 articles and book chapters on access and equity issues in postsecondary education. Nguyen holds a PhD from Michigan State University, a master's degree in college student development and counseling from Northeastern University, a master's degree in accounting from Syracuse University, and a bachelor's degree from Syracuse University.

Katherine (Katie) O'Dair is the university marshal at Harvard University. She has worked in higher education for over 30 years, including roles in student affairs at Tufts University, MIT, Boston College, and Harvard University. She has held leadership roles in NASPA, including as national chair of the Administrators in Graduate and Professional Student Services Knowledge Community and as a member of the 2019 Annual Conference planning committee. Her interests include assessment, organizational alignment, and strategy. She serves on several nonprofit boards and has been an evaluator for the New England Commission on Higher Education. O'Dair earned a bachelor's degree from Miami University, a master's degree from Northeastern University, and a PhD from Boston College.

Gage E. Paine is the associate dean for academic affairs and clinical associate professor at the Fran and Earl Ziegler College of Nursing at the University of Oklahoma Health Sciences Center. She was vice president for student affairs at the University of Texas at Austin, the University of Texas at San Antonio, and Trinity University. She has been president of the Texas Association of College and University Student Personnel Administrators and faculty member and director of the NASPA Region III/Southern Association for College Student Affairs New Professionals Institute. Her publications and presentations focus on legal issues in higher education, leadership development, and the role of creativity in leadership. Paine earned a BA in letters from the University of Oklahoma, a JD from Texas Tech University, and a PhD in higher education administration from the University of Texas at Austin.

Sofia B. Pertuz is an educator, consultant, and certified executive coach who has led organizational change and transformation in a uniquely varied career spanning over 25 years within higher education, nonprofit, and corporate organizations. Pertuz serves as managing director for diversity, equity, and inclusion for Billie Jean King Enterprises and is the founder of Mainstream Insight, LLC, partnering with organizations and senior leaders to help them foster workplaces where everyone can thrive. She has been an invited speaker for international audiences on leadership, change management, social justice, mental health, and LGBTQIA+ advocacy, including delivering keynotes in both English and Spanish. Pertuz earned a master's degree and PhD in higher education leadership, management, and policy from Seton Hall University; and a bachelor's degree in organizational communication from the State University of

New York at New Paltz. She is a senior certified professional by the Society for Human Resource Management and is a certified diversity executive.

Ana Rossetti is a consulting manager at Huron Consulting Group in the Higher Education Strategy and Operations practice. Before moving to consulting, Rossetti served in higher education since 2002 at Argosy University, Westwood College, the Chicago School of Professional Psychology, American College of Education, and Illinois Institute of Technology. She also was the director of the Aspen Young Leaders Fellowship program at the Aspen Institute and has taught at the undergraduate and graduate levels at Loyola University Chicago. Rossetti has been an active NASPA member since 2010, including leadership roles on the Region IV–East board for Knowledge Communities and several regional conferences. Rossetti also was national cochair of the Women in Student Affairs Knowledge Community. Her areas of research include cross-cultural and culturally grounded leadership development, racial identity, self-efficacy, and stereotype threat. Rossetti earned a bachelor's degree from The George Washington University, a master's degree from Loyola University, and a doctorate from the University of Pennsylvania.

Marcella Runell is dean of students and vice president for student life and lecturer in religion at Mount Holyoke College. Prior to Mount Holyoke, Runell held various positions at NYU, including founding codirector for Global Spiritual Life and the minor in multifaith and spiritual leadership. Runell has authored numerous books and articles on race, popular culture, friendship, and parenting. Her research interests include intergroup dialogue and critical pedagogy. Runell holds a doctorate in social justice education from the University of Massachusetts–Amherst, a master's degree from NYU, and a bachelor's degree from Ramapo College of New Jersey.

Baishakhi Taylor is the associate vice chancellor for student affairs at NYU, Abu Dhabi. She has served in higher education since 2003 at the University of Kentucky, Duke University, Middlebury College, Smith College, and now at NYU in Abu Dhabi. She has been an active member of NASPA in several regional and national capacities since 2009, including serving as a faculty member for the 2022 NASPA Institute for New Vice Presidents for Student Affairs. Her areas of research interest include gender, diversity and social justice, leadership, and organizational development. Taylor earned a bachelor's degree from Jadavpur University in Kolkata, India, a master's degree in women's studies from the University of Northern Iowa, and a doctorate in sociology from the University of Kentucky.

Lori S. White is the first female and first person of color to serve as president of DePauw University. Over a 40-year career in higher education, primarily in student affairs, she has worked at several universities, including the University of California, Irvine; Georgetown, Stanford, San Diego State, and Southern Methodist Universities; the University of Southern California; and Washington University in St. Louis. White's areas of emphasis in research and teaching include the student experience in higher education and the preparation and mentorship of new, mid-level, and aspiring senior student affairs professionals. She is the author of several articles and book chapters and has presented widely at professional meetings. Her most recent publications are coedited volumes titled *Keep Calm and Call the Dean of Students: A Guide to Understanding the Many Facets of the Dean of Students Role* (Routledge, 2019) and *Transformational Encounters: Shaping Diverse College and University Leaders* (NASPA, 2018). White earned an undergraduate degree in psychology and English from the University of California, Berkeley, and a

PhD from Stanford University in education administration and policy analysis with an emphasis in higher education.

Patricia A. Whitely is the senior vice president of student affairs at the University of Miami. She has served in higher education since 1982, including as vice president of student affairs since 1997 at the University of Miami, where she is also an adjunct faculty member. She has been honored by the University of Miami Faculty Senate with the James W. McLamore Outstanding Service Award in 2017, and by NASPA with the Scott Goodnight Award for Outstanding Performance as a Dean in 2013 and the Fred Turner Award for Outstanding Service to NASPA in 2020. She also was chair of the NASPA Board of Directors from 2014 to 2015. Her areas of research interest include crisis management, organizational leadership, and spirituality in college students. Whitely earned a bachelor's degree from St. John's University, a master's degree from the University of South Carolina, and a doctorate from the University of Miami.

Index

Figures and tables are indicated by f and t following the page number.

A

Academic advising, 44, 147
Academic capitalism, 286. *See also* Neoliberalism
Accountability
    accessibility of education and, 272–73
    organizational culture and, 247
    shared governance and, 280
    student activism and, 264
    as transferable skill, 277
    transparency and, 231
Accreditation, 81
ACE American College President report, 273–74
ACPA–College Student Educators International, 224
ADA (Americans with Disabilities Act of 1990), 136–37
Adaptability. *See* Resilience and adaptability
Adjunct faculty members, 105
Administrative positions, 167–82. *See also* Presidents
    career trajectory for, 168–74
    chaos theory of careers and, 174–75
    lessons learned for professionals interested in, 179–80
    in PK–12 education, 207–35. *See also* PK–12 education
    returning to, 177–79
    self-authorship theory and, 175–77
Admissions roles, 18–24
Advanced degrees. *See also* Faculty positions
    career advancement and, 31, 171
    consulting and, 85–86, 93
    curriculum relevance for, 6
    entry-level pay for, 3
    exploring programs for, 162–63
    faculty positions and, 160–61
    first-generation students and, 146
    growth in jobs requiring, 19
    non-education industries and, 100, 111
    PK–12 education and, 222
    race and ethnicity, 154–56
    transferable skills and, 2, 111
Advancement opportunities. *See also* Career trajectories
    burnout and, 116
    collective bargaining agreements and, 300
    consulting and, 83
    for faculty, 155, 158
    lack of, 5, 109–10, 114, 115
    mentors facilitating, 18–19, 56–57, 87–88
    norms of, 110, 117, 238
    values congruence and, 296–97, 299–300
    volunteering and, 117
Advocacy, 44, 136, 273, 292, 296–97. *See also* Empowerment
Affirmations and mantras, 222, 265, 270
African Americans. *See* Race and ethnicity
Alcohol consumption, 44, 189–91
Alfred University, 56
Allen, Ben, 35
Alpha Phi Alpha, 18
Alumni
    building names and, 59
    directors of alumni services, 131–33
    fundraising and, 132, 261
    PK–12 education and, 216, 222, 227

American Association of University Women, 183
American College Personnel Association, 184
American College President report (ACE), 273–74
American Council on Education, 184–85
American Psychological Association PsycTests database, 287
Americans with Disabilities Act of 1990 (ADA), 136–37
Angelou, Maya, 270
Arbery, Ahmaud, 106, 264
Arcadia University, Pennsylvania, 263–66
Ardoin, S., 239
Assessment skills, 111, 158
Assistantships. *See* Internships and assistantships
Associate vice president for student affairs, 30–31, 104, 134, 275–76
Association of Governing Boards Institute for Leadership and Governance in Higher Education, 37, 280
Austin, A. E., 144
Authenticity, 69–70

B

Baruch, Yehuda, 126
Baxter Magolda, M. B., 175, 177
The Board Chair Handbook (Creeden), 217
Board governance, 58–59, 216–17, 269
Boarding schools. *See* PK–12 education
Boston College, 49
Boundary setting, 239, 244, 249
Bright, J., 174
Brody, Jerry, 56, 71
Budget and financial issues. *See also* Fundraising
    COVID-19 pandemic and, 108, 277
    ethical practices and, 242–43
    growth opportunities, limits on, 114
    presidencies, preparation for, 269
    reimagined educational model and, 272
    as transferable skill, 111, 277
Building management skills, 77
Burke, Pauline, 55
Burnout and exhaustion
    boundary setting and, 244
    economic downturn and Great Reshuffle, 108
    emotional tax of student affairs work and, 116
    HESA pressures leading to, 4–5
    organizational culture and, 247
    serving students and, 5, 74, 104
    toxic work environments and, 63

C

Cabello, Constanza, 99
California State University, San Marcos, 257–61
Campus climates
    institutional policies and procedures, 67–68
    institutional values and, 63–64
    organizational politics and, 59–60
    for PK–12 education, 218
    quiet quitting and, 5
Campus service activities, 45
Canada, global work assignment in, 189–92
Carducci, R., 300
Career changes. *See* Career transitions; Changing institution type
Career counselors, 169, 287
Career fit
    feedback on, 268
    institutional fit and, 131–32, 240, 268
    job satisfaction and, 28, 74–77, 285
    outside of student affairs, 74–77
    person–environment fit theory and, 284–85
    values congruence and, 287, 297
Career realignment, 289–92. *See also* Values
Career trajectories
    in admissions, 18–24
    burnout and stagnation of, 5
    career shifts, normalizing, 114–15
    changing roles within institutions, 42–48
    conventional wisdom on, 123–24, 134
    global work assignments and, 187–88
    norms in higher education, 110, 117
    presidencies, 253–82. *See also* Presidential perspectives

reimagining, 239–41
returning to student affairs and, 128–32, 138–39
search for purpose and, 11–12
traditional and linear, 2, 11, 238
for vice presidents for student affairs, 56–57
Career transitions
   to administration, 167–82. *See also* Administrative positions
   away from student affairs. *See* Leaving student affairs careers
   to consulting, 80–96. *See also* Consulting
   to DEI roles, 99–108. *See also* Diversity, equity, and inclusion
   to faculty positions, 143–65. *See also* Faculty positions
   to PK–12 education, 207–35. *See also* PK–12 education
Carry, Ainsley, 183
Chait, Richard, 217
Changing institution type, 15–40
   administration changes and, 35
   calculated risk-taking, 18–23
   career goals and, 31–33
   COVID-19 pandemic and, 36–37
   experience opportunities outside expertise, 28–29
   lessons from, 37–39
   mentors and, 34
   opportunities to pivot, 26–28
   passion, following, 16–18
   stepping up as change agent, 23–26
   unique skill set, value of, 29–30
Chaos theory of careers (CTOC), 174–75
China, global work assignment in, 196–200
Christakis, Michael N., 55
Cincinnati State Community and Technical College (CSCTC), 29–30
Coffee conversations, 48, 50–53
Coleman, Karen Warren, 207
Collective bargaining agreements, 300
Colonization, 195–96, 203
Commencement ceremonies, 45, 257

Community colleges, xi, 26–30
Community connections, 44–47. *See also* Political involvement
Compassion fatigue, 247
Compensation. *See* Wages and compensation
Competencies. *See also* Skills
   global work assignments and, 199, 204
   organizational, 186
   presidencies and, 275–77
   returning to student affairs careers, 131–33
   shifting roles within institutions and, 50–51
Compton, Paula, 23–24, 33
Conferences. *See* Professional associations
Confidence, 69–70, 113
Consulting, 80–96
   advisor's role, 83–84
   beginning a career in, 85–89
   entrepreneurship and, 105, 115, 140
   to maintain connections to higher education, 105
   organizational structure, 83
   outcomes, 81–82
   professional development, 84–85
   project or engagement types, 80–81
   returning to a career in, 89–92
   roles compared, 93–96
   as side hustle, 241
   time allocation for, 82
Copy-and-paste approach to problems, 202–3
Costs of college, 5, 261, 272, 285–86
Council for the Advancement of Standards in Higher Education, 185
Counseling skills, 77
Covey, Stephen, 202
COVID-19 pandemic
   budget implications of, 108, 277
   career change during, 36–37
   commencement ceremonies and, 257
   consulting and, 88
   DEI roles, impact on, 107–8
   disruption of, 10–11, 102, 193
   family obligations and, 86, 102
   PK–12 education and, 217–18
   post-pandemic changes and, 74, 91

presidential responsibilities and, 269–71
self-reflection during, 284
social isolation and, 220
student recruitment and retention during, 10, 277
student support during, 64, 107–8, 261–62
workforce reductions during, xi, 3
Creating Sustainable Careers in Student Affairs (Renn), 239
Creativity skills
consulting and, 76
entrepreneurial mindsets and, 115
global work assignments and, 199
leaders promoting, 247
presidencies and, 255, 259
side hustles and, 241
values congruence and, 295, 298–99
Crisis management skills. *See also* COVID-19 pandemic
consulting and, 77
dean of students and, 275–76
PK–12 education and, 214
presidents and, 259–60
shared governance and accountability, 280
as transferable skill, 111
vice presidents for student affairs and, 66–67, 269
Critical thinking skills, 226, 229–31, 247
Croom, Natasha N., 143, 156
CTOC (chaos theory of careers), 174–75
Cultural humility, 266
Cultural intelligence, 280
Cyberbullying, 220

D

Data analysis skills, 111
Dawis, R. V., 284–85
Dean College, Massachusetts, 254–56
Dean of students
behavioral expectations for, 130
career advancement and, 27, 42, 209
challenges for, 104
networking with, 138
skills needed for, 132, 137, 275

Deck of disruptors (Feiler), 9–11, 9*f*
DeFillippi, R. J., 126
DEI. *See* Diversity, equity, and inclusion
DePauw University, Indiana, 267–74
Directors of alumni services, 131–33
Disruptors, 9–11, 9*f*
Diversity, equity, and inclusion (DEI), 99–108
accessibility of education and, 272–73
assessment and, 158
commitment in education, 226–28
COVID-19 pandemic, impact of, 107–8
economic downturn and, 108
job satisfaction and, 242
at NYU Abu Dhabi, 195
offices for, laws on, 273
pros and cons of leaving higher education for, 109–12
racial and social justice reckoning, 106–7, 264–65
risks and rewards story, 100–103
transferable skills in, 103–6, 110, 111
values congruence and, 294
Dual-career partnerships, 74, 88, 90
Duke Kunshan University (DKU), China, 197–99

E

Eastop, Dick, 22–23, 34
Eddy, P. L., 144
Ellis, Shannon, 55
Elmore, Kenneth, 253, 254
Emory University, Georgia, 263–64
Emotional intelligence, 111, 280
Employee recruitment and retention, 3–4, 243–44, 248
Employee shortages, xi, 3
Empowerment
belonging and collective responsibility, 246
career-building strategy, 8
institutional knowledge and, 60
leaving student affairs careers and, 104
organizational culture and, 246
sustainable workplaces and, 242
Engagements, consulting for, 80–81

Enrollment. *See* Student recruitment and retention
Entrepreneurship, 105, 111–12, 115, 140, 241
Equity. *See* Diversity, equity, and inclusion
Ethics
　consulting and, 82
　diversity and inclusion, promotion of, 226
　history of student affairs and, 184
　as organizational value, 293
　sustainable workplaces and, 242
Evans, Nancy, 30
Executive coaching, 105, 115, 179–80
Exhaustion. *See* Burnout and exhaustion
Exploitation, 117

F

Faculty advising, 163
Faculty positions, 143–65
　as a calling, 145–51
　challenges in, 172
　exploring doctoral programs for, 162–63
　interview process for, 171
　network and support for, 163
　presidencies, skill development for, 261, 276
　pull factors toward, 156–61
　push factors toward, 152–56
Faith-based institutions, 129–30
Family Educational Rights and Privacy Act of 1974 (FERPA), 200
Family obligations. *See also* Work–life balance
　career moves, timing for, 135
　consulting and, 74, 88, 90
　COVID-19 pandemic and, 86, 102
　dual-career partnerships and, 74, 88, 90
　global work assignments and, 201–2
　job satisfaction and, 243
　organizational culture and, 246
　prioritizing, 44
　support and leadership abilities, 70–71
　time management and, 240–41

Feedback
　on career fit, 268
　on consulting performance, 83
　critical thinking skills and, 231
　on job search materials, 79
　from mentors, 248
　for presidents, 265–66
　shifting roles within institutions and, 51
　from students, 265–66
Feiler, B., 9, 10
FERPA (Family Educational Rights and Privacy Act of 1974), 200
Financial consulting, 81
Financial literacy, 200–201
First-generation students
　challenges for, 169, 175
　completion rates, inequities in, 4
　graduate students as, 146
　institutional roadblocks for, 275
　mentorship of, 61
　support programs for, 157, 227
Fit, 131–32, 240, 268. *See also* Career fit; Job satisfaction
Florida State University (FSU), 152–54
Floyd, George, 102, 106, 264
Frankl, Viktor, 11
Fraternity hazing, 190–91
Fries-Britt, Sharon, 148
Fulfillment. *See also* Job satisfaction; Values
　consulting work and, 105
　protean career and, 124–25
　purpose-driven work and, 93
　reimagining career paths and, 239–41
　search for purpose and, 11–12
　strategies for, 6–8
Fundraising
　academic capitalism and, 286
　institutional fit and, 131–32
　networking skills and, 57, 76–77
　presidencies, preparation for, 269, 279
　for student scholarships, 261
　as transferable skill, 277
Funk, Michael S., 143, 145

G

Garcia, C. E., 294, 297
Gaston-Gayles, J. L., 144

George Washington University, Washington, D. C., 209
GI Bill (1944), 184
Gibson, Thomas, 253, 274
Global work assignments, 183–205
    in Canada, 189–92
    in China, 196–200
    history of student affairs and, 183–86
    lessons learned through, 200–203
    professional development and, 186–88
    in United Arab Emirates, 192–96
Goodrich, Alan, 25
Gordon, Stephanie A., vii–ix
Gray, Hanna Holborn, 230
Great Reshuffle, 108
Great Resignation, 108, 284
Greek life, 18, 190–91
Grellet, Etienne de, 168
Griswold, Selina, 25

H

Hammond, Amie K., 283, 285–86, 288, 291–93, 298–99
Handshake (job search tool), 17
Harding, Erin Hoffmann, 73
Harmon, Martino, 15
Harper, E. Royster, 36
Harper, Shaun R., 148, 163
Harvard College, Massachusetts, 49
Harvard New Presidents Institute, 269–70
Health Insurance Portability and Accountability Act of 1996 (HIPAA), 200
Hecht, Amy, vii, xiii, 1
Hecht, Cameron A., 275
Higher education and student affairs (HESA). *See* Student affairs field
Hill, Tom, 30–33
Hiring. *See* Interviews and hiring processes
Hispanics. *See* Race and ethnicity
Hobart and William Smith Colleges, New York, 208–9
The Hockaday School, Dallas, 209, 218
hooks, bell, 145
Hrabowski, Freeman, III, 148

Huron Consulting Group, 88
Hurricane Andrew (1992), 66
Hybrid education model, 5, 271

I

Imposter syndrome, 69–70, 146, 157, 160
Inclusion. *See* Diversity, equity, and inclusion
Independent schools. *See* PK–12 education
Indigenous people, 191, 193
Informational interviews, 48, 50, 77
Innovation
    career trajectories and, 239
    consulting for, 80–81
    crisis management skills and, 260
    entrepreneurial mindsets and, 115
    job satisfaction and, 242
    organizational culture and, 247
    startup opportunities and, 75
    student engagement and, 177
    student population diversity and, 5–6
    University Innovation Alliance, 32
    values congruence and, 290–91
Inside Higher Ed, on workforce reductions during COVID-19 pandemic (2021), xi
Institute model, 186
Institutional fit, 131–32, 240, 268. *See also* Career fit; Job satisfaction
Institutions of higher education
    administrative positions in, 167–82. *See also* Administrative positions
    board governance, 58–59, 216–17, 269
    consulting for, 80–96. *See also* Consulting
    faculty positions in, 143–65. *See also* Faculty positions
    global work assignments for, 183–205. *See also* Global work assignments
    job satisfaction and, 237–51. *See also* Job satisfaction
    organizational culture and, 76, 129–30, 245–47, 293–94, 298–99. *See also* Campus climates

organizational politics, 59–60
organizational structure, 201
PK–12 environments compared to, 211–14
policies and procedures of, 67–68, 74
presidents for, 253–82. *See also* Presidential perspectives
returning to student affairs careers in, 123–42. *See also* Returning to student affairs careers
role changes within, 41–53. *See also* Role changes within institutions
values alignment with, 283–304. *See also* Values
vice presidents for student affairs for, 55–72. *See also* Vice presidents for student affairs or services
Intelligent careers, 126–28
Interim roles, 27, 140, 173, 179
International students, 204
International work assignments. *See* Global work assignments
Internships and assistantships, 3, 127, 147, 152, 209
Interviews and hiring processes. *See also* Job searches
analyzing institutions during, 28, 63–64, 298–99, 299*f*
for faculty, 171
learning from, 89–90
mission and values of institutions and, 130, 294
outside of higher education, 77–79
questions for job seekers to ask during interview, 299
recruitment challenges and, 4
union and collective bargaining agreement as information sources for, 300
values of student affairs professionals and, 294, 298–99
Intrinsic motivation, 52–53
Iowa State University (ISU), 30–35, 158–61
Isolation, 104, 220

J

Jaffe, Sarah, 246
Job descriptions, 131, 285, 289, 293, 297–98
Job satisfaction, 237–51. *See also* Fulfillment
career fit and, 28, 74–77, 285
case study of student affairs professionals, 285–86
increasing responsibilities and, 3, 6
leadership skills and opportunities, 247–49
Macmillan Learning study on, xi
organizational culture and, 245–47
presidencies and, 255
reimagining career paths, 239–41
reinvigorating your career, 238
researching potential institutions, 28
sustainable workplaces and, 241–44
values congruence and, 286–89
Job searches. *See also* Interviews and hiring processes
advanced degrees, growth in jobs requiring, 19
faculty positions, 160–61
informational interviews and, 48, 50, 77
job descriptions and, 131, 285, 289, 293, 297–98
mentorships facilitating, 18–19, 31–35, 51–52, 56–57, 87–88
networking and, 154
online tools for, 17
paid leave for, 28
questions to ask during interview, 299*t*
résumés, 78, 153
search firms and, 30, 78, 134, 139
specialty work and, 137
values congruence and, 297–301
Jones, C., 126
Jones, Tamara Bertrand, 143, 152

K

Kapoor, Vik, 22
Kniess, D. R., 144
Knowdell Career Values Card Sort, 287
Kohler, Stephen, 238
Kratzer, Dave, 44

L

Lateral career moves. *See* Role changes within institutions
Lawsuits and legal issues, 67
Leadership skills and opportunities
   crises and, 66–67
   cultural differences and, 197
   job satisfaction and, 247–49
   leading from where you are, 258
   long-term positions and, 65–66
   for PK–12 education, 211–12, 226–32
   professional associations and, 22, 68–69
   resilience and adaptability and, 226
   shared values within employee teams and, 294–95
   for undergraduate students, 103–4
   values congruence of employees and, 292
Learning mindset, 52
Leath, Steven, 35
Leaving student affairs careers
   advice for, 96–97
   career shifts, normalizing, 114–15
   challenges and inequities in higher education careers, 115–17
   challenges in process of, 109–11
   for consulting roles, 80–96. *See also* Consulting
   for DEI roles, 99–108. *See also* Diversity, equity, and inclusion
   disruption of, 80
   finding next job opportunity, 77–80
   lifestyle upgrades, 112
   networks and, 77, 96, 105, 110–11, 113
   for PK–12 education role, 207–35. *See also* PK–12 education
   positive aspects in process of, 111–12
   reasons for, 74
   reflection questions for, 118–19
   social media group for, 184
   where to go, 74–77
LGBTQIA+ individuals, advocacy and support for, 44, 136
Lifelong learning
   as organizational value, 293
   passion for, 189
   in PK–12 education, 224
   role changes within institutions and, 47
   self-reflection and, 151
   transferable skills and, 111
   vice presidents for student affairs and, 67–68
Lifequakes, 10–11
LinkedIn, 78
Listening skills, 63, 230, 265, 295
Lofquist, L. H., 284–85
Love, B., 145
Lovett, Darryl, 237

M

Macmillan Learning, xi
Man's Search for Meaning (Frankl), 11
Mantras and affirmations, 222, 265, 270
Massachusetts Institute of Technology (MIT), 49
Mastrodicasa, Jeanna, 41, 42
Mathis, Joyce, 18–19
McKinsey & Company, 90–91
McMurry University, Texas, 127, 131, 138
McNair Scholars program, 157
Mental health issues. *See also* Burnout and exhaustion
   of college students, 4
   emotional tax of student affairs work and, 116
   job expectations and, 6
   of PK–12 students, 220
   quiet quitting and, 5
Mentorships
   career advancement encouragement and, 153–54
   as career-building strategy, 7
   career goals and decisions, facilitating, 34
   consulting and, 83, 92
   faculty positions and, 163
   institution changes and, 31
   job opportunities through, 18–19, 31–35, 51–52, 56–57, 87–88
   job satisfaction and, 247–48
   to maintain connections to higher education, 105
   organizational politics and, 59–60
   personal referrals and, 51–52
   preparation for new roles and, 31–33

by presidents, 280
professional associations and leadership opportunities, 68–69
professional coaching and, 179–80
race and ethnicity, 268
as support system, 70–71
vice presidents for student affairs and, 60–61, 209
Microaggressions, 146, 159
Mindset
career path explorations and, 52–53
career transitions out of higher education and, 110
for entrepreneurship, 115
jobs vs. careers, 126–28
student engagement and, 101, 197
values-centered, 295
Minnesota State Colleges and Universities, 125–26
Minorities. *See* Diversity, equity, and inclusion; LGBTQIA+ individuals, advocacy and support for; Race and ethnicity; Women
Mission-oriented organizations, 75, 105, 119
Mission statements, 294, 297
Mitroff, I. I., 275
Moffett, Raphael X., 183

N

Nair, Ajay, 253, 263
NASPA–Student Affairs Administrators in Higher Education
Conferences on Student Success in Higher Education, 178
founding and history of, 183
Minority Undergraduate Fellows program, 157
presenting at conferences of, 224
on trends in HESA, 4–5
National Association of Independent Schools (NAIS), 211–12, 217
Natural disasters, 66, 214
Neoliberalism, 285–86, 288–89, 293, 300
Neufeldt, Ellen J., 253, 257
New York University (NYU), 146–47
New York University (NYU) Abu Dhabi, 193–95
Nguyen, David J., 167
Nonprofit organizations
career transitions to, 104–5, 110–11
expectations and demands of, 112
presidents hired from, 97
transferable skills and, 110

O

O'Dair, Katie, 41, 48
Old Dominion University, Virginia, 260–61
168 Hours (Vanderkam), 240
O*Net Work Importance Locator, 287
Organizational change, consulting for, 81
Organizational culture, 76, 129–30, 245–47, 293–94, 298–99. *See also* Campus climates
Organizational politics, 59–60
Organizational structure, 201
Owens, O'dell, 29

P

Paid time off, 28, 248
Paine, Gage E., 123
Pandemic. *See* COVID-19 pandemic
Parental expectations and career influence, 16, 169, 176, 196
Parents of students
global work assignments and, 200, 215–16
PK–12 education and partnerships with, 214, 215–16
Patton, Lori D., 158–60, 163
Pay Up: The Future of Women and Work (Saujani), 246
People with disabilities, 136–37
Person–environment fit theory, 284–85
Pertuz, Sofia B., 99
Pew Research Center, 17
Pina, Jason B., vii, xiii, 1
PK–12 education, 207–35
academic environment, shaping, 221–23

educational environments compared, 211–14
leadership skills for, 211–12, 226–32
lessons learned, 232–34
motivations for transition to, 208–11
partnerships, importance of, 215–18
preparing for career in, 224–25
understanding institutions, 218–23
whole child approach, 219–21
Political capital, 59–60, 71
Political involvement, 43–44, 47–48, 58, 68
Position descriptions, 131, 285, 289, 293, 297–98
Post graduate degrees. *See* Advanced degrees
Power and privilege
 DEI initiatives and, 100–101
 empowerment and, 8
 international assignments and, 187
 organizational politics and, 59–60
 professional development and, 155
Presidential perspectives, 253–82
 Arcadia University, 263–66
 California State University, San Marcos, 257–62
 Dean College, 254–56
 DePauw University, 267–74
 University of Wisconsin, Stevens Point, 274–81
Presidents
 BIPOC talent for, 102, 267–68, 273
 career goals and, 37, 131–32
 from industry or nonprofit roles, 97
Principles of Good Practice for Boards and Trustees (NAIS), 217
Privilege. *See* Power and privilege
Professional associations
 career advancement norms reinforced by, 110, 117
 consultants' role in, 84–85
 founding and history of, 183–87
 leadership skills and opportunities through, 22, 68–69
 networking through, 104, 113, 178–79
 PK–12 educators and, 224
 presidencies, preparation for, 280

professional development through, 186
value of becoming involved in, 68–69, 138
Professional development. *See also* Lifelong learning
 for aspiring presidents, 279–81
 as career-building strategy, 6–7
 career shifts and, 102, 114–15
 career trajectories and, 239–40
 coaching and mentoring for, 105, 115, 179–80. *See also* Mentorships
 consulting and, 84–85
 global work assignments for, 183–205. *See also* Global work assignments
 job satisfaction and, 243, 248
 leadership opportunities in, 22
 learning mindset and, 52
 professional associations and, 186
 values congruence and, 299
Professional identity and reputation, 51–52, 130
Professional networks. *See also* Professional associations
 career-building strategies and, 7
 faculty positions and, 163
 fundraising and, 57, 76–77
 within institutions, 178
 job searches and, 154
 leaving student affairs careers and, 77, 96, 105, 110–11, 113
 networking résumés, 78
 PK–12 educators and, 217–18, 224–25
 race and ethnicity as factor in, 154–56
 returning to student affairs careers and, 138–39
 transferable skills and, 76–77
 vice presidents of student affairs and, 57–59, 68–69, 127
 volunteer opportunities and, 67
Professional standards, 184–85
Professors. *See* Faculty positions
Program coordinators, 48, 172, 295–96
Program development skills, 111
Promotions. *See* Advancement opportunities
Protean career, 124–25
Protests, 63, 263–65

Pryor, R., 174
Public speaking skills, 111

Q
Quality of life. *See* Burnout and exhaustion; Work–life balance
Quiet quitting, 5, 244

R
Race and ethnicity. *See also* Diversity, equity, and inclusion
  accessibility of education and, 272–73
  alumni, honoring, 59
  BIPOC presidents and, 102, 267–68, 273
  completion rates, inequities in, 4, 16
  diversity, equity, and inclusion commitment in education, 226–28
  global work assignments and, 191, 193
  institutional representatives for, 104
  legacy of inequalities and, 145
  marginalization and, 192–93
  microaggressions and, 146, 159
  misogynoir (racism/sexism intersection), 159–60, 159n2
  professional networks and, 154–56
  racism and racial justice, 5, 102, 106–7, 254, 264–65
  representation and, 273–74
  role models and mentors, 154–56, 158, 268
  Sisters of the Academy Institute, 154–55
  student activism and, 263
  student advising and, 147–49
  student programs for, 146
  student recruitment and retention and, 16, 21, 24–26
Racial battle fatigue, 146
Recruitment. *See* Employee recruitment and retention; Student recruitment and retention
Referrals, 51–52, 78
Reflection. *See* Self-reflection
Rejection, 133

Relationship-building, 57–59. *See also* Professional networks
Remote work, 88, 91, 242, 270, 277
Renn, Kristen A., 239
Resignations. *See also* Leaving student affairs careers
  career fit and, 285
  COVID-19 and, 278
  Great Resignation and, 108, 284
  to pursue advance degree, 32
  values congruence and, 292, 296
Resilience and adaptability. *See also* Transferable skills
  as career-building strategy, 8
  consulting work and, 85
  cultivating in students, 228–29
  diversity, equity, and inclusion commitment in education, 226–28
  leadership skills and, 226
  leaving student affairs careers and, 112
  networking and, 154
  presidencies, preparation for, 280
  skills for, 238
  student diversity and, 5–6
Résumés, 78, 153
Retention of employees, 3–4, 243–44, 248
Retention of students. *See* Student recruitment and retention
Returning to student affairs careers, 123–42
  benefits of employment outside higher education, 74–75
  career moves, timing for, 132–35
  competencies and skills for, 130–32
  entering, training, and advancing, 135–37
  individually managed careers, 125–27
  motivation and career paths for, 128–30
  networking and, 138–39
  unexpected career moves and, 139–41
Rhodes State College, Ohio, 28–29
Robert Morris University, Pennsylvania, 278
Rokeach, Milton, 287
Role changes within institutions, 41–53
  campus partners, relations with, 46
  community connections and, 46–47
  competencies, awareness of, 50–51
  lifelong learning and, 47
  mindset and intrinsic motivation for, 52–53

operational experiences and, 46
political involvement and, 47–48
professional reputation and relationships, 51–52
Role models. *See also* Mentorships
  advancement norms and, 110
  for organizational culture and change, 246
  organizational politics and, 59–60
  for prioritizing family obligations, 44
  race and ethnicity, 155, 158
  VPSAs as, 70
Ronald E. McNair Scholars program, 157
Rossetti, Ana, 73
Runell, Marcella, 237

S

Sabbaticals, 248
Salisbury University, Maryland, 260
Sanchez, Jamie V., 15
Saujani, Reshma, 246
Schein, E. H. & Schein, P., 245
Schlissel, Mark, 36
Scholarly practice principles, 177–78
Schwarzman Scholars program, 198
Search firms, 30, 78, 134, 139
Seggewiss, B. J., 293
Self-authorship theory, 175–77
Self-care, 102, 112. *See also* Work–life balance
Self-confidence, 69–70, 113
Self-doubt, 145, 268. *See also* Imposter syndrome
Self-efficacy, 112, 113, 145
Self-reflection
  career changes and, 100, 109
  COVID-19 pandemic and, 10, 102
  critical thinking skills and, 231
  on PK–12 education, transition to, 211, 214, 218, 225, 232
  questions for, 118–19
  student courses on, 61
  on values, 118, 284, 287–88
  Values Alignment Worksheet for Job Seekers, 300, 305–9
Servicemen's Readjustment Act (GI Bill, 1944), 184

Set Boundaries, Find Peace: A Guide to Reclaiming Yourself (Tawwab), 244
The Seven Habits of Highly Effective People (Covey), 202
Shalala, Donna, 59–60
Shifting roles within institutions. *See* Role changes within institutions
Side hustles, 241
Siner, Angela, 25
Sisters of the Academy (SOTA) Institute, 154–55
Skills. *See also* Competencies
  for assessment, 111, 158
  for building management, 77
  career-building strategy and, 6–7
  for counseling, 77
  creativity. *See* Creativity skills
  for crisis management. *See* Crisis management skills
  critical thinking, 226, 229–31, 247
  for data analysis, 111
  leadership. *See* Leadership skills and opportunities
  listening, 63, 230, 265, 295
  for program development, 111
  public speaking, 111
  for resilience and adaptability, 238
  for returning to student affairs careers, 130–32
  transferable. *See* Transferable skills
Social justice, 106–7
Social media and cyberbullying, 220
Social Mobility Index, 262
Society of University Planners, 279
Socioeconomic status and college completion rates, 4
Southern Methodist University (SMU), 134
Spock, Benjamin, 208
Staff recruitment and retention, 3–4, 243–44, 248
Staff shortages, xi, 3
Stephen A. Schwarzman Education Foundation, 198
Stereotypes, 146, 231, 268
Stevens, Heather M., 55
Stonehill College, Massachusetts, 55
Strategic planning projects, 80–81, 260, 271, 277, 279

Strengths, 50–51. *See also* Competencies
Stress, 80, 93–94. *See also* Burnout and exhaustion
Student advisors, 147–48
Student affairs field, 1–15. *See also* Advanced degrees; Job satisfaction; Values; *specific job titles*
    career-building strategies in, 6–8
    career trajectories and, 11–12. *See also* Career trajectories
    change, certainty of, 8–10, 9*f*
    in China, 199
    faculty positions in, 143–65. *See also* Faculty positions
    history of, 183–86
    lifequakes and, 10–11
    recent trends in, 3–6
    returning to, 123–42. *See also* Returning to student affairs careers
Student conduct, 28–29, 136, 183, 194, 198, 276. *See also* Dean of students
Student engagement and connection. *See also* First-generation students; Student recruitment and retention
    academic advising and, 44, 147
    burnout and exhaustion from, 5, 74, 104
    COVID-19 pandemic, support during, 64, 107–8, 261–62
    DEI initiatives for, 101
    feedback and, 265–66
    innovation and, 177
    international students and, 204
    listening skills for, 63
    mindset for, 101, 197
    political capital and, 59–60
    with presidents, 265–66
    protests and, 263–65
    quiet quitting and, 5
    race and ethnicity, 146
    safety issues and, 44
    student courses on self-reflection and, 61
    student diversity, adaptation and innovation for, 5–6
    of vice presidents for student affairs, 60–62, 276
Student-faculty relationships, 163, 261
Student groups and organizations, 18, 67–68, 103–4, 189–91
The Student Learning Imperative (ACPA–College Student Educators International), 185
Student newspapers, 63–64
The Student Personnel Point of View (American Council on Education), 184–85
Student privacy laws, 199, 215
Student protests, 63, 263–65
Student recruitment and retention
    admissions process and, 20–21, 24
    challenges in, 3–4
    consulting for, 81
    COVID-19 pandemic and, 10, 277
    declines in, 74
    presidents' role and, 270
    race and ethnicity, 16, 21, 24–26
Student scholarships, 63, 261

T

TACUSPA (Texas Association of College and University Student Personnel Administrators), 138
Tallahassee Community College (TCC), 152
Tawwab, Nedra Glover, 244
Taylor, Baishakhi, 183
Taylor, Breonna, 106, 264
Teaching assistants (TAs), 149, 158–59
Teamwork, 248, 294–95
Technological change
    adaptability and, 238
    consulting for, 81
    hybrid education model, 271
    remote work, 88, 91, 242, 270, 277
    social media and cyberbullying, 220
    startup opportunities and, 75
Telles-Irvin, Patricia, 44
Tennessee Tech University, 258
Terminations
    career fit and, 285
    COVID-19 pandemic and, xi, 285
    entrepreneurial mindset and readiness for, 115
    reduced workforce and, xi, 3
    values congruence and, 296
Terrell, Melvin C., 34

Texas A&M University, 157
Texas Association of College and University Student Personnel Administrators (TACUSPA), 138
Theory of work adjustment, 285, 290–92
Thompson, Lancelot C. A., 34
Time management, 240–41
Title IX compliance, 137, 259, 261
Toxic work environments, 5, 63, 133. *See also* Burnout and exhaustion
Transferable skills. *See also* Creativity skills; Crisis management skills; Leadership skills and opportunities
　advanced degrees and, 2, 111
　consulting careers and, 76–77, 94, 96
　critical thinking, 226, 229–31, 247
　DEI roles, transitioning to, 103–6, 110, 111
　global work assignments and, 200, 204
　for presidencies, 260–61, 275–77, 279–81
　reflection questions on, 118
　returning to student affairs and, 130–32
　shifting roles within institutions and, 51
　workshops on, 114–15
Transitioning out of higher education. *See* Leaving student affairs careers
Treadwell, K. L., 276
Triggers, 202
The Trustee Handbook (Orem & Wilson), 217
Trustees, 58–59, 216–17, 269
Tsinghua University, China, 198–99
Tufts University, Massachusetts, 48–49
Turnover. *See* Retention of employees; Terminations
Tyler, Bill, 18

U

Unions, 300
United Arab Emirates, global work assignment in, 192–96
United States Bureau of Labor Statistics, 19
University at Albany-State University of New York, 55
University committees, serving on, 22
University Innovation Alliance, 32
University marshals, 49–50
University of British Columbia (UBC), 189
University of California, Berkeley, 209
University of California, Irvine, 267
University of Chicago, 209, 230
University of Florida (UF), 43–48
University of Maryland, College Park, 158
University of Massachusetts Amherst Social Justice Education program, 148–49
University of Miami, 55, 66
University of Michigan, 35–37
University of Nevada, 55
University of Notre Dame, Indiana, 89–91
University of Oklahoma, 140
University of Tennessee at Chattanooga, 259
University of Texas at Austin (UT Austin), 134, 138
University of Toledo (UToledo), 16–27
University of Vermont, 209
University of Wisconsin, Stevens Point, 274–81
Upward mobility, 3. *See also* Career trajectories

V

Vacation time, 248
Values, 283–304
　assessments of, 287–88
　career changes and, 130
　career realignment and, 289–92
　case study of student affairs professionals, 285–86
　of employees, supporting, 292–97
　job satisfaction and, 286–89
　job searches and, 297–301
　organizational culture and, 76, 129–30, 245–47
　questions to ask during interview, 299*t*
　self-authorship theory and, 175–76
　self-reflection on, 118, 284, 287–88
　values congruence, meaning of, 284–85
　vice presidents and alignment of, 63–64

Values Alignment Worksheet for Job Seekers, 300, 305–9
Vanderkam, Laura, 240
Veterans services, 136
Vice presidents for student affairs or services (VPSA), 55–72
　career trajectories for, 56–57
　challenges of, 260
　confidence and, 69–70
　crises, leading through, 66–67
　future, excitement for, 64–65
　institutional values and, 63–64
　internships with, 209
　leadership choices and long game, 65–66
　leadership transitions, navigating, 61–62
　lifelong learning and, 67–68
　mentorship opportunities as, 60–61
　mentorships leading to, 31–35
　organizational politics and, 59–60
　presidencies, transitions to, 258, 260, 268–69, 276–77
　professional networks and, 57–59, 68–69, 127
　support system and, 70–71
　timing of career changes and, 134–35
Vice provosts, 276–77
Violence
　challenges for higher education, 5, 190
　challenges for PK–12 education and, 220
　fraternity hazing and, 190–91
　gun violence and stress, 220
　racial, 102, 106–7, 254, 264
Virtual education, 5, 271
Volunteer opportunities
　advancement opportunities and, 110, 117
　commencement ceremonies as, 45, 257
　for faculty, 172
　feedback from, 51
　leadership skills and, 66–67
　political, 43–44
　professional development and, 84
　program coordinators, 172
　student affairs events, 20
　student enrichment programs, 18

VPSA. *See* Vice presidents for student affairs or services

W

Wages and compensation
　advocacy for, 297
　collective bargaining agreements and, 300
　for consultants, 82
　employee retention and, 243
　for employment outside of higher education, 79–80, 105, 112
　equity issues in, 116–17
　at midcareer level, 74
　organizational culture and, 247
　recruitment challenges and, 4
　reflection questions on, 119
　stagnation of, 3
　values congruence and, 299–300
Washtenaw Community College (WCC), Ohio, 27–28
White, Lori S., 253, 267
Whitely, Patricia A., 55
Whole child educational approach, 219–21
William Penn Charter School, Pennsylvania, 218, 224
Wintersteen, Wendy, 35–36
Women
　American Association of University Women, 183
　BIPOC presidents, 267–68, 273
　helping professions, undervalue of, 246
　misogynoir (racism/sexism intersection) and, 159–60, 159n2
　racial justice and, 106–7
　role models and, 154–56
Work-from-home positions, 88, 91, 242, 270, 277
Work–life balance. *See also* Burnout and exhaustion; Family obligations
　flexibility and, 249
　inequities in higher education careers and, 116
　job satisfaction and, 243
　organizational culture and, 246–47

reflection questions on, 118–19
self-care and, 102, 112
sustainable model for, 238, 239
vacation time and, 248

Work relationships. *See* Mentorships; Professional networks
Work Won't Love You Back (Jaffe), 246